T0304727

Creating a Lean R&D System

*Lean Principles and Approaches
for Pharmaceutical and
Research-Based Organizations*

Creating a Lean R&D System

*Lean Principles and Approaches
for Pharmaceutical and
Research-Based Organizations*

Terence M. Barnhart

CRC Press
Taylor & Francis Group
Boca Raton   London   New York

CRC Press is an imprint of the
Taylor & Francis Group, an **informa** business

A PRODUCTIVITY PRESS BOOK

CRC Press
Taylor & Francis Group
6000 Broken Sound Parkway NW, Suite 300
Boca Raton, FL 33487-2742

© 2013 by Taylor & Francis Group, LLC
CRC Press is an imprint of Taylor & Francis Group, an Informa business

No claim to original U.S. Government works

Printed in the United States of America on acid-free paper
Version Date: 20120618

International Standard Book Number: 978-1-4398-0078-2 (Hardback)

Library of Congress Cataloging-in-Publication Data

Barnhart, Terence M.
    Creating a lean R & D system : lean principles and approaches for pharmaceutical and research-based organizations / Terence M. Barnhart.
        p. cm.
    Includes bibliographical references and index.
    ISBN 978-1-4398-0078-2 (hardcover : alk. paper)
    1. Research. 2. Lean manufacturing. 3. Pharmaceutical industry. I. Title.

T65.B345 2012
658.5'7--dc23   2011031366

Visit the Taylor & Francis Web site at
http://www.taylorandfrancis.com

and the CRC Press Web site at
http://www.crcpress.com

To Helen and Fiona and generations to come.

In loving memory of Dr. Leona Mae Barnhart.

Contents

List of Figures

Preface

Lean has a long and rich history of innovation and expansion. From some early efforts to improve a machine shop at Toyota, Lean's ability grew to where it could improve full production lines. Further effort enabled Lean to tackle the improvement of entire plant operations, and extended its value stream further and further back to its suppliers. Beyond production, Lean learned to improve strategy; to improve execution, technology, product development, and design; and to integrate these efforts into the growing learning capabilities of Toyota. From this expansion, it is clear that Lean is a learning, evolving platform—a research project whose goal is to explore the how and why of work and to devise ever-increasing capabilities to change work for the better.

I am very lucky to have been involved in the great research project known as "Lean." When I began my Lean experience in research and development (R&D), I was blessed with a new frontier to explore. There were, of course, and there remain, vast numbers of people engaged in improving technology, developing science, and pushing the frontiers of knowledge to create new products, technologies, processes, and capabilities. But at the time I began working in Lean, there were scant few people working to understand how to improve R&D, writ large, in a scientific and systematic way.

At that time, people were much more likely to imagine improving R&D productivity by giving it more (or less) money, organizing it into (or out of) functional or project teams, changing its location, scaling it up or atomizing it through outsourcing, or by changing the amount or timing of input from various functions. There were far fewer engaged in studying the thinking processes of R&D, the causes of R&D successes and failures, and the philosophies and assumptions about R&D, and in creating experiments to test, assess, and improve them. Yet there was, and remains, a need to answer fundamental questions that affect the capability of R&D in delivering valuable innovation. Can you learn to create "eureka!" moments that drive leaps in innovation, and if so, can you teach it? What are the barriers to innovation, and how can we remove them? In some areas, a key recurring question is: How can scientists better motivate themselves and each other to overcome the crushing odds against their eventual success? And always, R&D requires the synthesis of knowledge. We build on knowledge of past scientists; we collaborate with current scientists; and we share—through documents, objects, and so on—with other researchers, including those of our future. So how can we increase the quality and rate of integration of historic and emerging ideas so that knowledge can build more quickly into marketable innovations?

While there has been research into those and other critical R&D questions, most of these are philosophical or retrospective analyses without follow-on experimentation to prove their validity in changing R&D capability. Only a handful of people were actually doing experiments at scale to test new ideas in R&D and to prove and adapt them to enable real improvement. It has been my great joy to have worked with a number of these people, and to have had the opportunity to be involved in the research, testing, and implementation to prove (and disprove) and synthesize (and deconstruct) some of their ideas and my own into a coherent path to R&D improvement.

Along the way, it should not surprise you that Lean manufacturing tools cannot always transfer directly into other fields, for example, research biology. Some of the ideas presented will not feel like Lean, especially to those who have not spent time reading and exploring the history and works of the key Lean architects (in particular, Ohno* and Shingo†). Ohno, in an interview, stated that the pursuit of improved manufacturing productivity stalled in the 1930s, but that Toyota continued on in the spirit of Henry Ford, innovating in manufacturing efficiency.‡ These works stress the importance of thinking, the importance of experimentation, and the importance of learning to the development of Lean. Through these works, you can see the outcomes of this experimental endeavor, and what emerges is the strong impression of Lean as a decades-long and currently active research project.

Another, perhaps more subtle, message in these early works on Lean is the emphasis on people and community within the work environment.

---

* Taiichi Ohno and Norman Bodek, *Toyota Production System: Beyond Large-Scale Production* (Portland, OR: Productivity Press, 1988). Taiichi Ohno and John Miller, *Taiichi Ohno's Workplace Management* (Mukiteo, WA: Gemba Press, 2007).
† Shigeo Shingo and Andrew P. Dillon, *A Study of the Toyota Production System* (Portland, OR: Productivity Press, 1989). Shigeo Shingo, *A Revolution in Manufacturing: The SMED System* (Portland, OR: Productivity Press, 1985). Shigeo Shingo, *Zero Quality Control: Source Inspection and the Poka Yoke System* (Portland, OR: Productivity Press, 1986).
‡ Koichi Shimokawa and Takahiro Fujimoto, eds., *The Birth of Lean*, translated by Brian Miller with John Shook (Cambridge, MA: The Lean Enterprise Institute, 2009), 1, 13–14.

People at Toyota are expected to not only understand their jobs, but to experiment to improve their jobs. This is not merely true of managers of their employees, but of all employees at all levels. In this, there is a sense of community that is crucial to the existence (and in my view, the building) of Lean into the fabric of an organization. Realization of this connection to community came late to us, which is unfortunate, because the sense of community that is crucial *over the long term* in the production world is a necessary *precursor* for Lean in the innovation world. For this reason, it is presented front and center here.

Small improvements around the edges of R&D can be made by the application of Lean "tools" to the small number of manufacturing-like processes that exist within R&D. In contrast, by creating a sense of community purpose and research alignment and by building not merely an individual's ability to learn, but a community's ability to learn, an R&D organization can create leaps of innovation within its core responsibility of creating new products and processes. It can deliver nearly unimaginable improvements in R&D capability, perhaps as much as an order of magnitude or two.* Out of this community, new Lean tools, processes, and thoughts will emerge, just as they have done for decades in the manufacturing sphere, but it is important always to note that tools are not the answer in R&D any more than they were for Ohno in manufacturing. Just as in manufacturing, better thinking, better integration, and better community consistently deliver unexpectedly valuable results. It is into this realm that I invite you.

Finally, this book is but one more chapter in the research project that is Lean. Many other researchers will take alternative paths, some will build on this work, and others will find its flaws. Each case will expand Lean science beyond where it is today, and that is a good thing, for the more we explore, the greater is our ability to improve. I look forward to seeing where you take Lean on your journey.

---

* Those who doubt this should recall that Ford achieved a four- to tenfold improvement in labor productivity by introducing assembly line work (David Hounshell, *From the American System to Mass Production, 1800–1932* [Baltimore: Johns Hopkins Press, 1984], chap. 6, 217–261). Meanwhile, Toyota increased its *manufacturing* productivity tenfold in the decade from 1946 to 1955 (Koichi Shimokawa and Takahiro Fujimoto, eds., *The Birth of Lean*, translated by Brian Miller with John Shook [Cambridge, MA: The Lean Enterprise Institute, 2009], 13) and has obviously made significant progress since then.

Acknowledgments

I have far too many people to thank than I can list here. There are literally thousands of Pfizer colleagues whose work, experiments, and improvements have led to the thoughts embodied in this text (and none of them, by the way, are to blame). The number of colleagues who have directly redesigned their work as a result of projects I have supported is significantly more than 2,000. The number of colleagues who have implemented at least some of those changes in the wider organization must be close to 5,000. Each of you has my respect and thanks. It has been a joy to work with you every day.

Beyond the wisdom of my colleagues, I have been influenced by several individuals over the course of my time in Lean. Jim Luckman got me started on my journey with his excellent course in Lean product development. His subsequent coaching and thought partnership led to many of the "discoveries" that we developed into our own Lean practice at Pfizer. His colleague, Beau Keyte, provided the most breathtakingly important coaching moment of my Lean career when he mentored me to bring my first workshop back on the rails. We have continued to collaborate and to share methods and experiments as well as our lifelong love of Michigan football.

Jim introduced me to Bob Burdick, a former Lexmark/IBM engineer, whose research into physics, Taoism, Buddhism, and his dialogues about "have-do-be" (and nearly everything under the sun) created within me the ability to explore thinking in a way I'd never have imagined possible.

Monica Schroder worked with me in Agile R&D (Lean) and opened new pathways in thinking on an almost constant basis. Not just small diversions, these paths were big, wide highways of thought. She introduced me to Gary Hamel's work on radically different paradigms in business management. Not to be outdone, Adrienne Motion brought the personal touch to Agile R&D, creating a warm approach that negated the cold, calculated, tool-centric thought process that characterized its beginning. Similarly, Diana Galer introduced ideas like Nancy Kline's "time to think," which enabled us to build deeper reflection into our facilitation work, and thereby led us to much, much greater improvements.

Finally, Andrew Seddon was a part of nearly every project, every strategy session, every emerging development and experiment; and he had a special love and talent for creating, supporting, and engaging improvement in the most basic research in the company. Adrienne, Monica, Diana, and Andrew were a breathtaking group to behold in action, and I both honor and revere their capabilities and contributions.

I owe a large debt to the "Boyd" community and to the U.S. Marine Corps for supporting and nurturing that community. John R. Boyd was a fighter pilot, engineer, aircraft designer, and, most important, researcher into strategy, learning, community, innovation, and winning and losing. Although he purposely refrained from writing a text, his slide decks and briefings (many thanks to Chet Richards for presenting and explaining these and for being a mentor and friend for several years now) provide tremendous and unfolding insight. Jim Luckman's slide on learning loops led me to Robert Coram's biography of Boyd, which led me to Boyd's "Disciples." Chet Richards, who gives the authorized version of Boyd's briefings live, deepened and expanded my view of Boyd and his work and gave me direction. Frans Osinga's work gave me so much more depth and background into Boyd's thinking. The entire Boyd community continues to populate new ideas and insights. Boyd's work inspired much of the experimentation in community and fast learning, and provided early thought into what became the "wildfire" strategy. Within this community, several people stand out as mentors, co-creators, and inspirations, including Stan Coerr, its host; Scott Shipman, my friend and intellectual mentor; Michael Moore, a uniquely creative light; Marcus Mainz, the next generation; and Fred Leland, the relentless Lieutenant of Walpole, who tries and succeeds at delivering fast learning to communities near you.

In addition to the great colleagues across Pfizer, special kudos go to Pfizer's Strategic Management Group, which gave me the space not only to create thought pieces in Lean, but to actually test them in the real world of pharma R&D, and then to grow those experiments into a fully operating Lean R&D transformation group (Agile R&D).

Finally, I want to thank my family for their support through the always turbulent waters of personal and professional growth.

Introduction

MORE THAN MEETS THE EYE

People often ask what Lean looks like in research and development (R&D), or ask to see a site that is operating in a Lean way. This gives me pause because Lean in R&D doesn't necessarily *look* different than any other R&D environment, but it does *feel* different, and its operations might as well be on different planets for all of the similarities they share.

That said, I am left with the unenviable task of describing a feeling. Luckily, nearly every human has experienced this feeling and, therefore, we just need to link ourselves to it through analogy. For most of us, there was a time in our lives when we were a part of a group, perhaps a sports team, perhaps a choral or jazz ensemble, perhaps just a group of very close-knit friends, who achieved this state or feeling. Eventually, your group had worked together, been together, practiced together, performed together, and, perhaps, gotten into and out of trouble together long enough that each member felt he or she had intimate knowledge of what the other group members would do in a given circumstance. You just knew, without speaking, signing, or even looking at each other what would come next. Any emerging circumstance will fit seamlessly, naturally into the group's ongoing activities. The jazz band that pulls a yell out of the audience and distills it into a trumpet solo that then passes to the brass and on to the rhythm section has felt this. The hockey team that flows to the puck, passes without looking, adjusts to the greatest and least effort of its opponent, and scores seemingly without effort has experienced this. The friends who *just know* that, because it is Tuesday and the sun is out, Frisbee in the park is on (and bring extra water because someone will bring a new friend to join the group) has this feeling.

The feeling is an intimate sense of community, of belonging, combined with an indescribable but intensely energizing feeling of being "on." It involves trust and shared experience, a common purpose, and a sense of place. It involves a sense of personal commitment to others, and a group commitment to the person, but it neither involves nor requires a hierarchy, only shared capability, knowledge, direction, and common bonds.

Those grand words may strain credulity, and yet I watched teams at Pfizer build just such trust and confidence, collaboration, and capability, and do so in short order. Moreover, the same values that accrued to our group of friends, our sports teams, and our musical ensembles, when they reached that level of connection, accrued to these R&D teams. Their performance jumps to an almost ridiculous level. Following one example, a team's speed of scientific discovery increased by a factor of six; their newly developed scientific approach invalidated several disease hypotheses being actively pursued in the laboratory and, much more expensively, in the clinical trials of many global pharmaceutical companies. That same science identified likely causal pathways that no one had yet identified, creating uncharted opportunity for the team to pursue.

Other levels of performance changed just as dramatically. Scientific milestones were *never* missed. Progress was made on previously intractable problems. New paradigms of research, testing, and data manipulation emerged. New paradigms of project and scientific management were created, freeing up as much as 50 percent of management's time to invest in creating even more effective environments in which people and innovation could thrive. The whole *atmosphere* within the work area changed. It was noticeably calmer, happier, and more energized than other work spaces in the company. Conservatively, the level of performance increased a good two orders of magnitude in just five months.

That said, concrete outward signs of change were difficult to quantify, since, fundamentally, the differences between Lean and non-Lean R&D arise from different assumptions about how the universe works and how people work, interact, and flourish in that universe, as well as about how best to construct an environment in which people can create and deliver valuable innovations within that universe. These different assumptions have no outward physical component. The same people still read scientific literature, still design and execute experiments in the same laboratories with the same equipment they always did; they just think about their work in a radically different way, and that makes all the difference.

Author

Terence M. Barnhart, PhD, has worked as an academic and industrial research scientist, a strategy consultant, a plant engineer, and a project manager for some of the largest and best-known companies in the world, including Pfizer, McKinsey and Company, and General Electric. His professional passion is researching, developing, and implementing strategies to help people create environments in which they and others can flourish.

Dr. Barnhart received his PhD in inorganic chemistry from the University of Wisconsin and a bachelor of science degree and post-doctoral fellowship in chemistry from the University of Michigan.

1

Seeing and Removing Barriers in the R&D Environment

As I look out the front window of my house, I tend to absorb the beauty of the scene. There is a beautiful oak tree out there next to the dock. The dock juts out into a cove. If it is summer, there is a swim platform floating fifty or so feet across the inlet, and if it is daytime, people, especially children, can be found playing in the water. To the left, the inlet opens onto the river, a shallow half-mile-wide estuary with clamming and moored boats, posts with osprey nests, and navigational signs and buoys.

Depending on the day, it may be dreary or blindingly brilliant. I may see a sunrise that catches my breath, or snow and sleet. I may see violent weather that only wind, wave, and my own vulnerability can reveal, or depths of peaceful tranquility that only calmness and water seem to inspire within me. I will be annoyed when the geese come (their facility for turning green plants into fertilizer is somewhat frustrating), and I will be joyful when the swans appear, marveling at their beauty and the facility with which they run the geese out of town.

I am not a fisherman, but my neighbor is. He sees everything that I do, but he also sees that the bait fish are (or are not) running. He sees the waterway not merely as a place to swim or paddle, or to observe beauty, but also as a right-of-way to the ocean and the trophy bass that it may yield in future expeditions. The neighbor behind me, a retired commercial fisherman, sees the same channels as a source of employment, seeing the water—haven to many different species—by its seasons of harvest.

At the same time, none of us is a navigational engineer, so we do not see the changing depth of the channel and the consequent need to dredge, place markers, or remove obstacles. None of us is a biologist, who might note the changing levels of jellyfish and postulate something about river health, observe the horseshoe crab mating season and speculate on their future population, or a thousand other things. We are not shore-based contractors looking at pilings and assessing our year's business in dock repair.

Take a look around you right now. Are you in a room? How would that room look to you if you were an interior designer? How would it look to you as an architect, a stone mason, an HVAC (heating, ventilation, and air conditioning) technician, a building inspector, an ergonomist, or a child? How would a blind or deaf person perceive that room?

MENTAL MODELS

Each of us has mental models, lenses through which we perceive the world. Some call them neural networks; others call them paradigms. Bob Burdick, a retired IBM engineer, collectively calls these lenses our *be state*, while John Boyd, a famous military strategist and thinker,* called them our orientation. These mental models come from our genetics, our physical attributes, our experiences, our training, and our likes and dislikes. These mental models provide us with two very important things: the ability to see what is important, and the ability to suppress what is not. The separation of our observations into "important" and "unimportant" is an object lesson in a fundamental Taoist principle known as duality. When we observe something, and make a judgment about it, we immediately create its "dual" opposite (hence "duality"†). The Tao De Jing (Book of the Way) points out that there can be no "good" without its dual opposite "bad," no "beauty" without "ugliness." We cannot make something "observable" without making other things "hidden" and this duality is

---

* Lieutenant Colonel John R. Boyd published very little. Most of his work, which is legendary in military circles and within the community that researches fast-learning strategy, was developed on acetates for live presentations, or "briefs," which for Boyd might last 8, 12, or 16 hours. Nevertheless, two excellent references to Boyd include Robert Coram's biography, *Boyd: The Fighter Pilot Who Changed the Art of War* (New York: Back Bay Books, 2004), and Frans P. B. Osinga's excellent analysis of his sources, *Science Strategy and War: The Strategic Theory of John Boyd* (New York: Routledge, 2007).

† *Duality* is a Taoist term for separation or barrier between us and the "real" fabric of the universe—the Tao.

a core issue and opportunity for the scientist. When our mental models begin to lose their grip, and our dualities begin to dissolve, we open ourselves to that which could not be observed. We begin to access the novel, we begin to see pathways that had been hidden by our thinking—pathways to achieving things previously believed to be impossible. We create the opportunity for breakthrough.

We have created, through our mental models, the ability to see as we are—in my case a former chemist; a consultant; a researcher; a lover of water, light, and motion—but in doing so we create an *inability* to see as we are not, including the engineer, the architect, the biologist, and the person afraid of water and geese.

Now, look at your place of business. Do you see in it a place of joy? Of sorrow? Do you see it as a place of beauty? Do you see a place where people grow and thrive? Do you see a place where a community comes together to flourish? Surely some must flourish in the worst of places, and some languish in the best, but which ones and how many of each do you see? How many just put in their time and save their creative souls for their family, their friends, and their hobbies? How many of them bring their energy and beauty from home and use it to create in your business? How many take their enthusiasm from business back home to bestow it on their families? Do you flourish there?

Now, think about the best team, musical group, or organization you ever participated in. Do you remember a flow of energy among you during a game or concert, the flow that seemed to make magical every movement, sound, and feeling of the event? Do you remember your own ability to act in the knowledge that your teammates would react in kind, expanding on advantages you created, and covering for minor gaps? Do you remember the times when they instantly adjusted to your shot, your pass, or your block, the times that the audience just merged with the music, when the harmony was just right, where the other dancers held their pose just perfectly, giving new meaning to the music and the piece? Do you remember knowing what your teammates' strengths and weaknesses were, and how your strengths filled in where they were short, and how their strengths let you focus on the best parts of your game? Do you remember somehow knowing what the audience was feeling, what the opposing team was thinking? Do you remember that time that you knew what your team or bandmates were doing so well that you knew that if or when someone got caught out of position the rest of the group would not only cover, but use that slight awkwardness to create unexpected advantage?

How often have you felt those feelings at work? If you feel this only rarely, why do you suppose that is? If you feel it often, how did that synchronization come about? How will you maintain it, and, as your musical group did, improve it so that it is better and more sustained in every concert?

When was the last time you looked at your place of business in this way? If this is the first time, how has this new study of your business changed your perception of it? Did you see some possibilities that did not exist five minutes ago? Do you see things that you would change or do differently? Do you see things that are good and that could be expanded? If so, then your mental models have just loosened a bit, and your dualities have begun to blur.

Now think of those other teams you have been on. Teams that just couldn't put it together, teams whose members mistrusted each other, teams whose members would not support each other in a pinch, teams whose members were glory hounds on one hand and "Polaroid men" (people who watch the great player do most of the work and contribute little of themselves, as if they are cameramen at courtside) on the other. Think of the blown notes in concerts, the harmonies that just never came together, the stage fright that froze a band member or a late entrance by the musical's lead that unraveled the other players on stage. Think about how often you feel that your teams and team members at work act in this disharmonious way.

The difference between teams that synchronize and those that flail is another instance of duality, of separation from each other. We know that there are barriers between these people because we know from those teams, and from our loving relationships, what it is like to live, even for a few moments, without those barriers. The feeling of togetherness grows out of a *real* lack of separation between people, a oneness that flows from familiarity, from common purpose, from an ability to see and even be connected to that other person, without barriers. Teams that flail suffer from barriers that, for whatever reason, keep team members apart in the important ways that enable other teams to thrive. The flailing teams never seem to connect, never seem to bond or create that unspoken communication pathway that the best teams create. Their duality is not between people and their environment, but between themselves.

REMOVING BARRIERS TO INNOVATION

If nothing else, Lean is about seeing and removing the dualities that hinder people in their environments. When barriers between people and the physical world are removed, parts flow down assembly lines, work is done without error, and value accrues, almost magically, within a plant.

This property is valuable in manufacturing, of course. When we see that inventory is hiding our ability to see our problems, reducing inventory and its causes makes our manufacturing environment a better, smoother, easier place to work. When we believe that some aspects of work are "necessary" evils,* we separate ourselves from the ability to see other possibilities where that evil does not exist. We separate ourselves from the opportunity to live without that evil. When we believe that some workers are more capable of solving problems than others, we separate ourselves from the creativity inherent in each of them, and we lose the creative ability of those other workers to improve their own environment. And because we don't believe in those workers' creativity, we force other people, perhaps managers, to overuse their creativity to improve the workplace. In turn, they are overworked to compensate for our faulty mental model about people's creativity. When Lean begins to remove the self-imposed barriers on our mental models, manufacturing flows freely, workers' morale improves, quality jumps, and customers flock to products.

Toyota and others have proven how valuable the removal of barriers can be in manufacturing, but manufacturing is inherently a *physical* endeavor. It bends, shapes, drills, bolts, glues, paints, and shines things. But it is the people side of the business where thought, creativity, innovation and imagination, trust and enthusiasm, collaboration, and integration occur significantly in the minds of individuals and communities of people and only in the minds of those people. It is in these places where the ability to see and remove mental barriers[†] proves the only path to improvement. Imagine the value to a salesman of having no barriers between himself and a customer. He would be able to recognize his customer's precise product,

---

* Shigeo Shingo applies this same argument to overproduction ("necessary" stock) in his book, *A Study of the Toyota Production System* (Portland, OR: Productivity Press, 1989), 63–64.

† From here on, I will use the words *barrier, paradigm,* or some transparent synonym of these rather than the word *duality,* which, within my own mind, and perhaps within yours as well, seems limited or dissonant.

quality, and pricing beliefs as if they were his own. He would see emerging product needs and be able to address them with existing offerings, new proposals the company could provide, or a host of other ways to satisfy, in real time, the needs of his customer. He would prove a valuable, almost irresistible partner for the customer, so of course, sales organizations work very, very hard to create just such a relationship between their sales force and the customer.

IMPACT ON R&D INNOVATION

The value of removing barriers between and among researchers and their work is enormous. Science is not a solitary endeavor. Einstein famously noted that his achievements only came because he stood on the shoulders of giants who came before him. Much of the scholarly literature in biology has several, in many cases dozens, of authors, all of whom have contributed significantly to the scientific learning codified in a given research paper. In pharmaceutical research, biologists identify potential disease pathways, biochemical routes that, in misfiring, cause harm within the body. All of these are built on connections and knowledge amassed with and through the work of other scientists.

Chemistry is little different. Pharmaceutical chemists design molecules that shift, block, or enhance biological pathways highlighted by their biologist counterparts. These molecules, designed to remove or deflect the cause of disease and enable the body to function more effectively, are in turn synthesized by chains and sometimes armies of scientists, and even then, the work is not done. The effectiveness of these molecules cannot be predicted from a chemical drawing or computer simulation. They must go back to the biologists and be tested in Petri dishes and other models until, eventually, they are tested against the disease itself in clinical trials with suffering patients. In this progression, hundreds of researchers around the globe design and execute experiments to determine which molecules affect disease and which ones fall short. Coordinated like a winning football team, these scientific communities can achieve miraculous innovation in relatively short time frames. Disconnected and fragmented teams, hobbled by the barriers between people and processes, can suffer projects that drag on indefinitely. It is the ability of Lean to remove barriers

between people and the systems in which they toil that smoothly and easily converts the disconnected into the coordinated, the barrier-riddled
into the free-flowing R&D community, that enables innovation to build
and flow smoothly, almost effortlessly through time.

In our experience, the ability to find and remove barriers between people and their systems almost guarantees a doubling in performance, and
often delivers multiples of that. Teams that have smooth handoffs deliver
100 percent (and no more) of the required knowledge at those handoffs.
As a result, such teams do not lose critical information, have important
knowledge gaps appear unexpectedly in their projects, or have uncoordi-
nated knowledge transfers that lose minutes every day, days every month,
and months every year. They do not spend time or effort looking for missing information or re-creating it in multiple groups across the project.
Teams that have few barriers to communication make better decisions,
catch their early failures and convert them to wins, converse freely about
ways to go faster and achieve more, and invariably gain back lost time
and squandered innovation as the project progresses. Barrier-free R&D is
smooth R&D, it is fast R&D, it is effective R&D and it is ultimately satisfy-
ing and rewarding R&D.

An infinite number of things cause these barriers between people and
within their work systems. Physical barriers are a significant contribu-
tor, especially in an increasingly virtual world. If one researcher is in
China, another in Brussels, and a third in Kansas, time zone barriers,
shipping barriers, and communication barriers alone may keep them
from smoothly interacting. Emotional barriers, things that keep us from
trusting and interacting well with others, present another key impedi-
ment to building innovation rapidly. Observational barriers, the fact that
we cannot see crucial facts and circumstances needed for comprehend-
ing and answering key scientific problems, also hinder our innovative
progress. Thinking, the most important capability in an R&D enterprise, is hampered by its own set of barriers, which, when observed, can
be removed in ways analogous to the removal of the physical barriers
that hamper manufacturing.

A Lean R&D system will continually seek, recognize, and remedy existing and emerging barriers that hinder the smooth, rapid growth of innovation knowledge. These barriers come in four main categories: physical,
emotional, observational, and thinking.

Physical Barriers

Lean thinking can be used to affect the physical side of R&D. Experiments are run, prototypes are made, testing is performed—all of it in the physical realm. This means that the classic elements of Lean manufacturing that remove physical barriers to success on the shop floor have a valuable place within the Lean R&D realm. Physical laboratory work is hampered by the "seven wastes": overproduction, inventory, motion, waiting, transportation, overprocessing, and rework.

Just the transportation implications alone can be staggering. In a vibrant research community, laboratories are often spread across the globe. Biology may be done in Cambridge, Massachusetts, chemistry performed in Shanghai, China, and samples tested in San Francisco, California, with the results shipped back to an origination and orchestration point in London, England. In this common scenario, experimental design knowledge, testing regimens, raw materials, samples, and testing results will assuredly travel between locations. In addition, research methods are often difficult to reproduce, so scientists may travel to set up and run initial validations of a process. Even machines and test instruments may be shipped so that there are no changes from the originally proven design.

Transportation issues are not limited to international geography. R&D organizations are often located on campuses (academic and corporate) in which researchers and their supplies are distributed among many buildings, over many floors, and down long corridors. R&D instruments can be very expensive, so there are often shared services, and these, too, can be a great distance from the user or customer. Thought regarding the location of work within an R&D system can be quite helpful in eliminating barriers and ensuring that the work is done easily and in a short period of time.

Overproduction is just as prevalent in research as it is in manufacturing, and it occurs both in the ways people see it in manufacturing and also in ways rarely experienced on a shop floor. In the first instance, it is not unusual for chemists to design, for example, many more molecules than are needed to understand the properties of the chemical problem at hand. It is not unusual for designers of clinical trials to order more patient tests than are needed to fulfill the goals of the study. Sometimes these are "exploratory" tests; sometimes they are "just in case" tests. In both cases, the additional work clogs the system, slows down progress, and adds significant complexity to scientific analysis, the clarity of reports, and the delivery of knowledge to other researchers in the area. This overproduction also adds tremendously to the unused inventory of company knowledge that, lacking any other purpose, clogs computer databases and makes handling responses to safety and regulatory inquiries slower and more difficult.

These cases are similar to manufacturing, but R&D overproduction charts its own unique areas of waste as well. The most common form of overproduction comes from answering the same question multiple times. New knowledge is only new once. "Discovering" it a second time is just a waste of effort and resources. You can immediately see why this might happen through an organizational memory lapse or loss of documentation, but it actually happens on purpose as well. Academic publication standards differ from innovation standards. Often, in order to publish, a fact must be corroborated by multiple different scientific experiments. This is good if you want to *prove* something, but if you want to *use* that knowledge, it is completely unnecessary. Overproduction is costly, since it can take a lot of effort to deliver the same, already known answer through a different path. It also takes equipment and supplies unique to each method used. Worst of all, it consumes thinking time that could be applied to a valuable innovation.

Other manufacturing analyses translate exactly. Motion in the laboratory is just as bad as motion on the manufacturing floor. Flow is just as critical in maintaining the physical pace of work. Intriguingly, laboratories are normally laid out in cells, a practice used regularly by Lean practitioners. Often, laboratories are not laid out with the care that is taken with manufacturing cells, but the intent is exactly the same.

The list of potential physical barriers to the smooth creation of innovative knowledge goes on indefinitely, and there are as many ways in which the physical aspects of science can be improved as there are ways to improve manufacturing. In fact, there is an emerging field of study (called Lean Laboratory) devoted to this purpose.[*]

As a caution to manufacturing practitioners, there are also cases where R&D activities *look* like waste but are not. A scientist may repeat the same experiment many times or change many variables to establish process consistency, improve performance, and generally understand the interplay of variables. A researcher may test many different ways to answer a

---

[*] See the Wikipedia page: http://en.wikipedia.org/wiki/Lean_laboratory.

question in order to find one that is easiest and most effective before proceeding. In each of these cases, valuable knowledge is being sought, even if it appears on the surface to be redundant activity.

Emotional Barriers

Innovation is mental work and exists in the mental world where logic, intuition, and emotion merge. Emotional disruptions impact both the intuitive and logic channels required for innovation. Emotional barriers primarily inhibit trust and the smooth engagement and harmonious interaction between people. These barriers include beliefs and positive/negative experiences people have built up about other people, sometimes about people they have never met or done business with. Beliefs about these people from prior experience with their organizational function, with their professional background, with their ethnic origins, and so on, all contribute to difficulties in smooth collaboration. Cries of "Those people in that area don't work very hard" or "That type of scientist can't plan" are heard regularly, sometimes in reference to functions that have never interacted. In other instances, people have worked together closely and developed acrimony or distaste. These are two of the most obvious emotional barriers. Others are much more subtle and are often hidden, yet these hidden issues create just as much damage to the R&D environment.

People genuinely try to get along, so difficulties are often hidden or smoothed over; subtle personality conflicts that do not blow up into overt fights still inhibit the free flow of thought or even the deep consideration of new ideas that are required for real breakthrough innovation to occur. Whether the cause of emotional friction is visible or hidden, the negative impact on innovation is tremendous. Without trust, intimate collaboration cannot occur, leaving people to resort to authority, process definitions, and the like to do their communicating for them. Since innovation processes often cannot be designed with sufficient specificity to cover all possible scenarios, incomplete data packages often result. Delay in going through official channels leads to late deliveries and further angst. Late and incomplete delivery of results erode relationships, as does consideration of politics, which impacts the sharing of knowledge, which has obvious impacts to the clarity of scientific dialogue and planning.

Quite surprisingly, emotional barriers are often created by improvement efforts. Functional silos often work very hard to improve their work, but in so doing can make inadvertent (or intentional) demands on other functions. Dramatic or even subtle increases in the work of others caused by improvement projects will erode trust very quickly.

Although emotional barriers occur everywhere, they can be especially destructive in the R&D environment. We have seen lack of trust between a pharma company and a clinical supplier literally double the staffing requirements of both companies' efforts while simultaneously slowing project progression to a crawl. Untreated, emotional barriers, like the ones we experienced with our clinical partner, increase with repetition and familiarity, and the damage they can cause is immense.

Observational and Thinking Barriers

The value in removing observational and thinking barriers may be a bit more abstract, but it is just as powerful, as history proves time and again. Prior to the turn of the twentieth century, Newtonian physics held sway for 300 years. Mechanics, optics, and calculus—Newton's tour de force—created a unified paradigm of thought that enabled the industrial revolution not merely to come into being, but to explode onto the scene as mankind raced to develop new modes of travel, communication, commerce, and war. Yet for 300 years, gaps existed in Newton's theories; some were filled by scientists and engineers, but others remained unexplained for centuries. Importantly, the Newtonian paradigm defined what was correct (an inanimate, causally linked, clockwork view of the physical universe) and what was not (a messy, nonlinearly chaotic, gravitationally and time-warped universe). It defined which problems were important and which were not. Most importantly, it defined what people would see and what they would ignore.

Einstein was not hidebound by the theories of Newton. In fact, they affected him so little that his vision encompassed an entirely different way of viewing the physical world, a different paradigm known as *relativity*. The importance of relativity, and its different view of the universe, is made clear to me every day when I drive past the local nuclear power plant on the way to work, or watch a navy submarine steam past our workplace out into the ocean. In the Newtonian world, nuclear power cannot exist. In the relativistic paradigm, mass can not only be created and destroyed at will, as it is in the plants that power the submarines and supply our electricity, but, in fact, it happens on an unbelievably infinitesimal scale with each chemical reaction our scientists produce in the laboratory. Irrespective of how useful Newton's thoughts were, they are but a poor approximation of reality, which becomes glaringly obvious on the cosmic or atomic scale of the universe.

Of course, the fact that relativity was a big shift in thinking should surprise no one. What might come as a surprise, however, is that there were Newtonian physicists who could not, to their dying day, understand or even *see* the paradigm of relativity. They still saw everything through the Newtonian paradigm and remained locked, unable to shift their vision, their frame of reference, so as to see the Einsteinian viewpoint.

It seems that paradigm shifts—shifts in our mental models—can be very traumatic.* They can take moments to occur, or years, and in many cases, they can never occur at all. Einstein himself suffered the same frozen paradigm syndrome as the Newtonians he replaced. He famously could not bring himself to see the universe from the viewpoint of quantum mechanics, which is the theoretical basis for all current thinking in the fields of chemistry and particle physics.

Barriers to observing and thinking, then, are barriers to our ability to see critical data and circumstance and then to synthesize that into a new way of envisioning the universe. These are the most important barriers to science and innovation that exist. The Newtonians *could not see* the evidence that defined relativity. They had created such strong mental models of how the universe worked that they literally could not entertain one separate from their original pattern. Locked as they were, they could never innovate nuclear power, or create breakthroughs that power modern chemistry.

The lesson here is that our mental models distill the infinite universe into a finite vision of reality. As a result, anything that may exist beyond our models is *necessarily invisible to us*. Intriguingly, while our mental models are all but invisible to us, they present a solid-wall barrier that bars our observation and consideration of greater truths. On our own, we can only break these mental models with great effort. However, by exposing their existence and shining a light on the ones that hinder innovation, we can progress in literally unimaginable leaps. Lean R&D thinking revolves intimately around creating pathways that expose and remove these mental barriers.

---

* See Thomas Kuhn's *The Structure of Scientific Revolutions*, 3rd ed. (Chicago: University of Chicago Press, 1996).

LEAN AND THE REMOVAL OF BARRIERS

Through the ages, our human advances rode the coattails of people who were able to relax the barriers between themselves (or their way of thinking) and the reality that surrounds us. To do so, these people opened themselves to different ideas and possibilities, which, in turn, enabled them to attempt experiments and experiences that the rest of us would not have even dreamed possible. It would never have occurred to us to have such dreams because these possibilities were walled off by our beliefs, our mental models and the barriers we set in the way of our own innovative capability. In the economic world, the very breakthroughs that power our scientific advances and the innovations that drive new products and industries arise entirely from *someone's* ability to observe without the barriers that exist within *everyone else's* current thinking.

What Lean does in the manufacturing space is to expose the barriers in thinking that keep us from productive, capable work. That same philosophy that exposes barriers in manufacturing thinking can just as easily expose barriers in the innovation space. Once exposed, those mental models, those beliefs, can be shifted to enable newer, more flexible, more capable structures to take hold.

The trick is to go beyond seeing Lean as a box of tools and begin seeing Lean as a way of being, which, in turn, is a state of observing without bias, reframing those observations without imposing our mental barriers, experiencing a new reality that did not exist, and as a result, growing. Lean can be a state of being for an individual, a team, or an entire organization, as it is at Toyota. What it is not, however, is a static, rigid thing. The silver and green books of Toyota may codify their thinking, but Lean is growing, changing, and adapting all of the time. The ideas of Ford and Deming were surpassed by Ohno and Shingo, and their work has given way, under the weight of learning from the fields of chaos theory and systems theory, to the work of Fujio Cho in creating new paths to Lean. Aspects of Lean will likely never change; others will be unrecognizable a decade from now. Many workers, researchers like yourselves, will create those new Lean elements as you learn to overcome barriers standing in your path, your function's path or your company's path. Lean will change and improve as these barriers fall, and nuances to improve learning enter from new fields, disciplines, and research, and leave their mark.

2

Lean in Research and Development

Lean has proven to be a reliable resource for companies looking to improve themselves, particularly in their manufacturing functions. Lean has helped companies improve productivity, cost, reliability, and profitability. It has also helped companies to improve morale, create steady long-term profit growth, and facilitate many other useful objectives.

But what of research and development (R&D)? Can Lean help improve the innovation function of a company? If so, how? By how much? How long would it take? How would it differ from what we do now in R&D? How would it differ from what we do now in manufacturing? Where would we start? How would we progress? Where would we end?

These are all important questions, and the most strategic answer is that Lean can partner quite well with R&D, and powerfully so. Twofold, four-fold, even tenfold improvements and beyond have resulted, in surprisingly short periods of time, from the development of Lean thinking within the R&D function. Lean thinking applies to the most basic science and to the most routine production laboratory in biology and electrical engineering alike. It applies in the R&D manager's work and at the scientist's bench. It applies valuably across the entire innovation landscape.

But the Lean path is not a straightforward, linear translation of "Lean tools" from manufacturing to R&D. Like R&D, or Lean itself for that matter, the path to Lean R&D is a thinking, learning, experimental endeavor, and like many good approaches to better thinking, the path to Lean R&D begins with an understanding of cause and purpose.

PURPOSE

The purposes of R&D and manufacturing differ substantially, since they serve obviously different functions within a company. Manufacturing modifies and integrates physical things (raw materials and parts) until it delivers a coherent, valuable object for others to sell and buy. Successful manufacturing repeatedly produces the same objects, each of which can be sold for (more or less) the same amount of money to different customers. Successful manufacturing does all of this work at a total cost that is less than the sellable value of the product. The purpose of manufacturing, then, is to convert raw materials into valuable consumable goods that can be sold at a profit. The currency of value for the manufacturing function is the object that is produced.

Research and development, in contrast, generally creates and tests new ideas, building and integrating the results of those tests until R&D can deliver a coherent, valuable *package of knowledge* for others to use. That package might be a new object, the prototype of a product, that can be manufactured and sold at a profit. That package might be a new process with which to manufacture an existing product at greater profit. That package might be a new technology by which others can create or process their products, or it might be new knowledge needed to enable business functions (R&D, marketing, regulatory, and so on) to successfully support their business needs.* The purpose of R&D is innovation, and the currency of value for innovation is new, applicable knowledge.

There are many other differences between manufacturing and R&D, but the fundamental difference in their currency of value is most important to our thinking about Lean. These differences drive the many other differences that operationally separate manufacturing from R&D. Manufactured objects have intrinsic value, which means that identical objects can be manufactured and sold for about the same price. As a result, it is the rare manufacturing process that is run only once. In fact, it is customary for manufacturers to make as many identical copies of that object

---

* Academic research is only slightly different. Value there is measured in publications, grants, prestige, tenure, and, for graduate students, new jobs. Nevertheless, the currency of value in both academic and industrial R&D is not an object but, rather, is the relative value of the knowledge that is generated by the thinking and experimental activities of the researchers.

as the market will bear at a profitable price. Manufacturing is configured for repeatability that serves customer demand.

The same cannot be said for the value held in an innovation. Innovations are not physical objects but are, rather, useful knowledge or useful sets of knowledge. Once knowledge is created it can be forgotten, but it cannot be destroyed. This means that R&D, whose job it is to create valuable innovations, often needs to do a job just once (correctly) in order to satisfy the needs of innovation. The majority of R&D experiments deliver all of their useful knowledge the first time a test or experiment is run correctly. Running an identical experiment a second time typically adds no value whatsoever; hence, identical experiments are run only in special circumstances.* In all other cases, running the same experiment a second, third, or *n*th time yields no new value.

Variety of new knowledge, however, gives power and flexibility to valuable innovation. Similar experiments that test different options enable researchers, designers, and manufacturers latitude for greater value, lower costs, and greater reliability, among other benefits. As a result, R&D is configured for novelty and variety, and processes are designed to deliver one-time outputs cost effectively.

It follows that the physical tools used in manufacturing may not be entirely appropriate for use in R&D. That is why laboratory and pilot facilities look and operate differently than manufacturing-scale equipment and production trains. One merely needs to compare a chemical laboratory with a photograph of an oil refinery to appreciate the vast gulf that can lie between R&D and manufacturing. Manufacturing is configured for material and work flow at a scale commensurate with production at market demand. Laboratories are configured for flexibility, with scale as small as can be humanly created (smaller is generally cheaper) to still deliver the knowledge needed for other purposes. A specific flow of work often cannot be built into the process of R&D because the process of today is different than the process of tomorrow, obviating the value of a predefined configuration of equipment (within reason).

At the same time, there are many test instruments in the R&D environment that are never seen, let alone utilized, in the manufacturing setting.

---

* For example, experiments are repeated where statistical information or information about variations in the experiment itself will prove useful to the ultimate knowledge package R&D is trying to deliver. In these cases, the experimental *set* is the unique knowledge generator, not the individual experiment by itself.

These instruments provide knowledge about hypotheses under test. Once that knowledge is gained, it is possible (even likely) that the knowledge will not be needed in other settings. In synthesizing a new chemical, for example, we will need instruments that allow us to know what chemicals a given reaction creates. Once a chemical process is developed, with its side products identified and understood, and processes are in place to account for them, there will be no further need for such instruments. The principles and knowledge developed by that first instrument in the lab allow understanding of process conditions, of key tags for identifying impurities and their remediation, and so on. As a result, in a production setting, we may use less costly tools to assess structure and purity, and may need none at all; hence we put those less expensive tools—not the expensive, sensitive R&D instruments—into the production process.

CONTINUOUS IMPROVEMENT IN MANUFACTURING AND R&D

It follows, then, that if manufacturing and R&D differ in key ways, the same must be true of continuous improvement in each of these settings. If continuous improvement is defined as *Lean manufacturing*, then almost assuredly its range of concepts, and hence its greatest potential value, is reduced to its value to the manufacturing floor, or to things that, in other areas of business, appear manufacturing-like. If we followed this approach, Lean in R&D would be applicable only to those parts of R&D in which value is created by objects, or by processes that repeat the same or a similar thing many times.

Of course, this would make no sense at all, and there is strong precedent that Toyota never applied such a limiting thought process in the creation and development of continuous improvement. Even a cursory study of Toyota management philosophy and implementation shows that the *Lean philosophy* has been explored in a variety of venues across the company. Toyota has developed capability in *Lean product development, Lean planning and strategy deployment, Lean office,* and other areas. In developing Lean applications in this wider setting, Toyota has created a range of thoughts, applications, and tools not used in manufacturing. The Toyota Production System is a wondrous thing indeed, but so are the Toyota Product Development System and the other Toyota management systems and processes. Each of these has served its unique environment, delivering its own tools and thoughts to the body of corporate operational and continuous-improvement knowledge.

Precedent well in hand, we can begin building our own R&D improvement thought, our Lean for R&D, to support a simple notion: the creation of the most successful R&D engine possible for my company. To do this, I believe we will need to understand not only the value and purpose of R&D, but that of Lean as well.

THE PURPOSE OF LEAN

In an interview quoted in *The Birth of Lean*, Taiichi Ohno suggests that U.S. manufacturing productivity improvement ended, for all intents and purposes, in the 1930s.[*] In that same interview, he describes the ongoing push to explore new ideas and experiment in the science of manufacturing productivity. Toyota was, of course, struggling mightily, and that led to several issues that the company and its intellectual and managerial leaders had to overcome, while simultaneously putting organizational and emotional constraints on their actions. Ohno's focus on manufacturing productivity is partially explained by the financial struggles of the company, and partially by a personal bias that Ohno brought to the problem. But the broader implications of a labor agreement (lifetime employment) and capital scarcity led him to explore, very specifically, paths that would simultaneously release labor and overall manufacturing efficiency in the context of a strong humanistic/humanizing force.

This approach contrasts sharply with the experimentation done during the development of the Ford Motor Company in three key ways. Ford had nearly unlimited access to capital, had no formal agreement with the vast pool of (largely unskilled) labor it could draw from, and Ford had significantly fewer constraints on how he treated his labor pool. This is not to say that Ford deliberately mistreated employees, in fact the opposite was generally true. For example, the first assembly line was adjusted immediately

---

[*] Koichi Shimokawa and Takahiro Fujimoto, eds., *The Birth of Lean* (Cambridge, MA: The Lean Enterprise Institute, 2009), 1–20.

for height to improve worker ergonomics. But the labor was difficult, and the assembly line a harsh task master. By 1913, the labor turnover had reached 380 percent, and the remedy Ford turned to was to more than double pay, from $2.34 per day to $5.*

The purpose of Lean, then, could not merely be to raise labor or manufacturing productivity as had occurred at Ford. The social context at Toyota required a human touch as well. My synthesis from this history and Ohno's other early writings on the Toyota Production System† is that the purpose of the Toyota Production System is to improve the environment in which manufacturing occurs, not just to improve productivity, but to make manufacturing work easier, faster, and more flexible.

WHAT LEAN *IS*

A complete definition of Lean may be impossible. A definition of Lean that a large percentage of people agree on may be just as elusive. We can, at least, eliminate a few things, see what is left, and build from there a workable definition. First, we can rule out Lean as a set of tools for the improvement of manufacturing (or for the improvement of anything else, for that matter). While the "box of tools" definition is common, it fails even a cursory inspection. If Lean were a set of tools, it would have boundaries and a clear definition as well as, perhaps, a clear set of rules. But the "tool kit" of Lean practitioners keeps growing. In the early days, Ohno was experimenting with flow, machine layout, labor productivity, and cleanliness. Later, means for controlling flow of materials (the Kanban system) entered Lean. More than a decade later, Shingo would begin refining the Single Minute Exchange of Dies (SMED) system.‡ Along Lean's history, A3, value-stream mapping, and other tools were incorporated into the Toyota Production System. And as we described earlier, Lean exists in many, if not all parts of the company.

------

* David A. Hounshell, *From the American System to Mass Production, 1800–1932* (Baltimore: Johns Hopkins University Press, 1984), 256–59.
† Taiichi Ohno. *Toyota Production System: Beyond Large-Scale Production* (New York: Productivity Press, 1988); Taiichi Ohno. *Taiichi Ohno's Workplace Management* (Mukilteo, WA: Gemba Press, 2009).
‡ Shigeo Shingo, *A Revolution in Manufacturing: The SMED System* (Portland, OR: Productivity Press, 1985).

John Boyd, the twentieth century's greatest military theorist, once singled out the Toyota Production System as the only systemic embodiment of "maneuver warfare" theory in the business world.* I believe this is closer to the case, as maneuver theory rests significantly on principles analogous to Lean, including learning processes, certain management philosophies, and so on. However, it is not clear to me that the development of Lean was so much a weapon or theory of conquest as it was a means of survival at least in its early years, when Toyota was struggling.

Perhaps a useful starting point, based on historic precedent, is that Lean is merely a problem-solving philosophy. Such a philosophy would encounter similar problems many times over. To avoid having to reinvent answers to those recurring problems, a problem-solving philosophy would generate different tools to effectively handle those common problems with the least mental and physical burden. A general problem-solving philosophy could easily support many different types of activities, from manufacturing to management, from supply chain to product development. Along the way, it would throw off area-specific tools based on the purpose of the function and the recurring problems encountered there. This definition, if not complete, serves our purpose, because if Lean is a problem-solving philosophy, then it can just as easily solve R&D problems as it does manufacturing problems.

Moreover, problem solving is a knowledge-creating activity, so what Lean does is accrete knowledge that can be used to better operate a company. As noted previously, R&D is the corporate function whose purpose is to generate useful packages of knowledge. Since Lean is not a corporate entity per se, it is best described as an activity, actually an ongoing *research activity,* or *research study,* for the improvement of Toyota. In this respect, Lean can be seen to serve the same purpose as the R&D function. One could say that Lean is corporate R&D devoted to improving the company itself. In fact, at Toyota, Lean is a laboratory experiment encompassing every facet of the company—and a very large multinational manufacturing company it is.

Of course, Toyota's research study (Lean) is not bound by its own borders. By porting it wholesale into its Tier 1 suppliers and beyond, Toyota made Lean a much larger laboratory experiment, one that encompassed its

---

* Chester W. Richards, *Certain to Win: The Strategy of John Boyd Applied to Business* (Bloomington, IN: Xlibris, 2004).

suppliers. By starting its joint venture with General Motors (New United Motor Manufacturing Incorporated, or NUMMI), the Lean research endeavor crossed over to encompass competitors. The success of this research has spread fundamental ideas into nearly every aspect of our economy, from manufacturers to governments, from hospitals to advertising offices. Some estimates suggest that as many as 80 percent of all manufacturers employ the results of these experiments (some Lean tool or other).[*] Lean may be one of the largest research studies ever undertaken outside of the main body of academic science.

LEAN R&D

Within this vast research endeavor, there is a vanishingly small field of Lean R&D. Why this is so is not clear. Perhaps the newness of Lean in the R&D space stems from the dissimilarity between the purpose and methods used in manufacturing and R&D. Certainly there are barriers (social, language, and other barriers) to porting Lean into R&D. Perhaps it is because R&D (at least R) is often a very small percentage of the overall corporate budget of manufacturing companies.[†] Such companies, even having experienced success with Lean, may delay focus on the small part of their enterprise represented by R&D.

For whatever reason, the interest in making the transition of Lean into R&D has not been great, but there are intriguing implications and opportunities. Since the function of R&D is the accretion of knowledge into useful, valuable packages (products, services, enabling knowledge, etc.), Lean R&D can be said to be the *science of improving innovation*. This makes Lean R&D a recursive concept. It is research that endeavors to understand and improve the capability of research. Moreover, since R&D is populated by people trained to do research, it should prove a natural, even exciting new space for researchers to investigate, and this has proven true, in my experience, whenever researchers have embraced the core concept of Lean.

---

[*] IndustryWeek/Manufacturing Performance Institute, 2007 Census of U.S. Manufacturers.

[†] Average R&D expenditures comprised only 3.8 percent of sales for the world's top 1,000 R&D spenders according to Booz and Company. Barry Jaruzelski and Kevin Dehoff, "The Global Innovation 1000: How the Top Innovators Keep Winning," *Strategy and Business* 61, Winter (2010).

In the end, research may prove to be a breeding ground for Lean thinkers who will then populate back into the rest of the corporate world with new ideas and innovations that drive the next level of productive change.

IMPLICATIONS

Saying that Lean is a research enterprise is, I think, accurate but insufficient. What is the purpose of this research? *Improvement* is one potential purpose, but this begs the question of what the research is aimed at improving. We have demonstrated that Lean does not exist solely to improve manufacturing; otherwise, it would prove useless in other areas of corporate (and now even governmental) life. But if we believe that Lean is useful everywhere, that it is an active area of research, we must move deeper. We must delve back into the purpose of Lean itself.

Going back to Toyota, if we attempt to improve manufacturing, to what aspects of manufacturing was Lean applied? Operations, flow, communication, problem solving, inventory, quality, waste, changeover speed efficiency, cleanliness, machine availability, workload balance, speed, cost, worker training, problem-solving theory, management, strategy, strategic alignment—in short order it becomes clear that Lean was applied to improve *the entirety* of the manufacturing *environment*. Similarly, Lean's application in product development encompassed everything from gaining customer input to designing tools, from management structures to project reviews. Again, Lean was employed in the improvement of the *entire product development environment*. Intriguingly, where Toyota has applied Lean, it has done so holistically across the *environment* of the workplace.

CONNECTION WITH PEOPLE

I have had the great pleasure to have met and engaged at length several people who were trained as suppliers by Toyota Lean experts. Nearly every one of them has a story that goes like this: The Toyota trainer heard about the supplier's managers or management team solving a problem. Upon listening for a while, the Toyota trainer asks the manager, "How many people work in this factory?" to which the manager might reply, "One hundred." The Toyota trainer would then ask which employees solved the problem, getting the answer, "The management team." "How many of the employees are managers?" he would ask. The reply of "five" would then prompt the trainer to ask the manager, "Why do you waste 95 percent of your brainpower?"

For those steeped in traditions that imply, or outright state, that people have different talents, and for those who use such implications to build divisions of labor and hierarchies to maximize those talents, Toyota's belief in the ability of *all* people to operate at a level of sophistication and abstraction makes no sense, and is often written off as a slogan. It is only when their belief is seen up close in action that it comes alive. Respect for people at Toyota means something deeply and fundamentally different from what it means at other companies.

In his article "Decoding the DNA of the Toyota Production System,"[*] Stephen Spear describes the activities of a line worker in a Lean factory. This worker is doing the repetitive work of manufacturing, just like every other line worker in every other factory in the world. Unlike every other employee at every other company, however, this line worker has set up a series of changes to explore how to make his work faster, easier, and better. The employee Spear follows is an *average worker* on a normal production line doing scientific experiments.

The point of Spear's article is not (merely) to impress upon the reader that a company should routinely experiment to improve its processes. While this is incredibly valuable in its own right, the big part of this story is that Toyota line workers are scientists in the most fundamental way. They develop hypotheses about their work, design experiments to test their hypotheses, measure the results, and then codify what they learn into the greater body of manufacturing knowledge housed within the company. This reveals two amazing things about Toyota. First, Toyota has trained literally everyone in the company to think and act as a scientist. Scientific research exists everywhere, not merely in the loftiest halls of R&D, but those in the most modest areas of assembly and maintenance. Second, and maybe more astonishing, are the *assumptions* on the part of Toyota that (a) every employee *could* become a scientist and (b) having every employee become *and act like* a scientist in his own work *would*

---

[*] Steven J. Spear and H. Kent Bowen, "Decoding the DNA of the Toyota Production System," *Harvard Business Review*, 1999 (September-October), 97–106.

be valuable. Based on those assumptions, Toyota works to ensure that all employees are trained and capable scientists.

While most of us see differences among people and imagine those differences are large, Toyota's actions suggest that their underlying *mental model* of people is that *all* people are basically good problem solvers. This has important implications, since it means that Toyota assumes that the thinking contributions of every employee are crucial to the success of the company, and it goes to great length to cultivate that capability. As a result, Toyota is able to gain significantly from problem solving at every level of its operations, while companies whose theories in action suggest great differences in capability between people do not make such investments, and do not gain from each worker's ability to innovate.

We began our Lean journey with the concept of a philosophy for improving innovation. We believed that it could be taught, that work could be redesigned, and we believed that project teams could create dramatic improvements. With these beliefs in hand, we ran experiments, facilitated transformational change, and achieved doubling and sometimes quadrupling of innovation capabilities within very short time periods (usually 90–120 days). However, when we studied the depth of thinking on human capability that Toyota had established and compared their assumptions to our own, the stark difference started us down the path of rethinking Lean in the setting of research and development.

We began to back away from teaching and began to embrace a mentorship/collaborator model in which everyone (insofar as we could engage them) engaged their own problem-solving/improvement research in a commonly developed framework. This, in turn, led to much greater levels of improvement and far more integrated and capable teams than we could ever achieve with our original assumptions. This, finally, led to my belief that the purpose of Lean is the creation of environments in which people can flourish.

CONCLUSIONS

Just as our observations of Toyota's application of Lean led us to the idea of Lean as an evolving research study, inquiries into the improvement of innovation and creativity lead to the inescapable conclusion that such improvement requires the improvement of the human condition. A

Lean environment must grow not merely out of respect for people's ability to innovate, but from an understanding of what helps them develop and grow, and what helps them flourish. If we can create R&D environments in which people flourish, we will have jumped to a realm where *breakthrough* performance can be the norm of each new innovation project rather than—as it is now—a random occurrence where plodding improvement and regular failure is often our baseline expectation for R&D.

Innovation, the purpose of R&D, is the development and demonstration of valuable new knowledge. It is fundamentally a game of thinking. Likewise, Lean involves the development and practice of problem solving (which is a specific type of thinking) within a specific environment. Lean R&D takes that one step further, because the problem it seeks to solve is the problem of innovation. As a result, Lean R&D is devoted almost completely to the improvement of innovative thinking and practice as well as the environment in which innovative thinking takes place. Diving in here will require a bit of thinking about the creative process of individuals and about how to remove barriers to people's success in creating. It will require a bit of thought into the innovation process, which will require us to explore how groups develop and integrate knowledge. Finally, it will require that we build approaches to test, prove, and instill these thoughts at all levels through a company, from the individual technician to the most senior scientist, from the project team to the functional silo, from the bench worker to the senior manager.

Hopefully, by the time we are done, we will have built enough structure that a new area of Lean will emerge, one developed to create environments in which innovators can choose to flourish.

3

The Individual in the Lean R&D Community

A research and development (R&D) community performs only two things on the way to delivering useful knowledge packages: (a) Individuals within the R&D community create bits of new, potentially useful knowledge, and (b) the community itself integrates those bits into coherent, definably useful packages of knowledge. The community and individual are inextricably linked in this, as the individual gains perspective and direction as part of the community. The community defines context; that is

- What is valuable
- The boundaries of what is *known* and *unknown* in that value space
- How members of the community are arrayed
- How the community creates and sustains its culture to nourish or starve innovation

At the same time, the individual makes the community. It is through the collective, aligned intent of each individual that communities exist at all. Without envisioning and committing together to fulfill a higher purpose, individuals cannot coalesce into a coherent, operating community, let alone a well-functioning one. Individuals bring their own paradigms and norms together, and, somehow, within their shared community, create common norms and viewpoints, paradigms, and mental models that define a culture or an environment in which individuals exist and interact productively.

THE INDIVIDUAL/COMMUNITY CONTINUUM IN R&D

Individual and community are inextricably linked—in particular, within science, where the thoughts and ideas of the future depend entirely on the thoughts and ideas built, winnowed, changed, and absorbed in the present. A researcher cannot valuably function outside of the community, and the community cannot function without the creative efforts of its individual members. They are one. Therefore, if we want to create Lean R&D communities that exquisitely serve their innovation purposes, we need to consider the individual and community together.

With that in mind, the combined whole is somewhat intractable. Therefore, I will begin our discussion by splitting individual from community, separating the individual's commitment, contribution, and skills from the community's contextual roles of (a) creating purpose, alignment, and synthesis of individual contributions into the body of the whole, and (b) synthesizing environmental and cultural factors into a cohesive, functioning system. Since individual and community are inseparable in reality, there will be significant cross-fertilization of ideas throughout this book; however, in Chapter 7, I will begin to put the two together again in our discussion of creating and nurturing environments in which researchers can flourish. That will lead us to the wider discussion of implementing Lean R&D.

An Example of the Lean R&D Community

Some time ago, Jim Luckman showed me a video of a GM senior management visit to Delphi's Rochester Technical Center where he had been the senior executive. Leadership was coming to see something that had grabbed their attention: an R&D organization that had tripled its output in three years. But they were exposed to something beyond their original expectation. The employees lined the floor and mezzanine level of the atrium as the GM leaders came in, clapping in time and singing a song they had written and practiced for the event. It seems that every individual at the Tech Center had done something (including learning the song) to make that visit a special one.

This video is *amazing* to anyone who has been around large corporate entities for a while. It is true, of course, that people spend time and energy "sprucing up" a site when visiting dignitaries arrive. One large company I worked for spent almost nothing on grounds maintenance—until the CEO would make his annual visit. Then the whole place would get a big once-over: mown grass, new paint, and so on, all done by outside contractors in the space of about a week. It is also true that people in companies occasionally perform skits and songs. But these are almost always done in the waning days of very intense training programs, never by a huge group like the Delphi Tech Center staff, which had literally hundreds involved, spanning every function, every level, indeed, every person on site. In fact, that video reminds you of the outpouring of community pride that happens when a local high school football team wins a state championship, or a local son comes home from battle. It is an outpouring of the sort of simultaneous pride and camaraderie that only a closely knit community holds.

Of course, Delphi's Rochester Tech Center had been successfully running its own Lean Product Development System for three years or so, which brings us to this fundamental point: Lean R&D organizations *do* exactly the same kinds of things that other corporate R&D functions do. The products they deliver serve the same intended purposes, they explore the same fundamental areas of science and engineering; they build that science into new product designs; and they build and integrate the science and engineering needed to manufacture that product. Lean R&D communities have the same kinds of things as other corporate R&D functions. The buildings are the same; the technology is the same; the tools are the same; and the instruments are the same. To the casual observer, it can be difficult to tell the two apart, because Lean does not arise from what you do or what you have; it arises from *who you are*, and one of the things a Lean R&D organization *is* is a *community*.

Jim's video was the first time I saw with my own eyes the committed community that I have found common to Lean work environments. If you are attuned to it, you can observe this sense of community the moment you walk in the door. People have almost a palpable sense of purpose. The atmosphere is notably more egalitarian and inviting. The conversations are more collaborative. It is calmer, yet more active and driven than a non-Lean R&D site. In fact, the same thing is true within sites where Lean is starting to take hold. Pockets where people have become Lean feel different than other non-Lean parts of the site, a remarkable thing for people who pretty much have and do the same things as people in another part of a building.

How does such a community come about? How can it be developed and nurtured? To answer this, we need to start with the individual and with the common threads shared with others that form a Lean R&D community.

QUALITIES OF THE INDIVIDUAL IN A LEAN ENVIRONMENT

It is not clear to me that any particular set of attributes can define the Lean individual or her community, but several things seem to be common.* People who are Lean are invariably:

1. Committed
2. Deeply aware of their community
3. Skilled at learning (an explicit learning process)

Commitment

Commitment is an integral part of who a Lean person is. A member of a Lean community is committed to the purpose and overall success of that community, committed (at least implicitly) to the success of each of the community's team members, committed to overcome the technical and other challenges required for that community's success, and committed to the craft or art of research. The Lean individual is committed to filling his role with increasing ability, but is also committed to pitch in where others are struggling, to ask for help when struggling himself, and to advance with the others when things are going well.

This is exactly the same commitment one makes as a member of a musical ensemble. Everyone is responsible to play their part as ably as possible, which means not only knowing the music, but their instrument and its nuances. But music is not just a set of notes; it is a complex interplay of individuals with audience members, with the acoustics of the performance

---

* I omit basic competence in a given field for two reasons: First, because it is largely assumed that we engage people in fields of their interest and basic technical competence. Second, because a person with strong learning skills can develop competence in a wide variety of skills relatively quickly. Each of us proved this once by becoming biologists, physicists, engineers, artists, and musicians. Surely we could attain competence in a second, third, or nth field.

room, and with a host of intangibles. It is an emerging, flowing, interacting process in what might otherwise be thought of as a controlled environment. If one person increases tempo or shifts key, even subtly, everyone must adjust, or the group will veer into uncharted (and unfortunate) musical territory. But if the ensemble is connected and acting as one, the lengthening and shortening of phrase to subtly enhance meaning become more than just possible; they become inevitable. Even major changes—the insertion of a solo, or a spontaneous repeat of a phrase that is connecting with the audience, or the loss of another one due to a mistake—cannot negatively affect the musical outcome. For this to work, the individual must commit to the *harmonious* success of the team and, in so doing, gain the harmonious support of the team.

Of course, everyone who has experienced this in a musical ensemble or sports team (I suspect nearly every one of us has experienced this at some point in our lives) knows that, at the point where the group is acting harmoniously, much more than conscious individual commitment has taken place. People have actually stopped, in a sense, being individuals, and have begun to *be* the group. We have all, I think, been a part of a group or team that, in spite of technical skill, never "gelled" to *become one* in harmony.

The research teams I have had the pleasure of working with achieved this level of harmony in their research. Harmony proved to be an unexpectedly powerful driver in creating and integrating innovation.

Commitment to Craft

Just as simply joining a band or team is not enough for a player to contribute her all, commitment, in a Lean sense, is not simply becoming a harmonious part of the group. A Lean scientist will have a commitment to deepen and broaden her craft. Lean researchers will, among other things, observe things in their environment that exemplify or inform their research. They will use incoming thought to expand their research into new areas and deepen it to build more understanding of current knowledge. They will, of course, practice their craft, working not merely to improve the efficiency and capability of their experimental techniques, but, as important, to improve their ability to formulate, understand, and answer ever more difficult research questions with progressively fewer and more elegant experiments. They will work on the thinking and learning processes required of great scientific exploration.

I have previously used the terms *have*, and *do*, and *be*, borrowing from the thinking of a friend and former IBM engineer, Bob Burdick. He describes a *be state* as the complete set of paradigms whirling about in our minds that define what and how we observe and respond to the world. It is our experiences—mixed with the assumptions we use to make sense of those experiences, driven by our intentions and aspirations within our environment, and tossed with a bit of instinct and passion. Our paradigms determine what we observe and how we observe. It determines our viewpoints, how we interpret and react to our observations; it is the conceptual framework of *who we are.*

But who we are is not necessarily how we think of ourselves, which (Bob further elucidates) can emanate from a *be* or a *have* perspective. Analogies help here. For the sport fanatics among us, Roger Federer *is* a great tennis player. For the musicians, Louis Armstrong *was* a great musician. For the scientists in the crowd, Einstein *was* a great physicist.

The *have* perspective is exemplified by a 12-year-old boy with dreams of playing professional sports or becoming a famous musician or a Nobel-winning scientist. We often note of a 12-year-old boy that he believes that if he *has* a new tennis racquet and the latest sneakers, if he *has* a beautiful trumpet, or if he *has* a new computer, laboratory, or what have you, he *will have* all he needs to be a star. It is a belief that success emanates from the external, measurable qualities of his heroes, not the internal qualities that made them great.

Of course, that 12-year-old eventually meets someone who *is* a tennis player, scientist, or musician, not just a pretender with nice stuff. He finds that the local 12-year-old Federer could defeat him playing barefoot with a broom handle using his off-hand. Louis Armstrong demonstrated through the invention of "scat" that he did not even need words, let alone his famous horn, to express his musical talent. Einstein, and hundreds of talented scientists dating back through history, proved that great science does not require a computer, the latest atom smasher, or any other *thing* per se, so much as it requires good *thinking*, which perhaps best embodies the scientific *be state*. What you *have* means little compared to what you *are.*

Important to this dialogue is that a person can actively manage the screens and perceptions, filters, and assumptions that make up our *be state*. Managing the shift requires only two things: First, one must have some notion of something different to *be*; second, one must have an *intention* to be that. Richard Feynman, the Nobel prize–winning physicist, decided to *be* an artist. He enlisted an artist's help in learning the craft of drawing and painting; he practiced and experienced *being* an artist; and in the end, he proved a sufficiently capable painter that he was able to successfully exhibit his own work. He saw "artist" as something he wanted to be, and he put out his intention, which then led him, through apprenticeship and practice, to become an artist.

From our perspective, this means that people are not necessarily *born* great musicians, athletes, or scholars. Many, in fact, choose their *be state*, and toil and hone their skills, using great drive and intention to build exceptional capability into their *be state*.

Importantly, Feynman did not decide to buy artist materials and take lessons. Those are *haves* and *dos*. Instead, he decided to *be* an artist. In such a *be state*, lessons take hold, and materials take on a different meaning. An example of the distinction is that of people trying to exercise or lose weight. Rather than deciding to *be* a slender person, people *do* something, like dieting or quitting, or decide to *have* something, like a treadmill that will substitute for *being* slender. As you might imagine, *dieter* or *exerciser* is just not how anyone thinks of himself, but "slender" is, and so is "runner." A *have* or *do* orientation is not sustainable.

This simple shift, from focusing on the *haves* and *dos* of something to seeing the *be state* of that thing, is just another way of saying "reframing." Once we have reframed ourselves into seeing a new *be state*, change can be virtually instantaneous and lasting. Absent that new frame of reference, change is impossible.

Commitment to the Team

Real commitment means that membership in the team is an *integral* part of the researcher's *be state* or worldview. In addition, a Lean researcher will have a strong sense of the innate, innovative capability of others and an interest in discovering and encouraging that capability. A Lean researcher will be interested in the cleanest path to learning, not the politics of how learning arises. Lean researchers will commit to those things that make themselves and those around them better innovators, for in doing so, they improve the ability of their community to achieve its goals.

Awareness of the Community

A team member's commitment is of little use without the context of her membership in the R&D community. If the team member has only a vague idea what her role, or the roles of others on the team, might be, she will be unable to operate effectively as an innovator. The most basic elements of that context include

- An understanding of the set of research questions that will need to be answered by the community
- An understanding of who will likely answer those questions
- An understanding of when those answers will be needed
- An understanding of whose work those answers will support
- An understanding of whose answers will support her own progress
- The method by which new questions are identified and distributed among team members (since new questions invariably arise during the course of research)
- How each researcher will coordinate and synthesize her innovations with others into the community, so that all questions are answered and the answers are smoothly integrated into a valuable package

Often this most basic community knowledge is lacking in R&D projects. People roll on and off of projects, and must often learn their project work, team roles, and responsibilities by happenstance or self-designed inquiry. Teams often form and begin work without coming together at project inception to determine the knowledge and skills gaps, technical questions, and organizational and systemic problems that must be addressed. Roles can and must be flexible to enable a team to robustly answer questions and deliver innovation, but understanding of the basic scientific and social roles a researcher is expected to fill is crucial to an individual's smooth functioning as a researcher.

Roles are just the beginning. Once the roles are known, an individual may be hindered by not knowing the other players' capabilities, interests, and tendencies. This knowledge allows team members to align their efforts far more harmoniously, mentor those who are in a new role, capitalize on those with great experience, leverage the insight of intuitive and unexpectedly creative sparks, and so on. Absent this deeper understanding of the team, people are ill equipped to produce anything but generic results based on generic execution of often brilliant individual functional output. Products often fail from such disharmony. Great hardware saddled by poor software yields consistent market failure. Great chemistry against the wrong biology fails in disease treatment, and so on. What is lost is the harmony of a unified community *be state.*

In the current world of large-company R&D, this is an especially pointed opportunity. R&D teams are nearly always composed of members chosen from many different functional groups, but with globalization, it is not unusual for people on a team to hail from Europe, India, China, and the United States. In addition to the obvious difficulties in holding real-time discussions, such distances mean that team members may never meet one another in person. In such circumstances, gaining the intimate level of common understanding demanded by a highly effective community is difficult. Yet, for all of its difficulties, a highly integrated, functioning community composed of individuals with such diverse backgrounds will have a far greater wealth of creative experience to contribute. The problem is that making and maintaining deep individual connections in this environment takes time and special commitment on the part of each individual.

Finally, without a deep understanding of the team's purpose and direction, team members will be unable to smoothly integrate their creativity into that of the team's progress. This is important because the situation in science shifts constantly. A new product or process emerges in the market. A paper is published answering questions with direct or implied relevance. People leave the company, others join. Team skill sets are redundant in some areas, while other skill sets are missing. By understanding the team's purpose and direction, individuals in the community can always be contributing positively to the community.

This understanding is often sorely lacking in R&D and is, in my view, a primary cause of the R&D management problem commonly known as "herding cats." Scientists, engineers, and other researchers, being creative, independent-minded people, generate their own purpose and direction in the absence of a commitment to an easily identifiable and understandable aligning force. Absent such an aligning force, integrating individual creativity into a harmonious, valuable knowledge package is a challenge.

Synthesizing these elements into a sports analogy may help. In team sports, there are "stop and reset" sports, and there are what I call "flow sports." Football and rugby are largely the same sport,* but the former is played in stop and reset mode, the latter in flow mode. In flow sports, like hockey, soccer, and basketball, there is a free flow of action across the entire playing surface for indefinite periods of time. Teams that come together without knowledge of other players (pickup games) rely significantly on individuals to assess and interact on the playing field with whatever skills they came with, capitalizing on whatever clues and capabilities they can glean from other players in the short time they spend together. Without knowing something about the other team members and their potential roles and abilities, it is difficult for even accomplished players to maximize the capability of the team.

By contrast, teams who play together regularly and have had much longer to observe their compatriots can generate more complicated and, in all likelihood, more successful patterns of play, based on emerging events on the field. People who play together regularly are less likely to cover the same part of the field and are more likely to split, with one player going after the ball or puck and the other moving to a position to either block an opponent or become free to receive a pass. Real teams— teams that practice together, build strategies together, drill together, and spend real quality time outside of the play together—develop an intimate knowledge of where and when various scenarios will emerge. With *intimate* knowledge of the other team members' capabilities, far more valuable options are available. With community commitment to certain plays and strategies, new opportunities open up. Specific roles emerge and refine themselves. Individual understanding of, and *trust* in, other players enable a team to operate with "touch" that cannot be read by opponents, only marveled at in replay.

The reason for building on commitment and community first is that absolute player skill means less than community cohesion and synthesis. Take, for example, the following sports commentary about the 2004 U.S. men's Olympic basketball "Dream Team" on their loss to Argentina:

---

* With apologies to fans of both sports, who will rightly argue their intrinsic differences.

The Americans gave Argentina credit, but the fact remained that a big part of the U.S. team's loss was its fundamental weaknesses: a lack of familiarity with each other.

—**AP wire service**

More likely it [their loss] was because they simply aren't a team, but a collection of people with a lot of individual skill.

—**Mike Celizic, NBC.com**

You might think science was different. Sports stars, after all, make decisions and act instantaneously on physical things. But the sciences are exactly the same. If you know intimately what work is being done elsewhere, you can make immediate, pointed passes of knowledge emerging from your own laboratory. This enables the recipient to modify her experiments to capitalize on the best possible knowledge available at any given moment. Likewise, individual skill sets, especially those gained outside of work and otherwise invisible to you, are invaluable to progress, especially when gaining the most from younger researchers who have not yet established themselves. Young researchers invariably have skill sets unavailable to the older crowd. Right now, young researchers are wizards at social networking and "wiki" pages that allow fast transfer of information. If allowed to, these researchers will build methods of knowledge transfer that play at speeds unheard of in the days of electronic mail, let alone typewriters and onion skin. Tapping such skills creates three valuable outcomes: First, the science is enriched with greater capability; second, younger scientists gain valuable stature and confidence at a faster rate of speed; finally, the natural chasm between old and young is bridged or filled more quickly with far less disaffection, strengthening the culture.

Creating such a community, and making it inviting for individuals to join, will be covered in Chapters 7, 10, and 11.

Skill at Learning

Nothing can possibly take away from the talents and skills of the best and brightest, and this is the third element required of an individual working within a functioning Lean R&D team. In serving the wider R&D community's purpose (that of creating a knowledge package to answer a valuable innovation question), the individual must have some skill in generating knowledge that answers innovation questions. A portion of the individual's skill may be aligned with a technical niche, which can only be built up through experience in a field, but a greater portion of skill is an individual's basic proficiency in identifying and answering useful questions, that is, in *structured learning*.

Unfortunately, structured learning is not commonly taught in schools, nor is it systematically grown within most companies. Although interesting and valuable questions surround us throughout our lives, we are rarely taught a method for differentiating the valuable from the merely interesting. Worse, we are taught to order those things that we see into our worldview, so that we see questions, and their answers, from a narrower and narrower perspective. This has a certain type of value, in that we can generate quick answers to questions that present themselves, but as we grow older, we lose even the ability to see those wonderful, interesting, and potentially valuable questions. We are so used to categorizing and reacting to the *type* of question with rote processes that we do not recognize a new question when it presents itself. We are therefore poorly prepared to identify useful questions to answer.

An example is in order. Some time ago, I had the uncomfortable pleasure of watching a dialogue between a leadership team and a consultant. One of the leadership team members said how great their new organization and its processes would be. The consultant asked how he knew the organization and its processes would be great. The leader got a bit red in the face, because he heard that question not as inquiry, but as a specific denunciation of the team's plan. It took fully ten minutes for the leader to understand that the consultant was asking him to reflect on two completely different thought processes: how the leadership team was defining and measuring success ("great" is an indistinct measure of success), and what thought processes that leader held that would cause him to state something unknowable about the future as defined fact.

In the end, the leader's dialogue showed several disturbing traits. First, the solutions provided by the leadership team's plan were a form of *non sequitur*. They were solutions all right, but they did not address the problems facing the organization. Second, the leader (in fact, the leadership team as a whole) was not aware that their solutions were not connected to their strategic problem. Third, when going about creating the solutions, the leadership team had not set performance goals for the solutions to achieve. As a result, they could not devise measures to tell if their plan was succeeding, and by how much. There would be no way that the leadership team would know what had happened, positively or negatively, as a result of implementing their solutions. In fact, the leadership team did not have a hypothesis in mind for what the causes of their problems were, nor had they even considered proposing hypotheses. They had jumped straight from a problem to their internalized category of solutions and fired.

It has been pointed out to me that the creation of these problem-solution patterns is to allow highly efficient thought. It enables us to see "angry bear" and think "run" without muddling the process with intervening thoughts about how nicely the sun glints off the bear's fur. This is terrific when faced with an angry bear where *time efficiency* is the valued commodity. Mostly, when it comes to business or scientific problem solving or question answering, time efficiency is no match for *solution efficiency*. In other words, we often find that the right answer beats a fast answer.

Nevertheless, we often continue to believe that a fast answer is the best answer. Why we have come to think this way is largely irrelevant if we have a way to reverse the trend. It turns out that this is not only possible, but relatively straightforward through the application of learning loops.

Learning is largely done by a series of decision–action–assessment cycles, each building some new experience that, when integrated with other experiences, builds knowledge. These decision–action–assessment cycles are known as "learning loops." The scientific method is the most famous of these. It connects a scientific problem with some background knowledge of the problem; develops hypotheses on what causes that problem and considers how these hypotheses can be tested, understood, and/or addressed; and then executes those tests to illuminate the validity of those hypotheses, which then, if all goes swimmingly, allows us to resolve the original scientific problem.

Getting back to our example, the most intriguing thing to me is that every member of that leadership team came with impressive scientific credentials. Some were chemists; others were biologists; still others were material scientists of one description or another. Every one of them had a PhD. Some had been admitted to rarified international scientific bodies. Yet not a single one had set up their business problem using anything remotely resembling a learning loop, let alone a rigorous, experimentally based scientific approach. They were using fast thinking, not good or structured thinking, and they had the results to prove it.

The scientific method is one well-established learning loop, and there are many other structured learning methods as well. Lean practitioners will recognize Deming's learning loop, the so-called Plan-Do-Check-Act (PDCA) cycle. Military types will recognize Boyd's Observe-Orient-Decide-Act (OODA) loop. Nearly any learning loop that forces a reflective, empirical structure on problem solving will work to sharpen thinking. Our leadership team could have used PDCA, for example, or OODA and created vastly different results, because their structured thinking would not have led to a *belief* in their future success. They would have been thinking instead about leading assessments, alternative approaches they might consider if certain outcomes appeared, and so on. Belief would have been replaced with capability, and capability would have served them in matters strategic and tactical.

It is my strong belief that structured learning is structured learning. People who use PDCA, OODA, and the scientific method are engaging in the same thing. Which method you use is largely unimportant, with a few exceptions. People have different reactions to language. Different words create subtly, or even greatly, different understanding in the minds of different people. As a result, the language and mechanics (if being structurally rigorous) of each learning loop create nuances of thinking. We resonate with some, and others leave us cold,* but understanding and practicing different forms of structured learning bring a different level and subtlety to our thinking, and this brings me to the point of this section. As a member of a Lean R&D community, my most valuable contribution is my ability to think well. If I study and practice nothing else, I must study and improve the quality and the speed of my learning as defined by problem solving or question answering. The faster and better I can answer complicated questions related to my community, the more likely we will be to deliver high-quality innovations at a rate faster than our competitors.

I am almost agnostic on the point of where anyone should start in developing this practice. Every learning loop provides valuable insight and capability to your learning processes. Every one of these loops will

---

* I am notoriously incompetent with Deming's PDCA loop. The language trips me up when I try to think through it, and this causes me to describe it poorly, hence I use it infrequently. For other people, PDCA is as natural as walking, and they use it religiously and well. I invite you to find your own structure and style, it will work beautifully.

make you a better thinker, *if you practice it explicitly*. Again, a quick metaphor may prove helpful. Musicians practice scales early in their career. This gives them quickness on their instrument. It gives them feel. It gives them the structure of the scale itself, helping them remain on-key during complicated passages. It generally builds skills by providing structure. Athletes do drills. Drills help tennis players set their feet in positions that allow them to hit the ball well, allow them to recover for the next shot, and so on. In both music and sports, there are many people who are just naturally talented. For those people, it is very easy to attain or demonstrate considerable skill. It is consequently easy for these same people to rely on talent rather than practice or the technique that it engenders. Later, people who have spent the time and effort to develop good skills surpass these talented but unpracticed people.

But as the scientific method is not explicitly directive, it is easy to *say* you followed it, without actually doing the hard work of writing things down and following them up. The same is true of PDCA, OODA, and the rest. Like lifting weights carelessly, we can easily fall into bad habits, which allow our skills to deteriorate, or to develop in ways that stunt our overall capability.

With this in mind, I suggest starting to practice and deepen your already considerable learning skills by using the A3 format. An A3, as we will learn in Chapter 5, is not a learning loop, but a structured learning format on a single piece of paper. Following the A3 format is like doing the scientific equivalent of musical scales. It is explicit practice for our thinking processes. It exposes areas where our skills are weak. It helps us learn good thinking skills, perhaps slowly at first, but with time, we will accelerate to the point where the scientific thinking process is ingrained within us, where we use it in our everyday observations and engagement with the wider world, where it is, in the end, a part of our *be state*.

PULLING IT TOGETHER

Lean can only really exist within a community setting, and when it does, those communities invariably operate at much higher performance levels than their peers. In manufacturing, Lean companies eventually overtake their rivals, almost no matter where, in terms of size or initial performance, the rivals begin. In R&D, Lean communities outdeliver their counterparts by astonishing margins, delivering double, triple, and greater levels of performance compared to their peers.

But a Lean community is composed of individuals working harmoniously toward common and universally understood innovation goals. In order to serve that community well, each individual must understand the framework of innovation needs required by that community, must bring exceptionally capable thinking skills to answer those innovation needs, and bring a commitment to the success of that community and those within it. In the next chapters, we will dive first into structures and drills that individuals can use to support their thinking and innovation; then we will spend some time on how to create community structures that support identifying and communicating existing and emergent community need, so that individual innovation can link seamlessly across the community. Finally, we will dive into structures that can transform communities and, for large organizations, strategic approaches to build Lean communities and systems across the global locations and functions that comprise modern conglomerate R&D enterprises.

4

Lean Exercises for the R&D Professional

SEEING

If you have ever seen an exceptional scientist or engineer in action, you probably noted that the person could just "see" things that you could not. Such people see problems that others miss, causes that seem to be removed from the immediate problem, implications of observations that others just cannot comprehend, and so on. This ability to see need not be unique to them; it can be learned by anyone and is crucial to becoming a Lean researcher.

Seeing in this sense requires the ability to observe without assumptions. As we saw in Chapter 1, our mental framework and assumptions put our raw observations in context. It tells us that one observation is important, but that another one is insignificant. It tells us that this observation builds to a conclusion, that nothing useful can be gleaned from a different observation. Our mental models create the context in which we winnow apparently useful from apparently useless observations. The observable universe is so large and complex that our mental models serve mostly to help us focus on a narrow set of observations that allow us to take action. It enables our ability, more than anything else, to tune out the din of the observable so that we can focus our limited observational capability. If that narrow capacity observes the right things (tigers about to pounce), we can take meaningful action. If it observes the wrong things (flowers near the tiger, but not the tiger), then our actions will be meaningful, but ultimately disastrous. In essence, our mental models are there to focus observation on information that leads to problem solving. Using the important information, we can quickly identify and pursue the best possible option(s).

For obvious reasons, this winnowing is incredibly valuable. It is also exceptionally limiting, because it means our problem solving is limited entirely by the scope and inflexibility of our mental framework. We are in big trouble, for example, if that tiger has a full belly, but the flower is camouflaging an enemy with a blow gun.

The problem is that our mental models, like Newtonian physics, are exceptionally condensed visions of reality that we carry around in our heads. Useful as they may be, their simplicity, which is the result of this condensation of reality, means they are *always* massively incomplete, hence subtly or substantially wrong, depending on context. Newton's mechanics, for example, are sufficiently precise for most walking-around work, but they break down to pure uselessness outside of their limited range of time, speed, and scale.

Importantly, the usefulness of our models often leads us to forget that they are only useful in a narrow range and, therefore, we often use their winnowing implications to eliminate observations that would otherwise lead us to greater insight. Einstein was not swayed by the assumptions of Newtonian physics ingrained in other physicists' minds and was able, therefore, to absorb rather than cast aside as unimportant observations that had been building among other scientists for decades. By accepting the importance of these previously discarded observations, Einstein was able to synthesize the science of physics in an entirely new and valuable way.

A few examples from polymer science might be useful. More than a billion kilograms of polycarbonate plastic are synthesized every year. Because of its scale, it is manufactured in large plants that cost hundreds of millions of dollars to build. In these plants, powders and (usually) pellets of the plastic are formed, which are then shipped to plastics customers who melt, cast, or extrude these pellets into shapes and forms for final use.

If we lock onto these original assumptions—big plants, big chemistry, pellet forms, etc.—we limit ourselves to improving the existing process. We could, for example, go from "solution" phase synthesis to "interfacial" synthesis of the polymer. These two approaches use the same basic infrastructure. We might look at different chemistries but, again, assume they need to be scaled up to megaton production rates. This assumption might result in the choice of melt processing as an answer to the problem. However, this approach fails to consider the opportunity of utilizing the end user as a manufacturer. In this case, truly ingenious chemists identified ways that a plastics parts manufacturer could insert the right raw materials into its extruder, where polymerization would take place, and out would come high-quality polycarbonate. Connected directly to a part mold, the extruder could go from raw material to a completed product at need on the customer's production floor and eliminate entirely the need for a polycarbonate manufacturing plant.

Meanwhile, "composite" parts, like fiberglass and carbon fiber pieces, are not made using polycarbonate plastic (they are not made using thermoplastics in general). This is largely because composite manufacturing often involves workers handling steps that are suited to room-temperature work, while the formation of thermoplastics, like polycarbonate, requires melting and manipulation that can only be done at high temperature. If we stick to that assumption, we will never use polycarbonate in the manufacture of composites. However, if we are open to the idea that other forming opportunities are possible, we will see that there are chemical routes to fluid polycarbonate precursors that could be used in composite manufacturing.

By being open to other areas of thought—in this case, adjacent clues from customer infrastructure or customer needs—we can identify pathways to new, potentially valuable innovations. If we believe exclusively in a single viewpoint, then we will continue to pursue the same means and deliver the same ends.

The best scientists and engineers "see" without the baggage of mental models that lead others to pursue false, limiting, or damaging actions. Seeing without the baggage of mental models reduces the chance of making automatic decisions that might otherwise lead to potentially incorrect paths. Operating with fewer or less rigidly attached mental models enables the best engineers to see more potential paths than the rest of us, one or many of which might prove an easier, better, or more robust path than our current thinking allows. Our first skill-building exercise, then, is to create the ability to see as these scientists and engineers, the ability to see without the baggage of mental frameworks that narrow and interfere with our ability to observe holistically.

Toyota does this exact skill-building exercise by making new managers and pupils of Lean stand within a circle on the shop floor. The pupil is to observe closely the action on the shop floor, capturing the context of the work, the work itself, nonessential and essential observations alike. Unsurprisingly, the difficulty faced by these students is that they come with mental models that limit their ability to observe well all of the actions and nuances going on in front of them. By sending the pupil back to observe from within that same circle for day after day, the teacher brings the student to the point where his mental models no longer hold sway, and he is open to observing everything before him. He is open to the widest possible understanding.

Skill-Building Exercise 1: Seeing without Prior Mental Context

Most of us cannot be brought out of our regular jobs for two to three weeks to do nothing but stand in a circle observing, so the Toyota model probably will prove impractical. However, we have the advantage of knowing the purpose (learning to observe without prior mental context), the mechanics (do nothing but observe intently), and the time it takes to achieve the exercise's purpose (perhaps eight hours a day, five days a week, for two to three weeks, or about 100 hours). Armed with this knowledge, we can create hypotheses in identifying new exercises that may achieve the same or similar results. For example, if we just observed the same thing intently for 2 hours a day over 50 days, we might achieve the same result.

This approach might be fairly straightforward for most people. For example, you could try this exact experiment if you commute one hour to work by train. You could observe intently the goings on of the station, the train, the rail employees, and the commuters as they go about their business. You could write these things down; measure times, spaces, and conversations; make diagrams about flow and activity; and absorb without being judgmental. At some point, I believe the whole thing will begin to unravel your mental models about trains and commuting, the reasons *you* imagined to be right and good or wrong and bad about trains and rail commuting. Simultaneously with the removal of your imagined rules and thoughts, you will suddenly see actions and interactions, assumptions and underlying capabilities that limit, enable, and define rail transit. You will see things that no other person has observed, and you will suddenly be in a position to think and act completely differently about train travel. At this point, you would have made the breakthrough that the Toyota trainers were building in their students. You would have attained the skill of observing without prejudice, and you will be able to apply that new capability literally anywhere.

To build this skill, then, identify something that recurs daily in your life, and observe it closely for an extended period of time. Keep this up until the day that the whole thing shifts, the day that you see it very, very differently, the day that you can no longer believe you thought your prior thoughts about that part of your life and a new sensibility takes hold. It will take a while.

Since this book deals so much with the barriers that separate people, hence hinder our ability to create collaboratively, a similar exercise is worth considering in "seeing" our beliefs about other people. To tee this exercise up, I would like to remind (or introduce) readers to an episode of the once popular television show *M*A*S*H* in which two of the main characters, Hawkeye Pierce and B.J. Hunnicutt, who are best friends, decide that they would fake arguments between each other as a present to their much detested tent mate Frank Burns. Since Frank detests them in equal measure, they believe (correctly) that this prank will put Frank in a good mood. In order to pull this off, Hawkeye and B.J. argue about the mundane things that normally annoy people with whom you share close space. How you brush your teeth, the way that you clean your side of the tent, and so on.

Normally, by labeling someone as a "friend," our mental models filter out, or label as harmless, those traits of a person that annoy us. Similarly, labeling someone as an "enemy" or some equally distasteful descriptor sensitizes our mental model to the foibles of that person. Every annoying trait is amplified, and things that are not normally annoying to us are raised to the point of irritation. Hawkeye and B.J. continue the ruse for a significant period of time. They eventually tell Frank it was all a ruse, but by the time that has happened, each has offended the other and sown doubt as to the depth and quality of their friendship. They not only eroded the mental model "friend," but began to put in place mental models associated with enmity and incivility.

It is my experience that the Hawkeye/B.J. experiment, which created a certain enmity and eroded friendship, can be reversed and used to create friendships and erode enmity. It can be used to remove barriers to seeing people negatively and enable the observer to begin creating pathways to closer working relationships.

To connect with others, you could do an analogous exercise to the commuter experiment suggested previously. By creating in your mind a completely new set of mental models about a person, and observing behaviors that *support* your newly composed mental models, you will eventually see that person very differently than you do now. Take someone you currently detest. Consider everything you believe about that person. He is unkind, uncaring, not trustworthy, etc. Now change completely your mental models of that person. Assume that you like that person. Imagine that person is a good, humane, caring, kind, and trustworthy person. In fact, take every one of your negative perceptions and reverse it. Then, observe all of the actions the person takes that support your new belief system while closing off observations that undermine your new beliefs. For example, if you believed the person to be unkind, assume the person is kind, and only allow the person's kind actions to filter into your consciousness. If you believed the person to be stupid or thoughtless, assume the person is brilliant and caring, and allow only those observations that support the new assumptions to enter your mind. When the new assumptions start to take hold, you will have learned to see aspects of someone you hadn't recognized before, and, at that point, you can try dropping your assumptions about that person entirely in order to see that person as a whole.

As we saw in Chapter 1, the power of assumption is rarely more clearly demonstrated than in the sciences. Newton's laws, the mental models of physics from the time he enunciated them until Einstein's relativistic theories were adopted early in the twentieth century, were clearly stated. Everyone could look at them and examine them. They were explained in very simple, easily comprehended mathematical terms. In those intervening hundreds of years, people could not imagine their fundamental incorrectness. They were not merely believed to be correct in the main, but, in fact, any other set of assumptions were necessarily believed to be *incorrect*. Further, if other assumptions *must* be incorrect, we stop seeing them as assumptions at all. Our ability to operate as thinking beings in this space begins to fail.

"Seeing without prejudice" is only one of two main seeing skills necessary to Lean. The second is the ability to see the assumptions by which we separate ourselves from the wider universe. The Newtonian example shows the effects of subsuming our ability to see assumptions about science, but the same applies with people as well. In the earlier exercise of seeing someone we dislike as the whole person, I suggested that we adopt the opposite of the negative beliefs we hold about that person. In essence, I asked you to identify your assumptions about that person and reframe them.

It is often easy to identify what we don't like about someone, and note that we formed those beliefs based on a set of observations. By examining what we believe about that person, we can identify how those beliefs color our observations, how that coloration affects our actions, and how those actions might affect our relationship with that person. This is not to suggest that we will or even should like everyone, but to note that our beliefs *affect how we see people* and that we can, by analyzing those beliefs, come to see them more holistically, and, one hopes, interact more appropriately with them. To even start down this road, we must see our beliefs.

Skill-Building Exercise 2: Seeing Beliefs

Most of us have beliefs about research and development (R&D), its operations, and its capabilities. For example, you may believe that innovation cannot be scheduled. If you believe this, you will not attempt to schedule innovation, which may, given other assumptions, be a pretty good idea. Importantly, however, you will not look to see where and how innovation scheduling has been attempted, where those efforts have succeeded and failed. You will not wonder why those failures occurred, nor will you believe that actual successes have occurred, let alone look to understand what might have contributed to those successes. You will not build experiments in scheduled R&D, whether to create a new way or to address those potential causes of failure identified in old ways of scheduling. You will not seek relentlessly to find a new way in which innovation can be delivered on time every time. You will not fail, but far more importantly, you will not succeed.

As researchers, we hold many different, often untested or poorly tested assumptions about R&D. These assumptions hold us back from improving R&D. They hold us back from even *seeing* what in R&D could be improved, and by how much.

Thus, in thinking about R&D, I suggest taking 30 minutes to an hour to write down every assumption you can imagine having ever held about R&D. For example, many people believe that R&D is inherently risky, or high risk. Other people believe that risk and reward are related, and that high R&D risk means high reward.* You might assume that R&D is slow or that it is fast in creating value, that R&D drives growth or diminishes opportunity, that R&D absorbs necessary resources or that it is valuable to your company. Do this again the next day until you have done it for a full week running, asking yourself each day, "What other assumptions do I hold?"

---

* This is, of course, one of the silliest mental models of all time. There are many things that are very high risk, even impossible, which, if overcome, will yield no appreciable value. There are other things that hold great value that can be done easily and simply (little or no risk) if someone merely thinks to do them.

After you complete this list, begin a follow-up exercise to see how your assumptions affect your worldview. For each item on the first list, build a second list describing how that assumption affects your vision. How does it affect your selection of projects? How does it limit or focus your improvement efforts? How does it support or diminish your interactions with others? How does it affect your decision making? Be as detailed as possible, and come back to it again and again during the following week. When this is complete, create analogous lists for manufacturing, then for sales, then for marketing, and so on.

Once you see these assumptions, it will be time to begin removing those assumptions that, by the reckoning of your second list, most affect your ability to grow the kind of environment in which your people thrive and your company succeeds. It is not quite time (yet) to act on your new ability to see, but we are getting there.

REFRAMING TO INNOVATE

Reframing is the art of shifting your mindset from its present configuration, in which a problem currently exists, into a mindset in which either the problem no longer exists, or the problem can be addressed in one, or perhaps many different ways that do not yet exist. Einstein, for example, shook off the Newtonian mindset. Thus freed, he was able to frame several current problems in physics in ways that had not previously existed. In these new frames, Einstein could explain different aspects of observed phenomena previously ignored by the Newtonian viewpoint, and as a result, the entire science of physics expanded enormously.

The engineer who can see the broken machine without assumptions can see the problem in context, and, from there, easily frame the problem in a way that it can be solved. The Lean thinker seeks to attain a state of mind that is open to many ways of perceiving human activity and human thought. In so doing, she may access one or many different ways that may hold the key to an easy solution or approach to a problem, issue, or opportunity at hand.

Reframing requires three things: First, it requires seeing the actions and underlying assumptions that lead to the current way of believing and operating. Second, it requires deconstructing the current circumstances, the states of mind in which they exist, and the experiences of the thinker, so that the associated parts can freely recombine in different and more valuable ways. Third, it requires synthesis of these parts into myriad possibilities that can then be compared (for potential value) against an aligning purpose, so that a better path can be charted.

Deconstruction and Synthesis to Increase Value Content

Most of us know our purpose when we set out on a problem-solving expedition. It might be a faster way to make something, or it may be a need to reduce resource burden, so that people can spend their time more productively elsewhere. One way to attack such a problem is to free your mind of everything you believe about it, and leave yourself only with your observations surrounding the problem (this is why seeing is so important). Keep only facts; remove any judgments, beliefs, or attitudes. Next, tear apart everything that is left. Deconstruct all of those observations and bits of fact, leaving only those items that connect, however remotely, to the purpose you are seeking to fulfill. Then, using *only* those elements connected to the purpose, synthesize a new flow of those elements. This is a new *frame* which, ironically, has gained dramatic improvement without fundamental innovation. The result you wanted was already there, all you have done is stripped away everything that was not giving you the intended result.

Done well, *value stream mapping*—a Lean manufacturing technique—is a form of deconstruction in which an entire system is distilled into elements—for example, actions, flows, and metrics. Elements that do not create value are essentially torn from the picture. Synthesis of these value-creating elements into a future state completes the value stream mapping exercise (at least the design phase).

Making Snowmobiles

The mechanical value stream mapping approach outlined here may deliver a breakthrough in terms of value creation in an existing context, but in terms of innovation, it leaves something to be desired, as no new value-creating steps have been envisioned. To create *new* value, as required for innovations, deconstruction must not merely enable removal of nonvalue steps, but it must be combined with synthesis to enable something new to emerge. Boyd calls this "building snowmobiles," his term for simultaneous destruction and creation events. Boyd, for example, suggests that creativity is linked to deconstruction into elemental pieces of things from every part of your experience, followed by the reconnection of these things in new ways or the synthesis of these elements in new contexts. Boyd suggests deconstructing a motorcycle into wheels, transmission, light but powerful motor, handlebar, control devices, and so on. A tank can be deconstructed into tracks and track drives, turret, gun, heavy motor, armor, optics, and so on, while a water ski show can be deconstructed into people, skis, ropes, boats and motors, wire and cable steering, and so forth. Synthesis of skis, light powerful motor, tracks, and handlebar controls yields a snowmobile.

In his example, Boyd is engaging the thinker in pulling apart and rebuilding his experiences of different objects, but it can equally be applied to thoughts and theories to create something new and previously unimagined. Boyd deconstructed ideas from complexity theory, thermodynamics, military history, Eastern religious teachings, his experience as a fighter pilot, psychology, quantum physics, and philosophy. From these, he synthesized, among other things, a theory of winning and losing, an "organic design" for command and control, a theory of strategy based on interaction and isolation, and the famous "Observe-Orient-Decide-Act" learning loop.

The much-heralded iPod by Apple is a prime example of innovation, combining both physical and conceptual destruction and creation. Nearly every company in the high-technology arena had access to small, high-density hard disk and solid-state storage elements. Likewise, each had access to battery power supplies and controllers, and electronic hardware, firmware, and software to operate the on-demand musical storage and retrieval functions required of the device. Further, each company had access to sufficient capability to put up a web page, or access to market digital files to users. Finally, licensing and protection of content, while difficult and time consuming, is something that has been handled by legal and software specialists in several arenas. What Apple did was to synthesize these smoothly into a new value-creating unit. They built snowmobiles.

The trick in building snowmobiles is finding the right purpose, the right direction to build snowmobiles as opposed to airmobiles (Ford's airborne flivver never became a serious mode of personal transportation). Success is complicated because, to a certain extent, it involves predicting and delivering against an unknowable customer need, and then transitioning customers from their existing value frame (what they want now) into the future value frame (where they want the new product). Thus, you can do what marketing attempts to do—figure out what current customers want that they do not already have, or you can figure out what people *will* want, even things that they cannot currently comprehend valuing (e.g., the personal computer to people in the 1960s, the Internet for people in the 1970s, etc.). The former stays within your current customers' frame, can be very valuable in new product development, and it potentially brings you outside of your own current frame of reference. The latter brings both you and your customers outside of your frames of reference into unknown areas of potential value.

To chase such an unknown frame, as Apple did with its Newton, is fraught with danger unless you can test this new frontier in low-cost, high-repetition ways. Internet service is a classic example. Thousands of businesses were tested in wild varieties of formats and web pages. Many of them succeeded, many failed, but the cost was so low that many companies could open and close with little risk until a winner emerged.

Another clear downside to breakthrough innovation is the regular success of fast followers in a given field. Many companies find that they spend a lot of time and effort, both in R&D and in marketing, developing a new idea in the global marketplace. This expensive development platform serves to define what the real market is, so that their competitors can capitalize on it quickly and cheaply. The opposite effect can also be seen. A nimble, effective, low-cost R&D effort can bury its competitors by shifting the market unexpectedly. This effect was caused by Honda in the Yamaha-Honda wars of the early 1980s, in which Honda produced, in 18 months, several times as many new motorcycle models as Yamaha. This redefined the market, rendering Yamaha's entire offering, and its installed manufacturing base, obsolete.*

As Boyd makes clear, victory accrues to the side that learns to deliver innovation fastest.

The Role of Language in Reframing for Innovation

Both value stream mapping and building snowmobiles are exceptionally useful approaches, but even taken together, I find they lack something. In

---

* George Stalk Jr. and Thomas M. Hout, *Competing against Time: How Time-Based Competition Is Reshaping Global Markets* (New York: Free Press, 1990).

the first case, the skills of value stream mapping are wonderful for increasing value content in an existing context, but don't especially build innovation. While the second case is wild with creativity, it is lacking a structure to ensure the success of innovation. You could imagine building skills around deconstructing things you come across and rebuilding them into different, never-before-envisioned things, and many of the very brightest innovators did just that starting at very early ages. Thomas Edison and Ford, for that matter, are excellent examples of people who pursued the snowmobile creation approach. But this seems a bit undirected, and one can easily envision creating dozens of "Frankenstein" contraptions of no value for every innovative object valued by other people. Enough failures, even cheap ones, will prove costly.

An alternative is to "reframe" directly through the recontexting function already built into the brain: language. When we describe problems, activities, and thoughts, we nearly always build them in the form of statements. That is, we state something like, "I drove to the store." This statement is pretty innocuous, but if we state and follow that statement many times over months and years, we will find that when we run out of food, or more precisely, one or more ingredients for the dish we wish to eat, we immediately get in the car and drive to the store to replenish our stock.

We rarely, in such cases, see these statements for what else they inevitably represent, namely, the answer to questions small and large that we come across every day. The statement, "I drove to the grocery store," is the direct answer to two questions: "How will I nourish myself?" and "How will I access that nourishment?" If I merely convert the statements into questions, then I immediately see that I can nourish myself with a different menu out of the larder, nourish myself with bar or restaurant food, nourish myself through the grace of neighbors, friends, family or strangers (e.g., charity soup kitchen), or any of a host of other options from fishing to thievery. If I then have the answer to that first question in mind, the means available to access the food will shift. If I maintain my fixation on the grocery store, I could drive, walk, take a bus, hitchhike, beg a ride from a neighbor, call parents, or any of a number of other means. If I choose to eat fish, I may kayak out onto a lake or ocean and get it directly, wait at the docks for the fishermen to come in, or, again, I could go to the grocery store.

Now, think about the most basic things we do in R&D. We analyze or test samples. I will bet that in your R&D department, you have a set way of analyzing or testing prototypes of a given type. In pharmaceuticals for example, we run a battery of assays that test newly synthesized chemicals. One assay will tell us how well it "hits" the intended protein target. A second will tell us how it hits a certain toxic trigger (a sign that the molecule is poisonous). A third assay tests for another aspect crucial to our understanding of drug treatment, and so on. We go through this same battery of tests for every molecule we make, but is that needed? What question are we trying to answer with this new molecule? Are we trying to eliminate a certain toxic factor? Then the toxic screens are most crucial, but others may not tell us anything useful. Are we trying to get a lower dose? Then our "potency" assay will be crucial. While the parameters that a molecule must hit are multifaceted, the learning required is often centered in specific areas. By not assuming we need to run all tests, but instead asking "what do we need to learn?" we can devise different paths (some potentially better, some potentially worse) to get to our end result.

This is one of the simplest examples imaginable in R&D, but we have mental barriers even at this level. Without thinking about the opportunity to change even such simple pathways to knowledge, it will never enter our minds that we can make even small breakthroughs in the speed of learning.

As in the previous example, we find very quickly that our early testing designs, our earliest experiments, even the language that we use limit the options that we are able to see and select. The implications of even the *simplest* statements are immense, but we don't see them because the statements themselves have been loaded with answers and their inherent assumptions. By converting statements directly into questions, we can immediately and effortlessly reframe nearly anything, opening our minds to meaningful innovation options; inviting us to bring in our experiences, dissected or whole; inducing us to consider our current circumstances, deconstructed or synthesized as they sit—all without once engaging our assumptions.

Consider our polycarbonate example. How many different ways can we think of to synthesize polycarbonate? What is the smallest manufacturing footprint I can envision? What equipment do we have available in the laboratory? What equipment is available in the manufacturing plant? What equipment do our customers have? What kinds of products do other plastics serve? What other materials are not replaceable (yet) by plastics? None of these questions has a single answer. None of these questions has even a static set of answers. If Ford buys our plastic, then surely they have different equipment coming and going in every plant nearly every day of the year. This dynamic adds to the opportunity space opened by questions.

Answering any of these questions could yield a new product or a new process. Answering any of these questions with better or even different quality of answer than our last answer could yield a new product, process, market, or an increase in market share. A friend of mine, Michael Moore, noted that "questions bypass the censor." Indeed, questions bypass our basic thinking filters, opening our thoughts to many options otherwise closed to us.

Skill-Building Exercise 3: Reframing by Converting Statements into Questions

This exercise is quite simple: Just identify things about you and then convert their presence into the underlying questions that they answer. A pickup truck is the answer to what question(s)? What question is a garage the answer to? The CEO's new initiative is the answer to what question? Our newest product feature is addressing what question asked by our customers? My new experiment answers what question that will ultimately allow us to deliver an innovation? Do this many, many times, and keep a list of intriguing questions that cross your path.

The next step in reframing—the need to answer some questions is obviated by answering a different, perhaps simpler question or set of questions—will eventually leap out at you. For example, if you have an electronic car door opener, you do not need to answer the question, "What door handle design will be required?" If you have a new extruder-based polycarbonate synthesis, you will not be asking where to build a plant, but instead, you will be asking how to get raw materials into and out of your customer's facilities.

The final step in reframing is to convert the remaining questions into robust sets of alternative answers. What other answers could be formulated to answer that same question?

Skill-Building Exercise 4: Seeing and Reframing through Value Stream Mapping

On a sheet of paper, use three steps to map the activities associated with performing a complicated task. First, name all of the activities you perform in doing that task. Second, arrange them in the sequence that these activities are performed (show arrows between activities to make the flow obvious—sometimes there are rework or learning loops). Third, add three simple metrics for each activity. Note the cycle time, which is the total amount of time that step took, from incoming work available to hand off to the next step. Next, note the processing time for each step, which answers the question: "How much time was actually spent doing the work of that step?" Finally, note the first-pass quality of each step. That is, what is the percent of time the work is fully complete and accurate, multiplied by the amount of completeness and accuracy of the work itself. This metric is an indication of how often the customer step gets exactly what it needs to do its work—no more and no less—based on one pass through your process.*

In this exercise, practice mapping processes around you. They can be as simple as mowing your yard or as complex as mapping the activity in the company cafeteria at lunchtime. They can be as concrete as our mowing or food service work examples, or as abstract as the thought processes you used to create the last monthly report or develop the last switch mechanism. The more practice you get in identifying the elements of physical and knowledge work and their value in supporting others, the more easily you will be able to configure them into a new paradigm of quality and speed.

In reframing, analyze the map. Identify barriers to easy progression of the work, barriers to completeness of the work, barriers to work accuracy, places where work stops or pools. Then see if you can configure the work to double its speed or deliver 100 percent accurate and complete work on the first try. Try to think about ways that you can get it done with half the work. Finally, try to think of something that, if done, would eliminate the need for you to engage in that value stream at all. Mowing, for example, could be eliminated if you had Astroturf, a stone garden, a meadow, or a maintenance-free ground cover. This does not mean you want to remove your lawn, but as a thought exercise, it provides fodder for thinking differently about landscaping than if you just went out to buy a few shrubs.

Skill-Building Exercise 5: Reframing by Making Snowmobiles

This exercise requires mentally or, better yet, physically deconstructing items and thought processes around you. If you have children, they come with a built-in mechanism for making snowmobiles. Deconstructing their

---

* See, for example, Mike Rother and John Shook, *Learning to See: Value Stream Mapping to Add Value and Eliminate Muda* (Cambridge, MA: Lean Enterprise Institute, 1999).

broken toys has the advantage of no downside loss and tremendous upside gain if you can synthesize (repair or modify) the parts at hand to make a working toy (not necessarily exactly like the one your child broke in the first place) and make your child happy. Just seeing how things go together will give you new ideas about how to synthesize other things in your life.

In the absence of toys to rebuild, nearly anything can serve, but some things, like motor vehicles, have potentially expensive repercussions. If you are a tinkerer, you know this already. For those without this bent, care is in order, but breaking things is a great way to learn to fix them and build confidence at the same time you build experience in reframing.

Making "mental snowmobiles" is less costly, but nonetheless valuable. It is easy to absorb new ideas because you can find them literally everywhere. There are, for example, a host of different approaches to government that have been tried. The Quakers use a model of 100 percent consensus to govern their order, while the autocrat requires consensus of exactly one person. Anarchy has no government, while the myriad economic models, both micro and macro, provide mechanisms for the control of markets. Meanwhile, there are myriad ways of influencing people, from the coercive to the passive; there are myriad religious models and theologies—the potential list of conceptual fodder for snowmobile synthesis is endless.

By observing these models with as much context as possible and then taking them apart—considering their elements and how these elements and systems worked in their context, how these elements connect to one another and, hence, possibly to other different concepts, and so on—a rich tapestry of ideas around social environments will emerge. This tapestry of ideas and contexts will prove invaluable not only in the dismantling of unsuccessful and damaging elements in the environments around you, but it will prove invaluable in designing, testing, and building successful, flourishing environments as well.

Reframing is the element of life (and Lean) that is most crucial to *change*. You must see to be able to reframe; you must reframe to be able to change. It is also the most crucial element of innovation and especially breakthrough innovation. Without reframing, Einstein is just a guy with wild hair, not an icon of physics. Without reframing, Ohno is just a machine shop manager, not the person who saw manufacturing as an experimental playground, and certainly not the person who saw a flow-based rather than scale-based paradigm for efficiency. Your ability to reframe, as scientist or R&D manager, defines in many respects the trajectory of your company's innovation level. Reframe well and often, and your company will soon find itself in unexpectedly valuable places. Maintain the same frames of reference, and your company's R&D will stagnate and wither.

THE VALUE OF EXPERIENCE IN INNOVATION

Experience holds a twofold meaning in this context. The first is straight-forward: Experience is the stored and accessible things that happened to you and around you. Musashi, the legendary swordsman of Japan, stressed the importance of studying (through hands-on experience) as many different aspects of life as possible. These experiences help the swordsman see other things useful in battle while enriching his life. Musashi himself studied art, calligraphy, as wide a variety of weapons as possible, as wide a range of martial arts styles (methods of using weapons) as possible, agriculture, music, and so on.*

A much more modern example, Richard Feynman, the Nobel Prize–winning physicist, studied physics of course, but he also traveled and studied other sciences like chemistry and biology; he studied arts and became an accomplished (and commercially successful) painter; he studied bongo drums, and a host of other subjects. Sports, art, music, engineering, mechanics, horticulture, building and repair, travel, writing, literature, and so on contribute different things to our experiences, building a broader, thicker tapestry of ideas and knowledge for us to synthesize when we reframe our world. The broader the experience base, the more radically the frame can shift in scale, dimension, and perspective.

But this is only half of the picture. Experience is also what we create. We design our travel schedules to see wonders and beauty. We design our studies to ensure we get a deep understanding of Gregorian chants and a broad understanding of their role within theological music. We study the successes of our company and its failures in an effort to understand how we might repeat or surpass our successes and avoid our past mistakes. Reframing gives us the hypotheses to test; experience provides us the means and activities to develop valuable, tangible understanding that we can use to continue shifting and improving our frames of reference.

---

* Miyamoto Musashi, *The Book of Five Rings*, trans. Thomas Cleary (Boston: Shambhala, 2000).

In this respect, it is important to consider a few of Ohno's concepts that might prove valuable in the development of experience. First, consider scale. If an experiment costs $1 billion, the work of the entire R&D staff, and five years to execute, it will hold a lot of risk unless the experiment delivers useful value under all possible outcomes. (It is possible, if not necessarily straightforward, to design such experiments, but just because they can be done does not mean these are the best use of your time.) As a result, it will not only be very difficult to gain experience in this way, but, first, you will only gain experiences around this single concept and no other, and, second, you will have a hard time justifying all of the costs in work, funds, and opportunity that this experience will require.

By contrast, it is very easy to design an experiment that you can do today, this hour, or even this minute that will yield some valuable insight. Moreover, it is pretty easy to convince yourself to try the low-cost, low-effort, and still valuable experiment. If it does not work out, there will be no political risk and little loss of time or money. Meanwhile, if it does work out, much could be gained. This concept is exactly the same as Ohno's vision of one-piece flow (taking the smallest, most elegant route to an answer) for the innovative engine. If you design the smallest possible experiment to build the knowledge required, then you will be much better positioned than someone else designing a much larger experiment. Experiments often deliver learning that was not predicted by their designers; hence, the designer who has the most opportunity to experiment, learn, and change direction will invariably succeed over the one whose experiments are based on slow, high-risk approaches. More experiments means more practice with this thought process, and that will yield additional benefits because a search for the smallest and simultaneously most informative experiment teaches experimental elegance. Your experiments will become increasingly insightful, easier, less costly, and more fun to do.

Velocity is another important aspect of Lean R&D. While it is true that one-piece flow implies taking the smallest, richest, and most elegant route to an answer, capacity results from the rate of flow itself. Analogous to takt time, the rates at which an experiment is designed and tested, observations are made, and the mental frame reassessed determine the *speed* of innovation. Answering the right questions supports the *direction* of innovation. Taken together, the vector of speed and direction gives the velocity of innovation. The depth or quality of your answers is akin to the *mass* of the innovation. The momentum of your R&D efforts is no different than the Newtonian momentum vector, which is the product of speed and mass in a given direction. In R&D, momentum is the speed at which a project team answers the right questions in the appropriate depth to yield value.

Skill-Building Exercise 6: Improving Innovation Experience through Daily Experimental Practice

If we continue in our assertion that it takes practice to develop skills, and that more practice delivers better results, then designing and running experiments—skills that scientists use regularly—can be dramatically improved through daily use. If you have been doing the seeing and reframing exercises, use your seeing and reframing output as fodder for an experimental-design exercise. Once you have something reframed, say, the path of a barista in a coffee shop or the quality of bolt tensioning in videogame consoles, then you are well positioned to think of three or five or 100 different ways to perform that task or deliver that piece of knowledge (if reframing has brought you to a question). This exercise is to see *how many* different ways you can design a way to test your new frame, which can then lead effortlessly into selecting several good ones that you can test and experience in the physical world. Test as many as you can, and hone your ability to design the elegant experiment well, so that you can more quickly learn and grow.

GROWING YOURSELF AND YOUR ENVIRONMENT

Growth is entirely about stretching. When we grow, we stretch our capabilities. We become faster or more facile at something. We gain nuances of understanding and expression we did not previously imagine. We stretch our ability to communicate and influence others. We stretch the depths of understanding we can produce. We stretch the elegance of our thinking.

For me, this leads inexorably to the question, "Where to stretch?" The answer, again, is the same as before: toward an environment in which people can choose to flourish. If I build my capability to see things as they are, I will set myself up to find the most insightful concept or observation, no matter how insignificant it might first appear. If I build my capability to generate hypotheses, devise critical questions, and reframe my assumptions, I will have set myself up nicely to try experiences that yield breakthrough learning against my own and my community's purpose. If I pursue those experiences and measure their progress against my new frames, I will generate the most valuable possible learning toward our purpose. In sharing that learning, I will have provided my best opportunity to improve the environment and our ability to flourish within it.

Ohno was faced with a company in a cash crisis. To improve the company's ability to flourish, he did whatever he could to help out. He thought about cash flow and saw that inventory was tying up working capital. By ruthlessly eliminating inventory, he freed up capital to enable more finished goods to roll off the line. He thought about cash flow and saw that scrap and damage meant both cost of materials and cost of rework. By ruthlessly pursuing quality, the amount of scrap and damage dropped and, again, the cost of materials and rework fell along with it. He thought about demand fluctuations and saw that if he arranged machines in certain configurations, one worker could execute each machine operation one at a time at a slow rate, while two could operate half the machines at twice the speed, and so on. A factory with fixed equipment could operate at variable levels by dynamically balancing staffing in a "cell." He thought about manufacturing variety with small inventory, and connected his studies of supermarkets to come up with new ways to supply production. Ohno observed his company's situation, he observed his available resources, and he reframed them in a way that his environment could be successful. In so doing, Toyota could, and did, flourish in a time of great stress, and as a result, Toyota grew.

Growth is the fulfilled promise of connecting *seeing, reframing,* and *experience* to the improvement of environments so that people might better flourish. *Growth* is creating environments in which you can better flourish, environments in which your family can better flourish, and environments in which your community can better flourish, preferably all at the same time. It provides a "true north" against which learning and doing paths may be reliably, almost unerringly selected.

For those of us in the pharmaceutical field, you can imagine developing your skills to enable you to better pursue experiences that enhance our ability to treat or cure cancer, Alzheimer's disease, tropical infections, or even the common cold. Successes in building knowledge in any of these areas improves the environment for the world's people to flourish, the ability of your company to flourish, the ability of your team and function to flourish, and the ability of your own career to grow.

To "practice" growth, think about ways that you can connect your selection of experiences (experiments, researches, practice elements, focus of reframing) in ways that help your growth and the growth of those around you. What does your environment need to improve people's ability to thrive or for your ability to thrive? What experiences can support that? As these experiences present themselves, they will be easier to select and pursue.

Practice to Grow

There are an infinite number of mental exercises that can be imagined to improve your ability to see without prejudice, to reframe, to experience, and to grow. The important thing is to find something that really opens your consciousness to things your mental models have hidden from you and to open your vision to seeing your mental models themselves. It is essential to find things that work with your life, that help increase your facility at reframing and experiencing things that will help you and others grow, but like exercises for sports, the things you choose should not be chosen merely because they are easy. Instead, they must serve the purpose of creating higher and deeper levels of capability, which enable you to more effectively be Lean.

Think about and try the exercises outlined previously. As you work through them, think about how well they do or do not work for you, and think about how you might imagine helping others exercise their skills. What better ideas do you have, and how much more elegant an exercise can you devise?

PULLING IT TOGETHER—SEEING, REFRAMING, EXPERIENCING, AND GROWING: A LEARNING LOOP FOR INNOVATION

The exercises I have outlined provide practice in the individual *elements* of an *innovation* learning cycle: see, reframe, experience, and grow. The key, of course, is reframing. Our mental frames are the single biggest and, in fact, only barrier to innovation. If we cannot reframe, we cannot think fundamentally new thoughts. What is more, our current frames are *axiomatically* incorrect. No matter our other beliefs, this is the fundamental tenet of science. Whatever we believe correct today is merely useful. Something bigger or more precise, something more general or more capable, can and eventually will take its place.

This makes clear that the more capable we are at creating viable but very different frames, the more capable we will be at *breakthrough* thinking. That this should be difficult is no surprise. We rarely, if ever, delve into the most deeply held assumptions of our fields of research, let alone those of how we work, interact with others, and so on. This blindness to our assumptions is what makes breakthrough thinking so rare. Once the ability to step dramatically away from the boundaries of current thinking has been lost to an organization, the only innovations left to it are those that fit within the bounds of current thought. We will be able to build better coal, gas, and oil engines. We will be unable to split atoms or build supercomputers.

Luckily, the reverse is true as well. By training ourselves to see and reframe together, we can actually *learn* breakthrough thinking. The ability to generate a eureka moment is a learnable trait. It is something we can practice; it is something that we can teach to others.

Of course, reframing is not enough. There are an infinite number of frames that do not work, and perhaps can never work, and the only way to differentiate between really interesting and seemingly correct new frames and workable frames is to run insightful experiments. The farther a frame is from current thinking, the more experience (testing and knowledge building) is required to ensure that the frame is a viable innovation and not something fragile, unworkable, or ultimately useless to the people we imagine might want it. As a result, each of the four elements I have described—seeing, reframing, experiencing, and growing—is required for us to successfully innovate.

So, while the experiments that I have outlined in this chapter (and the better ones you will undoubtedly find on your own) are like the passing, dribbling, ball-handling, and shooting exercises that basketball players drill with every day, they are only the most basic, individual skills needed to play the sport. These exercises do not constitute the play itself or the thinking that a player must engage in dynamically to support his team. These exercises do not even represent the entirety of skills required to excel within the sport. In fact, they are only the most basic skills that, when brought together, allow the individual player to do naturally that which is *physically* required of him.

We want to be able to smoothly connect the skills discovered previously in this chapter into a more complicated, integrated skill for the individual scientist. We want to be able to engage the entire learning loop, from seeing to growth. Interestingly enough, Lean provides such a framework in the A3 format. Practicing seeing, reframing, experiencing, and growing through use of the A3, or the *explicit* use of the scientific method, provides just the integrated practice we are looking for. Practice in this integrated skill will increase the scientist's capability of seeing, reframing, and resolving problems in a smooth and, soon, seemingly effortless fashion.

In addition to A3, a few other exercises that integrate various parts of the learning loop, including "good-better-best" and value stream mapping, can begin to rapidly improve our individual and community's ability to think in ways that support breakthrough innovation.

INTEGRATED EXERCISES

Skill-Building Exercise 7: The A3 Format

A3s, which are described in detail in Chapter 5, are quite easy to do but, at the same time, are very difficult to do well. They are deceptively awkward when you first attempt them, but they help you learn very quickly to think well. An A3 has the seeing, reframing, experiencing, and growing all rolled into one easily sharable page. The thing that makes the A3 so useful is that its conciseness engages the simultaneous mental challenge to shorten something to its strictest elements while still covering the subject in its entirety that is, it teaches elegance. Equally valuable, the A3's requirement to record thought processes exposes poor or uncritical thinking, providing a platform for very rapid, self-directed learning. Meanwhile, an A3's insistence on proven completion and sharing of the work means that the author cannot rest until the A3 is concluded.

While these attributes can make the A3 a difficult exercise, they also make it an unparalleled learning exercise as well. Practice concise language, and you will build precision. Practice good thinking, and you will build good analysis and design skills. Practice good execution, and you will develop good experimentation skills. Analyze and design repeatedly until a barrier is firmly removed from the workplace, and you will gain deep knowledge of your work and have learned much about your workplace, its culture, and the thought process that created it. Do a good A3 on any given topic, and you will only need to do an exercise on this topic once.

Skill-Building Exercise 8: Good-Better-Best

If scale is the enemy, then large, intractable scientific questions are screaming to be disassembled into actionable subquestions. A Pfizer biology research team noted that people often froze when considering very large scientific questions with vast areas of unknown space. Barbara Tate, the leader of the team, broke these mental blocks by asking her team members to accept that where they were was *good*, but to imagine what would improve that level of capability just a little bit? What would make our position *better*? She would tell colleagues that often we cannot see the path to a big scientific solution because we cannot see over the first hill of innovation. By achieving a better level of knowledge, we can, perhaps, think of another idea that will get us to an even better place and from there—or from a long series of *betters*—get to a place where the scientific question has been answered, her definition of *best*.

This is akin to Ohno's idea of one-piece flow and rapid, continuous improvement. Barbara is just suggesting to her team that where we end up cannot always be determined, but as long as we are taking steps in the direction of our goal, we will get there more rapidly than we can imagine at the start.

Skill-Building Exercise 9: Mapping

Full critical-question and value stream mapping exercises (going from current state, or critical question, all of the way to future state and plan) are not just for teams.* A friend of mine, who is admittedly something of a Lean nut, has value-stream-mapped the mowing of his lawn. He identified barriers to time, storage space, fuel usage, and so on. He tested them and found they helped his life around the house and reconnected him with his inner geek. It was a simple exercise, but he *saw* barriers in his yard work,

---

* You will find detailed descriptions in Chapters 10 and 11.

reframed his work in a way in which he could operate with fewer barriers, *experienced* the different approaches he could devise, and *grew* his family time. You may see that as a bit overboard, but like the A3, it provides a platform on which to practice and become really good at seeing flow and systems issues, reframing them into new work flows and dynamic systems, experiencing life without those barriers, and seeing subsequent growth.

The value stream mapping process is, in its typically large, glorious format, just an A3 with lots of boxes, arrows, and metrics. Because value stream maps are activity based, and my work is so innovation based, I do much, much less of this and far more Critical Question Mapping[(SM)] (CQM), because CQM[(SM)] *requires* me to reframe before designing experiments and makes it difficult to design just one approach. That said, both are highly valuable approaches to synthesize your new skills. I recommend them to anyone wishing to gain integrated skills in Lean.

Apply Liberally

We get measurably better at whatever we do when we practice it. The more times we set out to observe barriers in our lives, the easier the process of observation becomes, and the less of our conscious effort will have to be applied to making valuable observations. Reframing is very difficult when you first try it, but with practice, it becomes almost a natural extension of how you interact with the universe around you. When coupled, observation and reframing merge, and new ways of seeing and operating will begin to form without conscious effort.

Again, with practice, with an identified purpose in mind, and with the solid belief that there are no solutions, just hypotheses to be tested—*experience* becomes an almost personal requirement for assessing what has gone before and what you intend to do. To the emerging Lean thinker, the more you learn to see mental models and assumptions, the more proposals and solutions that are presented to you will appear to just be the untested hypotheses that they are. Some will dawn on you instantly, and you will work to probe them in your environment to see whether they hold true and, if not, what needs to be done to gain the value of that proposal without its unintended side effects. Others will prove more subtle. It takes longer to see beyond the presented face value of proposals that make intuitive sense. Creating "accountability" in your management systems, for example, would immediately appear to be something good for a flourishing environment. But "accountability" is an amorphous concept with a lot of subtlety in language and emphasis (it means different things to different people). The subtleties and depths of the mental models buried within such amorphous concepts take time to unravel so that we can begin to see how they affect (whether to promote, inhibit, or are neutral) the smooth running of our work environment.

With practice, however, new proposals of any depth of subtlety will trigger a conscious or an unconscious analysis of the underlying beliefs and the reasoning behind them. You will no longer accept as "known truth" or "given" that a proposal to change your environment will have the intended effect. You will instead look to identify a way to probe what the effects of that proposal are in your world, assess them against their design, and modify them to succeed. You will become a scientist of management and thought as well as the scientist of your chosen technical specialty.

Apply in Your Work, Start Small, Grow in Scale, and Spread Outward

People often try to improve other people's work first but, of course, your own work is the best place to test new ideas. There are many ways to do this, but start with your current project. Map the questions that, if answered, will deliver success in one small aspect of your work. Plan the next two days with the experiments you will do and the targets you hope to achieve. Every four hours, check against your intended progress. Did you hit it? If not, spend some quality time observing. What physical and mental barriers got in the way of your four-hour plan? What caused those barriers to exist? How will you remove them before starting your next four-hour experimental set? Your first two-day experiment may take you a week this way, but the next one will take three days, and the one afterwards a day and a half.

Once you have begun relentlessly removing barriers from your own work, begin removing barriers that cross the boundary between yourself and your immediate work neighbors. Start by observing. Do you know what your common objectives are? Do you know what each person is specifically working toward and how that fits with your own efforts? Do you have explicit understanding of how to communicate emerging results? Do you know when your emerging results will impact your coworkers? See if you can map important interactions and handoffs. See if you can map the work. When you have identified barriers that these "seeing" exercises uncover, try one of the reframing exercises to identify a suite of possible paths to remove each of these barriers, testing the easiest, fastest, least politically sensitive ones, and begin to make your interactive environment better.

As you progress in your work, people will begin to notice two things: First, your work is getting done faster and with higher levels of innovation, and your stress level and even your working hours may be dropping as you progress. People like this trend and want some of this sort of progress for their own. It is not unlikely that your friends will start to want in on the action, which will enable you to enlist others in your own Lean journey. Second, so long as you keep as your goal the creation of an environment in which everyone flourishes, people will notice, subconsciously or explicitly, that you are becoming easier to work with, more collaborative and more supportive of the overall effort, and they will begin engaging you in more of their problems. Their barriers to working with you will diminish, and people will seek you out for collaboration.

You can, of course, proselytize Lean. This can help or hinder the spread of the philosophy, depending on how you go about it and how your culture accepts such things, but it should be noted that proselytizing often has little effect unless tangible results are evident for people to see. In the end, you will be unable to control whether those around you begin to engage in Lean thinking, but your example will draw others toward you. New colleagues will want to learn how you are so much more effective than others. People on other teams will want to sign you on to their efforts, and so on. There is a reasonable chance that people, especially those who are under stress or having difficulty meeting objectives, will begin to engage you openly in spreading Lean, but if not, you will at the very least have created within your circle of friends a more effective environment and a more attractive place to work.

This is how Taiichi Ohno began Lean at Toyota. The company as a whole did not begin with his philosophies on a Lean workplace. His effectiveness and the capability of his immediate working area were appreciated, but were not generally applied until Toyota came under great corporate stress. At that time, his effectiveness was seen as a potential path to return Toyota to good graces, and Lean began to spread rapidly. Time, as they say, is the master.

5

The A3 in Developing R&D Thinking

DESCRIPTION OF THE A3

The A3 report, named after the A3 size of paper[*] on which it is written, is nothing more than an explicit, single-page format for solving problems or answering questions using the scientific method (Figure 5.1).[†] The A3 has five main sections. The first section is devoted entirely to defining the problem or question being posed. The second is devoted to understanding the circumstances surrounding the problem or question. The third section helps reframe that understanding into a possible path, process, or future state in which that problem no longer exists. The fourth section defines an experimental path (the learning plan) to test and achieve this future state, including the parameters that define what success would look like in that future state. The final section describes the results of the experimental section compared with the success criteria, describes open or unresolved issues, and, where possible, describes potential approaches to resolve those issues.

These five sections contain all of the elements of the scientific method. As such, it enables deep problem solving on one easily created, shared, and digested sheet.

---

[*] For those not familiar with the A3 paper size, it is fairly large. A3 is approximately double the size of a standard U.S. letter-size sheet. (A3 measures approximately 11 × 17 inches.)

[†] Although all A3s have the same basic sections, there is no "official" layout for the A3. People and organizations have developed variations to suit their specific problems and their own organization's needs. In this chapter, I use a format developed at Pfizer. It is similar to a standard Toyota format (see John Shook, *Managing to Learn: Using the A3 Management Process* [Cambridge, MA: The Lean Enterprise Institute, 2009]), with language altered slightly to avoid confusion with other Pfizer terminology.

Title (the critical question to be answered or problem to be solved)

Value (also business case or background section)

. . . .

Current State

. . . .

Analysis/Synthesis

. . . . . .

Goal/Target Condition(s)

. .

Future State/Proposed Countermeasures

. . . .

Learning Plan

Experiment	Expected Outcome	Owner	Due Date
1			
2			
3			
...			
n			

Results/Countermeasures/Future Implications

. . . .

FIGURE 5.1

A typical A3 layout as described in the text and used in R&D projects.

PURPOSE OF THE A3

At one page, the most obvious purpose of the A3 is to facilitate concise rapid communication. Interestingly, it is not primarily the communication of results that the A3 is designed to convey. Instead, the A3 is designed to communicate the *thinking process* that someone is using to solve a problem. Showing the A3 author's thinking process has four main values:

1. It facilitates practice in (and reflection on) thinking and problem-solving skills by the author.
2. It facilitates engagement of others in the problem-solving process.
3. It facilitates mentorship of the author by others engaged in the problem-solving process.
4. It provides a simple format for archiving in-progress and completed learning cycles.

In the previous chapter, we stated that one of the commitments that Lean scientists have is to continue to explore and improve their scientific problem-solving/question-answering skills. Just like a journal provides a practice environment for writers to sharpen their ability to convey meaning through words, the A3 provides a practice environment for researchers to practice scientific thinking. By writing down and making explicit their approaches to solving individual problems, A3 authors can easily see their muddled or incomplete thinking. They can identify new areas of inquiry, gaps in rigor, and opportunities to explore alternative possibilities that would not otherwise occur. In a way, scientific problem solving is a lot like doing higher math in a car. It is possible to "carry the two" while driving, but it is a lot easier to stop, pull out a sheet of paper to write down the equations, and work through the problem with visual reminders. The A3 provides those visual reminders, supporting the scientist's need to roll things around in his mind, plugging together, removing and adapting ideas as they flow through his mind. It is a powerful self-learning tool.

A very intentional purpose of the A3, the power of which proved surprising in R&D, was the ability of the A3 to engage others in problem solving. It is not unusual in the corporate world to go through reorganization, and we were not immune to such events. During one such reorganization, I had been working with a team that had developed a robust set of A3s to help guide the science behind their project. The team lost 40 percent of its researchers in the change, but because they had A3s outlining their scientific goals, thinking process, and proposed paths to reach those scientific goals, other scientists were easily recruited onto the project and engaged in the science. The project proceeded with almost no reduction in speed through what might otherwise have been a tumultuous experience.

Another type of engagement that the A3 facilitates is the potential mentorship of the author by nearly everyone who reads the A3. New scientists who come on board a project, when they see an A3, can volunteer new perspectives on what is missing, new approaches that might be taken, and so on. By seeing their thought processes laid out in detail, experienced colleagues can mentor fresh recruits, again by pointing out areas where the new colleague can build depth of understanding, can establish a stronger fact base, can do more sophisticated analyses, can define more incisive experiments, and so on. They can hold the new researcher to established goals, noting when results fall short or analyses do not support a likely successful outcome.

Finally, the A3 facilitates storage, retrieval, and sharing of problem-solving results. In addition to being brief, the standardized format facilitates fast absorption of knowledge and thought process, reducing the inherent barriers people have to accessing archived information. And better than just a round-up page, an A3 will show *how* those results were obtained, what was also tried (hence not valuable to try again without new thinking), the gaps that remain, and so on. Anyone picking up a series of A3s addressing problems in a given space will have at his fingertips a mountain of easily digestible knowledge to help him quickly define a new, untried path to success.

SECTION 1: PROBLEM STATEMENT, BUSINESS VALUE, PERFORMANCE GOALS—DEFINING THE PROBLEM AND THE TERMS FOR ITS SUCCESSFUL RESOLUTION

The First Step in Creating Thought Clarity—Separating Problem and Solution with a Well-Constructed Problem Statement or Valuable Question

In Chapter 4, I described a leadership team that had hopelessly muddied thinking. In particular, I noted that their solutions were *non sequiturs*. In no way did their solutions address the problems facing the organization. Formulated correctly, the very first A3 element, the problem statement, would go a long way to addressing this gap in their thinking process.

The title of an A3 ("Title" in Figure 5.1) is a single sentence describing a problem or question that, if solved or answered, would provide a valuable improvement to the performance of the project or company. While this would appear to be the easiest part of an A3 (it is certainly the briefest part of an A3), it is conversely the most difficult. For whatever reason, we have become almost hardwired to provide an answer to every problem that pops into our heads. In fact, it is very difficult, without considerable practice, to state a problem without stating an answer to that problem at the same time. To see what I mean, consider the following two statements:

1. There is no system in the company to codify, store, and retrieve our research knowledge.
2. The company spends significant resources repeatedly developing answers to the same technical, managerial, and organizational questions.

These might appear to both be reasonable problem statements, but their implications are vastly different. Consider what you could do when faced with the first problem, and ask yourself this: "Would I successfully solve the stated problem by creating a knowledge management system that codifies, stores, and retrieves our research knowledge?" The answer is undoubtedly "yes." Then ask, "Could I create that knowledge management system with such properties that it takes longer for people to use than if they went to the library and looked up old laboratory notebooks?" If you could do that, do you also see that you could successfully "solve" that first problem without creating anything of value for the company (in fact, while destroying company value)?

The point is even more subtle here, because no matter how good the embedded solution might be (no matter how skeptical I am, an information technology [IT] system *might* be the answer), it still colors the thinking of every aspect of the project. If an IT system is assumed in the problem statement, will people try to identify paper-based solutions? Would they try to identify simple solutions that require no paper, electronics, or thinking of any kind? Would they try to identify anything except an IT system?

The point is also less subtle in this respect. I have noticed that whenever solution-free problems are identified, it opens people's thinking to a wider scope of possibilities. It opens them to observe new places and things and to address problems at a more strategic level. In the end, separating problems and solutions just supports good thinking.

By contrast, it is virtually impossible to answer the second question without improving the performance of the company. If you can find a way to not have to re-answer questions, then you will have either found a way to reuse knowledge that the company has already created (solving the implied, but actually unstated, problem in statement 1), or you could find an even more clever way to address the problem that would prove less resource intensive. At any rate, you would have eliminated a vast amount of rework that most companies engage in daily.

Even if you tried to game the system and said, "We will succeed by just never answering the same technical, organizational, or managerial question, even if we need the answer to succeed," you would have had to do something (create a way to know what problems had been answered) that could prove valuable. Damage done would be offset, at least in part, by gains elsewhere. In fact, it is almost impossible to imagine how you could game this and not find yourself in a position where you succeeded at most, or in part, in delivering against the spirit of the problem.

Back to our muddied leadership team example: If our leadership team could have clearly articulated the performance problems they were experiencing and separated their solutions (organizational structures, new processes, new standard operating procedures) from those problems, they would have gone a long way to improved performance. Once separated, they could see that an organizational change does not, in itself, change the process by which science is progressed, how knowledge is captured, or how people are coached and promoted. Likewise, process change does not, a priori, improve the performance of the projects that process supports.

In the end, clear problem solving begins with a clear articulation of a problem, nothing attached, nothing embellished. Spend some time on this first point, because it will color and enable (or hinder) all of the work to follow.

Business Value—Creating a Stage for Buy-In

The next element of the A3 is to describe what will be gained when the title problem or question is solved or answered. This section need not consume vast amounts of energy, because if you have identified a problem of sufficient value to warrant an A3, then the value in its resolution should be pretty straightforward. In our example statement 2, if we have eliminated the waste of developing new answers to the same question more than once, then several things will be apparent:

1. We will be able to apply the resources used in "developing answers to previously answered questions" to valuable scientific and managerial pursuits
2. Colleague and manager frustration with "reinventing the wheel" will be eliminated.

Obviously, I tend to think of this in fairly simple terms. I could easily build in an estimate of how large the problem is (but that will appear in current state anyway), and there may be other more specific things that will be addressed, but in the end, we are just establishing a solid base by which we can engage others who will want to know, "Is the problem big enough for me to care about?" and "Is it big enough for me to spend a few hours of my time, or commit people or resources to its resolution?"* If, as a problem solver, I have made that case clear in the Business Value section, then I will have generated enough engagement for someone to read further and understand (or to help me understand) the circumstances around the problem as we know it today.

Things to consider for this section:

- Value in terms of cycle time
- Value in terms of resources (cash, people, floor space, etc.)
- Value in terms of colleague satisfaction, ease of work, career growth, capability improvement, and so on (and don't forget the people part of problem solving)

---

* There is, I believe, reasonable justification that *any* problem identified is worth working on, in fact, Steven Spear's *Chasing the Rabbit* (2009, McGraw Hill) is based entirely on this premise. I invite you to decide for yourself.

To the extent necessary, sufficient rigor needs to go into this to show a positive value proposition.

Goals—Defining Criteria for Successful Completion, a.k.a. "When Do I Stop?"

Defining goals for the successful resolution of the problem naturally coincides with a description of business value if the problem is solved. If the problem (a lack of performance) and the business value (what should be improved if the problem is solved) are clearly defined, then the performance goal—what our new performance level should be when the problem is solved—should be straightforward to define. The goal should, as far as possible, describe the condition in which the question has been answered or the problem solved. In our example, it might be very simply stated, "The company answers a question, or solves a problem only once." Immediately, you can see a set of significant implications for our example A3. Our topline goal implies that we will need to know in an instant whether a question or problem has been addressed, and how it was addressed, so that an answer or solution can be reapplied.

Of course, problems come in all shapes and sizes. There is not always the limiting case (questions answered only once), and there are many cases in which the limiting case is not possible to reach. There are three approaches to setting valuable performance goals:

1. Set goals with the company's needs in mind. If our survival means that we need to deliver a product with twice (or ten times!) the performance of our current model, there is little use in setting a goal beneath that.
2. Set goals with the aspirational end state in mind. In our example, we don't really want to spend *any* time reinventing the wheel. Zero rework seems like a good goal, but it means that this A3 may never be retired.
3. Set goals with an understanding of what is achievable.

This third option is the least desirable method, especially in R&D. Most scientists recognize the difficulty in predicting what is possible. They have all seen one good thought upend an entire area of science, and we have all heard stories of the same thing happening to industries. Nevertheless, many organizations use the third approach as their standard method. This appears regularly when a company's human resources (HR) policy puts people's careers in conflict with what may be in the best interests of the company or its customers, that is when people are rated on the basis of achieving goals, rather than assessing progress against company needs.

When we measure people against achievement of their goals and reward them for success and/or punish them for failure, moral dilemmas arise. For an extreme but very real example of this, hospitals are staffed by humans and run using human-designed processes. As a result, mistakes occasionally occur. Usually, these mistakes do no harm, but occasionally they result in injury to a patient, and on rare occasions, they cause accidental/preventable deaths. As patients, of course, we all hope that our hospital has processes in place to identify potential failures and remove them, with the goal of *zero* accidental or preventable deaths. It may not be possible to reach zero, but is reducing accidental deaths by half, no matter how achievable it might be, an acceptable goal? At no time do we want to pit a hospital employee's career against the welfare of a patient, because the cost of a moral lapse is so high.

The business value and the end point of problem solving must coincide, so check the two against each other. Our goal so far is to answer a question or solve a problem only once. We also have a business value that states colleague frustration from having to answer the same questions repeatedly will disappear. An allied goal, then, would be something like "zero colleague frustration from having to answer the same question more than once." Our business value also states that we will reapply the current effort in reinvention to something more valuable. This one is trickier. We do not yet know how much effort is applied to reinvention, nor do we have any idea what we are to apply it to. We might need to make estimates, poll some people, or do some research to inform this goal.

An A3 is a living document. As a result, we can either go through those research efforts or put in a stop-gap goal to be replaced later. A stop-gap goal might look like: "A process to identify, quantify, and reapply work from second through nth answering of questions."

Other Types of Stop-Gap Goals

Although I cannot speak for the experts at Toyota and their use of the A3, in R&D, we cannot always deliver countermeasures that we believe will solve the A3 problem. At the time the A3 is developed, science may not be sufficiently advanced to accomplish the goals outlined. As a result, sometimes the analysis/synthesis portion serves merely to deliver us from the current state to a slightly better one, which we can call a *good* state. Continued work on the question will eventually bring it to a *better* state, and, finally, when the future state demanded by the A3 is achieved, a *best* state. By breaking their *go for the win* thought process, a scientist following a *good, better, best* ladder of improvement can create a few quick scientific wins. Often, these modest wins improve the scientist's perspective sufficiently, that a path to the desired scientific breakthrough becomes clear.

The value from a corporate perspective is that projects are often incredibly complicated. The point, in many cases, is to make a dent in the problem, so that other aspects of the project can create a viable product. For example, so many technical issues interact in the creation of a new pharmaceutical treatment that *full* understanding of any given biological or medical problem is just not possible. What is necessary is getting *enough* knowledge in wide-enough areas of a project that fast, sure progress toward its conclusion can be made. Indeed, only a sufficient amount of progress that a viable treatment can be designed and proven is required.

In engineering circles, the same should hold true. In the emerging edges of engineering, many things are tried that are quite new and immature. In these cases, having something useful and effective beats having something perfect, because just as in pharmaceutical development, the useful can serve as a thought starter in future generations of innovation with increasing levels of perfection.

The goal, then, is sometimes what we would like to achieve, and the requirements of the team will determine how precise this needs to be at any given time. Make it your own and work within your culture to define your own trajectory.

Section 1 Summary

The problem-definition section helps the A3 owner, company managers, and other stakeholders understand what the problem is, why it is valuable, and how we will know it has been solved to the company's satisfaction. These three elements will go a long way to setting up the problem-solving team for success.

SECTION 2: CURRENT STATE

Now that the problem has been identified, its value described, and its successful resolution criterion established, we are actually ready to develop an understanding of the problem itself. This section is all about "seeing" or "sensing" the relevant circumstances surrounding the problem so that *easy* and *complete* resolution of the problem can take place, and the business value can be realized. At a minimum, we need to explore several things about the problem:

- Where does it occur?
- When does it occur?
- In what form does it occur?
- How often does it occur?
- To whom does it occur?
- What is known about the problem from the literature?
- What is currently known about the problem from within the company?
- What are the process steps that create, support, and surround this problem?
- Are there discernible dependencies?
- Who is affected by this problem?

What we are looking for in this section are facts, as plain and bare as we can make them. We want the facts to be colored as little as possible by interpretation or even "gathering bias,"* so that the problem is fully described and its circumstances agreed to by as wide a range of stakeholders as possible.

Our example is wildly complex, covering almost every area of a company, so it will be difficult to do it justice in a few sentences. However, think for a moment about how your company answers questions, knows that it has answered prior questions, and ensures that it uses those answers when the same question appears in future. What would you want to observe about

---

* Gathering bias is when someone or a group gathers the information that is easy for it to obtain, either because it is close to those facts or has access to the people who own those facts. Bias occurs when different or relevant facts available through other channels do not come to light. Facts alone can cause interesting political discussions, but facts colored by gathering bias can cause quite a stir.

the system? An extremely short list of observations I have had about this problem in my R&D lives includes

- Solutions to technical problems are stored in laboratory notebooks.
- Active notebooks (often going back several years) are kept at a scientist's desk or laboratory area.
- Old notebooks are archived in the library.
- Solutions to technical problems are presented to the business unit in PowerPoint slide format. These slide decks are not officially archived. Scientists often (poll of 12 scientists show that 9 retain them on their laptop) maintain these slides. Business managers often (poll of 6 business leaders show that 4 retain these slide decks on their personal laptops) maintain these slide decks. Legal does not maintain technical slide decks.
- Solutions to technical problems in our processes are kept by manufacturing support on 11 × 17 summary sheets in two-ring binders.
- Solutions to business problems are archived:
  - In process maps if they are process related
  - In organizational design documents held with line managers if they are organizationally related
  - Not consistently maintained in other circumstances
- There is no comprehensive archive or list of solved technical problems.
- There is a partial list of solved technical process problems residing on a page in two-ring binders noted previously.
- There is no list of solved business problems, either organizational, process, or otherwise.

This section of an A3 is almost always given short shrift, if for no other reason than most problems are a lot more complicated than they appear at first blush. Even very simple problems are surrounded by myriad circumstances and observables. It is also easy to overlook elements of a problem and to miss critical context needed to solve a problem. There is an exercise described in Chapter 4, in which a person is asked to stand in a circle (known as an Ohno circle after the father of Lean, Taiichi Ohno) and observe a process for an extended period of time. A version of that exercise might prove useful when completing this part of the A3, by having someone stand and observe the area where a problem occurs as it occurs.

At this point, it should be noted that an A3 is a living document. The *point* of beginning an A3 is that there is not yet enough knowledge to solve a problem. Just looking at my list of current-state observations, you can easily imagine a dozen (at least!) other things you would want to know. This is the opportunity to *note the gaps* in the current state, as you see them, and build into your learning plan (see Section 4) a path to learn the answers to fill those and other gaps.

Each A3 typically supports a business or technical problem with some level of organizational or technical complexity. As a result, early iterations of an A3 should seek to build large and detailed descriptions of the current state of the problem gathered from as many stakeholders as possible. This research will give the most inclusive perspective on the problem. It will also deliver unintended but invaluable problem-solving information in the form of revealed biases, hidden agendas, and other organizational traps. Done right, a good current-state description will provide the broadest and most comprehensive understanding for the problem solver, as well as lower barriers to engagement once analysis and countermeasure design gets under way.

For very large systemic problems, such as those tackled by our value stream mapping workshops (see Chapter 9), current-state value stream (activity) maps create an excellent detailed understanding and high level overview of the system's activity and issues. Do not imagine that an A3 is just about words. Graphs, maps, charts, and photographs typically condense and convey information far better than sentences ever could.

Section 2 Summary

Section 2 is about the facts and just the facts. Unimpeachably established facts usually do not cause conflict. It is only when these facts are interpreted that conflict arises. By ensuring thorough investigation and clean separation of fact from interpretation, the A3 author generates credibility for analysis. When the facts are presented in easily digestible form (through graphs or simple statements), the widest range of audiences can understand, identify with, and support further learning within the A3 process.

SECTION 3: ANALYSIS/SYNTHESIS—FINDING THE ROOT CAUSE OF A PROBLEM AND DEVELOPING COUNTERMEASURES TO ADDRESS ROOT CAUSE

Analysis/synthesis comprises two subsections of the A3. *Analysis* is where we interpret the current state. Why does it work the way it does? What are the barriers in the current state that keep us from achieving our goals, delivering our business value, and solving our A3's stated problem? Analysis is where we understand the root causes of parts and pieces of the problem and, hopefully, the problem as a whole. Analysis is where we separate the current state into subsections so that we can see the connectivity between all of the various parts of the system and assess how those connections affect the system when things progress. When something goes wrong, what step does it dent, and which section gets completely flattened?

This is the place, in classic Lean work, where people use "five whys" very effectively. If we understand why A occurs and get an answer of B, and then we ask why B occurs and get an answer of C, and so on, then we drive back from symptoms A to progressively root-cause drivers of the problem. Far enough removed from the original problem, a root cause can be addressed removing the problem with almost no adverse impact to the current state of operation.

Analysis and current state occasionally overlap and, in fact, our learning plan often has, as a result of analysis, some new thing to understand in the current state. The A3 is a living document, so we should expect to go back to observe, but also go back to think through our analysis. Do we know enough yet that we can identify all of the value called for by our goal? If we are to deliver a twofold increase in speed and we have not yet identified half of our work time that can be eliminated, we have more analysis to do.

Synthesis is an unstated process whereby we reconnect some or all of the bits we tore apart in *analysis* and then combine them with new ideas, thoughts, objects, and so on. This is where we not only have license, but a duty to wild flights of fancy. We want to be asking and answering all kinds of provocative questions: "What would we have to do to eliminate this entire process?" "What would the world look like if this problem never existed?" "Where is the point in the system where the smallest change creates the biggest impact?" "How can I leverage that point to increase quality, speed, or innovation (where that point had, in past, caused quality and speed problems, researcher angst, and innovation problems)?"

These flights of fancy will result in a set of hypotheses that we will call "proposed countermeasures." Ideally the set of proposed countermeasures should have three attributes:

1. There should be several hypotheses for removing each root cause; hence there should be several countermeasures that eliminate each root cause identified in analyses. We want a lot of shots on goal.
2. Each countermeasure must be directly traceable to the root cause of a current-state problem as identified in analysis. We don't want solutions to nonexistent or unrelated problems.
3. Each root cause must be accounted for, *in full*, by the set of proposed countermeasures.

Remember our misguided leadership team? Part of their muddied thinking was that their solutions did not address *any* problem in the current state. A second part of their muddied thinking was that they did not assess whether their solutions would provide enough improvement to meet their goals. Of course, they did not have articulated goals, so perhaps I am wrong on this point, but you get the picture.

The first attribute of the proposed set of countermeasures is valuable in all areas of business, but it is *crucial* in innovation work. Having only a single approach to a technical problem is to risk *everything* on an untested hypothesis. Having three, ten, or a set of fifty different approaches to a technical problem ensures that you will have the opportunity to test many different lines of thinking in low-cost ways. One, and perhaps several of them, will prove easier, faster, and less costly than you first thought. One or more will no doubt cost more and take longer. The idea is that if you do not take the time to create a set, you will not go through sufficient rigor in your thinking to create a breakthrough. This is a huge leverage point for innovation. Take time here.

Incidentally, this is the area of problem solving where exceptional engineers (and we all know one such person) make the whole process seem like magic. These are the guys who can walk up to a production line and just about put their hand on the part that is creating a problem others have been trying to find for weeks. I have seen engineers come up to a broken machine, ask a few questions, poke in the machine for a few moments, and know, almost as if through divine intervention, the machine's problem and its immediate and long-term solution. Like their engineering brethren, scientists often have eureka moments in which the scientist seems to see an elegant solution to a problem without any apparent input beyond the problem itself.

This unconscious approach to problem solving or answering critical questions often leaves the rest of us (a) scratching our heads, wondering how that person could possibly accomplish that feat of thinking, (b) imagining that such leaps of intuitive ability are somehow divinely inspired, and (c) thinking that they cannot be taught or learned.

Far from it, the activity that goes on unconsciously—what a friend refers to as "sitting in the fields while the problem speaks to you,"* or as I describe in this book as "reframing"—is an activity that encompasses all of the parts of the A3 through synthesis. What the A3 does is provide a framework that clearly articulates a problem and its surroundings, then *demands* that the author imagine/create paths to its resolution. "Reframing" is something special, but it is by no means unique. We all do it; in fact, we all do it all of the time. It just occurs for those exceptional people more quickly under certain circumstances than it does for you and me, who perhaps have a less complete understanding of the underlying problem or a less complete set of options for its resolution than those people can generate almost at whim.

Without having thought through it in great detail, my hypothesis is that "sitting in the fields" is something akin to being an accomplished musician. The instrument just becomes a "part" of the player. It takes no conscious effort to play; it merely takes picking it up and manipulating it as if it is a part of your body. This capability comes through practice. The A3 is not only a frame, but provides a type of practice for scientific problem solving. Do it even a few times and you will notice your thinking and imagining process change. Do it a lot, and I believe you will find problems speaking to you more often.

Considerations in Analysis/Synthesis

Allen Ward mathematically described the value of the *multiple options* approach, but raw experience illuminates this far better than any

---

* "Sitting in the fields," a phrase used by Robert Burdick, a retired IBM engineer, can occur immediately, or it can literally take sitting in a field somewhere for the problem to provide its answer. Relying on this method, which we all do at some point or another, is tricky. We can help it a great deal by practicing A3.

mathematical approach can. Two examples from my personal experience arise from work at GE on catalysis and work at Pfizer on the structural determination of proteins. During my tenure at GE, R&D had a long-standing project to synthesize a polymer (resin) precursor from its constituent parts. This turned out to be a difficult proposition, so the process used at the time combined different starting materials, and then substituted a second set of starting materials to deliver the desired precursor. Each step required additional pots and pans, pressure pumps, piping, and the like, which in turn created the need to hold additional inventory and attendant holding tanks, and so on. Since we were dealing with chemicals, this approach added hazards and pollution opportunities that a direct synthesis would avoid.

At the time I arrived at GE, the team working on a direct process had a catalyst that worked, but very, very poorly. Moreover, the catalyst itself was composed of one of the rarer metals in the Earth's crust, meaning that the catalyst cost hundreds, if not thousands, of dollars per gram. The chemistry of that process was, more or less, assumed to be understood, but despite years of effort, the efficiency of the catalyst remained stubbornly low; in chemical terms, catalytic efficiency held at six turnovers. This means that every catalyst unit produced only six molecules of desired product. We weren't going to get a cost reduction if the catalyst cost more than what it could make.

A second team was commissioned to try alternative approaches. In a fit of inspired randomness, they tested potential catalysts that made no sense chemically but that happened to be lying about the laboratory. Some of these potential catalysts yielded the expected result, which was exactly nothing. Others, however, showed unexpected catalytic activity (they worked), and *at a much higher rate* than the catalyst possibilities that made chemical sense. Given a result they could not understand, they began trying many, many different types of catalysts to see if they could figure out some chemical principles in order to design a successful catalyst on the basis of rational design. Six months later, the team had moderately priced catalysts with turnovers up to 60,000 and calcium catalysts showing turnovers in the tens of thousands. Calcium, as you may know, is a key component of limestone and other rocks. Within months, the new team found something that was literally made of dirt and far more effective than what had gone before.

Another example from Pfizer illustrates the same point. To function, the body suppresses or stimulates production of proteins. This proves a delicate balance, because over- or underproduction of a normal protein is a typical cause or effect of disease progression. That is, a disease can often be traced to incorrect protein action within the body. In treating disease, it is crucial to know what proteins exist where, how they are produced, and, from there, to figure out how to selectively stimulate or suppress their occurrence to block or enhance their ability to act in the body. In figuring out how to create the desired effect, it often helps to know the structure of a protein, since structure can show pockets where potential drugs could dock to change the protein's action in the body. Unfortunately, it is quite difficult to determine protein structure, since every step of the process—from cleanly expressing the protein (its manufacture in sufficient quantities), to purification, to crystallization for X-ray analysis—is tricky.

In their initial approach, the team at Pfizer would scour the literature in order to find and begin with an already successful process for expression and purification. Unfortunately, the protein literature is notoriously irreproducible, and first-pass success rates to replicate the literature at a successful scale were exactly zero. No team had *ever* had a first-pass success. As a result, the team would make a first attempt, observe the failures, and develop process changes to remediate those failures, often going through many, many learning cycles, never knowing after a failure if the next revision would succeed. Using this approach, their fastest ever structural determination took nine months. Many projects were just abandoned, leaving the research teams they supported with a knowledge gap in their attempts to modify disease.

After some consideration, it was concluded that trying multiple expression options, followed by multiple purification options, would give them at worst a deeper understanding of what might work on their second try, and might in fact prove capable of generating a first-pass success. This approach brought first-pass success rate to 75 percent (from zero), while cycle time decreased from a best of nine months to a repeatable three months. Moreover, the teams knew after their first pass whether they would succeed (75 percent of the time) or that their science would not support their success (25 percent) and that they should abandon the project. This latter knowledge had never been available to them before, and it proved a valuable cost-, time-, and resource-sparing piece of information.

Section 3 Summary

Analysis is where understanding of the causes of current-state performance are explored. Root-cause analysis is best supported through unimpeachable fact. An experiment that establishes cause for a process error, a methodological issue, or a quality problem—and that establishes many hypotheses (potential countermeasures) for its removal—creates engagement for testing of those countermeasures. Thorough testing of countermeasures in nonthreatening environments creates engagement for adoption of those countermeasures. Again, a solid job of separating the elements of thinking, and not reaching conclusions in advance of facts, supports the continued success of the A3 author in solving underlying problems, even in contentious areas. We have observed very junior researchers gaining high-level management support in solving very sophisticated problems because they used the A3 effectively.

At this point, it is important to note again that the A3 is a living document. It cannot be written in one day, because the analyses needed to understand the current state, establish the validity of countermeasures, and demonstrate the resolution of the problem cannot be accomplished at the outset. At each stage, some part of analysis will either be labeled as "unknown," "to be determined," or "in progress." These elements will be supported in Section 4, The Learning Plan.

SECTION 4: THE LEARNING PLAN

If the other areas of the A3 are more intellectually challenging, the learning plan is the least understood of any. We invariably understand what a problem statement *is* even if we don't do it well. We can dissect problems and provide potential solution paths, but a plan in R&D is *not* the same as a plan in deterministic areas of work. Reflecting back on the purpose of the A3, which is to improve our ability to think, and the nature of R&D, which is to build and integrate innovative knowledge, an R&D A3 has some structural requirements that we do not usually associate with plans. To support our thinking, its structure is set to provide *predictions* against which we can test our thinking. To support our R&D purpose, an A3 is specifically designed to explore a variety of thinking before settling on one path forward.

Learning Plan Structure

In order to learn, we must be able to contrast what we think against what is really there. This is the essence of a scientific experiment. We predict (hypothesize) that something will be the case. We design an experiment with that expected outcome in mind. If the outcome of the experiment matches prediction then we are, at any rate, not demonstrably wrong. Our thinking is not inconsistent with observable reality.

So, what sort of predictions do we want to make? In my view, there are two main learning points that produce business-valuable predictions. The first is a target condition (a prediction) of the outcome of each activity that we undertake. If we are going to learn something about the current state through a survey of stakeholders, then the prediction should include what we believe we will learn from the survey. If our survey, when filled out, meets that expectation, we move forward, but with only the expected knowledge we had hoped to get. If we *fail* to get our expected result, then all kinds of interesting things could happen. Let's say that people did not fill out the survey: That gives us some insight into our company's culture. If people did not believe those were the correct questions, it says much about our ability to design surveys or our lack of understanding of our problem. If we get a completely different result than expected, our thinking process that generated our prediction is wrong, and we can ask ourselves what that implies and how we would remedy it in future.

So, for each activity, I require my teams to post a predicted outcome, no matter how mundane, such as

Activity	Expectation
Design survey	Survey completed
Send survey with cover letter	Everyone receives, fills out, and returns survey
Tabulate survey results	25 percent of respondents agree, 50 percent disagree, 25 percent I don't know

Although we require this level of prediction, it is surprising to me that this request meets with such resistance, because prediction is an absolutely critical piece of scientific thinking, and when it gets lost, science gets lost with it. An absolutely astonishing example comes from medicinal chemistry. Medicinal chemists *design* the molecules (chemicals) that become drug candidates, and eventually drugs. Skillful medicinal chemists design several molecules around a given hypothesis about different chemical properties and how those properties will enable a molecule to interact with a disease-causing protein (for example) and not interact with any other proteins (which can, for example, minimize drug side effects).

When the molecules are synthesized, they are tested to see if they interact in the expected way; then new hypotheses are formed, and another set of molecules is designed and tested, until enough predictive power is generated that the designer can design molecules that exquisitely interact in the desired way. These molecules will do exactly what is desired, affecting the disease, without doing anything else, especially things that might prove toxic, harmful, or uncomfortable to the patient.

When medicinal chemists follow this path, they are invariably successful, if not in designing a successful treatment, at least in hitting the properties they were aiming for. Medicinal chemists who follow this approach tend to deliver high-quality compounds after testing between 400 to 800 different molecules.

But medicinal chemists have been "helped" by the ability to make "libraries" of compounds. That is, they have the ability to make not just 10 or 20 compounds at one time, but they can make hundreds or even thousands of compounds at a time. This would appear to be a boon to the trade, but two things happen. The first is that, with all of those compounds, writing down every hypothesis proves arduous, and people stop doing it. The second thing that happens is that testing of compounds was pretty fast in the small-number scenario—no more than two weeks. But when dozens of chemists are dumping thousands of compounds into the system, the testing regimen times balloon outward, and pretty soon it is nine weeks, then twelve weeks, then twenty-some weeks before results come back. When these two effects are combined, chemists lose track of why they designed their compounds in the first place. They lose their inherent connection to hypothesis-driven science.

In this high volume world, the *demonstrated* effect is that the number of compounds synthesized goes up by a factor of 20–50, with a significant *reduction* in the quality of the compounds developed. Interestingly, this effect can be reversed by the simple act of writing down hypotheses again, and only designing new molecules when data come back from the first set to inform a logical next step. Making predictions and checking results is all-important, and all that it takes.

Predicting Plan Timing

The second type of prediction concerns our own ability to plan and execute the plan. In our planning process, we require that, for each activity, we have an owner of the activity (this may or may not be the person who completes the activity, but it is the person who is tracking and ensuring its on-time completion) who is responsible for a start date and an end date. These dates are predictions in exactly the same way as the activity content prediction. If we meet the prediction date, then we have learned nothing of particular interest. However, if we deviate from plan, this tells us a lot about our ability to predict how long something will take. It can inform us of the unexpected complexity (or simplicity) of an approach. It can tell us we are overtaxed. It can tell us that we need to think more carefully about estimating or managing time. Observing the deviation from the time element of the plan is useful in project management. If we are ahead of plan, we can apply the unexpected speed to something of value; if we are behind, we can rethink our approach to ensure that we deliver the problem's solution on time.

Building Fast Learning into Our Planning Process

In a deterministic environment, like manufacturing, every activity has consequences. Stamping stamps, milling mills, welding attaches. These consequences are predictable with great certainty. Thus, a plan to stamp, mill, and weld a piece of metal will likely result in an output with those three traits imposed on it. By contrast, an experiment is, by design, an uncertain thing. You can bet that *some* learning will come of it, but not necessarily the learning required to advance your project. As a result, there should literally be *no expectation* that any aspect of the A3 plan will succeed. This is a valuable and freeing assumption, because then we will create plans that do not depend, sequentially, on every step to succeed. We can, in fact, we must plan plans that succeed in aggregate but not in specificity.

Since the success of R&D is not in the completion of activities, but in the attainment of a specified quantity and quality of knowledge, the learning plan is built with precisely the same qualities in mind. Since success of any given plan *activity* cannot be predicted, the importance of generating multiple options in the analysis/synthesis stage cannot be overstressed. The synthesis section should have generated *many* different approaches to answer a given technical question. If the learning plan is not built to test one but to test at least several of these different approaches, the likelihood of the plan failing, both in timing and in quality of answers, drops very quickly.

Multiple options build a *variety of thinking*, not redundancy of action, into the plan. The same experiments are never repeated, but different approaches to solve the underlying problem represent exploration. By comparing different approaches, the plan can inform the quality and stability of each approach. This, in turn, delivers choices to the researcher, not merely on solution options, but in a broader sense on how to prosecute the next steps of the plan itself. If a single thought process were tested, there would be nothing to compare to, and nothing to inform future direction, should the results come up short.

In addition to the obvious choice of which experimental approach to try first, second, third, and so on, a plan with multiple learning approaches allows the researcher to stop whenever the quality of answer meets the requirement of the A3, or if time or knowledge needs permit, to continue with deeper inquiry that could lead to a breakthrough or significant improvement beyond what was originally targeted. The researcher can choose problem-solving speed and move on, or choose problem-solving depth and inquire further.

Additional implications exist for those teams and individuals pursuing good-better-best approaches (see previous discussion). In these cases, early successes can be used to both redirect future efforts along the path to best, but also enable the same researcher to push the boundaries *beyond best*, until her research capacity is needed on another part of the project.

It is important to note that neither the ability to increase success nor the ability to flex with knowledge generation exist without the pursuit of multiple options.

Thinking and Cadence in the Learning Plan

Cadence, or the tempo of learning, is important in creating progress. The faster knowledge can get into the system, the more aligned the system will be and the faster the system can operate. In this regard, a very strong

Batch Processing

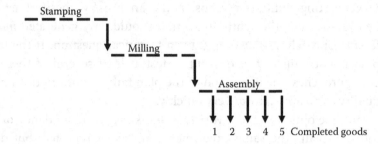

One Piece Flow

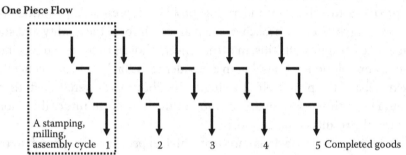

FIGURE 5.2

A graphic depiction of batch vs. flow processing. In the batch processing case, the first sellable product is complete only after all stamping and milling, and one cycle of assembly is completed. In the flow processing case, the first sellable product is available after only one cycle of stamping, milling, and assembly. While the last item is completed at approximately the same time in both processes, the availability of usable material occurs much earlier in the first case. The R&D analogy is that usable information is available much earlier when experiments are designed and executed in a flow rather than a batch mode. Flow is supported by smaller scale, lower cost experimentation. By engaging both methods (flow plus smaller scale), learning is greatly accelerated, usually two- to tenfold.

analogy to Lean manufacturing is the idea of *one-piece flow* (see Figure 5.2). In manufacturing, a process with three steps—for example, stamping, milling, and final assembly of a part—could be accomplished in one of two ways: (a) *batching*, in which all of the parts are run through the first process step, then all run through the second process step, and finally all run through the assembly step, or (b) one-piece flow. In the flow process, stamping, milling, and assembly are done on one part, then a second cycle of stamping, milling, and assembly is done on the next, until the entire set of parts is made.

The obvious downside of batch processing is that release of value takes *much* longer than in one-piece flow. In the batch process, the company must wait until all of the parts have been stamped and milled, and the first part assembled, before it can release a finished product to be sold. In the world of one-piece flow, the first product is ready to be sold in less than one-third the time. This is important because if anything happens in the marketplace—a product update, a market shift, or a product recall, etc.—the batch process will have a significant wasted investment in work in process (WIP), whereas the one-piece flow process will have only raw materials, and, at most, one part in WIP.

One-piece flow is about creating the fastest path to value, which in R&D is new knowledge. The same thing is true in R&D. Small, fast experiments run and release knowledge quickly, confirming successful hypotheses, and enabling researchers to quickly redirect their work when hypotheses prove baseless. This is true not merely for the primary researcher, but for all of the researchers in the community who may, even down the line, be affected by the emerging data. The faster the cycles, even on partial data, the more an individual or team can keep its experiments running in a positive direction. Much less time is spent in blind alleys and nonvaluable research than on progress toward the goal.

This has a strong, positive psychological effect as well. Teresa Amabile, in her groundbreaking work on innovative environments,* showed that progress was a key element in researchers having *good days* at work. What is more, researchers, she found, have more *innovative events* on good days. She showed that good days have an extended effect, with an elevated number of innovative events occurring on days *following* good days as well. That means that progress makes for better days, better days mean extended periods of innovation, and a positive spiral of confidence and capability ensue.

Thoughts on the Learning Plan

Of course, like many things in Lean, the positive effect of breaking experimental scale is not obvious until it is tested, at which point its value astonishes even experienced Lean R&D types. A case in point revolves around a printer manufacturer with a three-year product development cycle. Their normal approach had been to learn, from marketing, the key features that their next product needed to have in order to really excite the marketplace. Marketing typically suggested 18 to 20 new features to

---

* Teresa Amabile and Steven Kramer, *The Progress Principle: Using Small Wins to Ignite Joy, Engagement and Creativity at Work*, Harvard Business Review Press, 2011.

the team, and the team would diligently design those features into the next pilot build. Given the product development cycle, they had time for three experimental prototype builds, the last being a preproduction model. As many of the new features as possible would be built into the first prototype, along with software and other changes intended for the new model. In fact, so many changes were designed that the prototype would invariably fail in testing, and it would fail in such a way that very little could be learned about any of the features or changes the team had designed. A second prototype would be designed with changes based on what was known and hypothesized about the first failure, and, again, with so many changes, little could be learned. The third, preproduction prototype, *had to work*, so the team typically scaled back to the two to four improvements they knew would work, and built those in.

By contrast, a team using A3s with learning plans broken into two-day learning cycles was able to answer the most important technical questions within 20 days. With each technical answer, a new question, with its own A3, was brought on board. Within 60 days, all 18 of marketing's desired features were designed and tested at the subsystem level, leaving proto-typing to test integration. Software updates were also tested on mules in advance of prototype testing. As a result, the effect of bringing the sub-systems together successfully in a full prototype demonstrated issues and opportunities for integrating all of the new parts. Because individual con-tributors were required to break the project down into small, easily exe-cuted pieces, the integrated rate of learning jumped more than fiftyfold.*

Breaking very large, complex problems into small, bite-sized pieces is crucial to aligned progress and to the success of the individual in meeting objectives. It enables the researcher to deliver more value more quickly, which leads to a happier life for the researcher. The takeaway: Create experimental plans that read out *something* every day. Daily progress from such a cadence will make you happier, and that alone will translate into increased innovation. If nothing else, progress is a real career builder. By contrast, imagine the angst experienced by the researcher who builds massive, complex research projects that read out after long hours of toil

---

* Two months of effort yielded 18 new features (9 features a month), where, previously, approxi-mately 24 months of feature design effort would yield about 3 to 4 new features, yielding some-where between 54 and 72 *times* the learning speed of the original process.

performed over years. If a project does not yield the hoped-for learning, the blow can prove devastating.

Scale is the enemy, and breaking a problem into small bits is an excellent approach to improving the rate of innovation. However, it is not the only excellent approach. Good thinking is often just as good or better, which is the reason the analysis section is *so* important. In R&D, *a new question* can eliminate the need to even ask questions previously thought crucial to success (see the section, "Developing Critical Question Maps" in Chapter 8). A friend was advising a furniture manufacturer on Lean product development in a case where an engineer was gearing up to prototype a new assembly, a process that would have taken months and a relatively large amount of money. My friend asked, "Is there any other way to get that knowledge?" The engineer thought for a moment and said, "I could model it on my computer." It turns out that modeling could be done that evening at no additional cost. Thinking beats activity every time. Spend time in the analysis section, and the plan will yield magical results.

Ganging a large number of experiments together into one big batch slows R&D in exactly the same way that batching does in manufacturing. The printer manufacturer was ganging many *different* types of experiments into one prototype; other R&D organizations, like our medicinal chemists, have tried to batch *similar* experiments into one in order to take "advantage" of robotics and scale. The result of batching is that timelines increase dramatically and complexity ramps up unexpectedly. Meanwhile, knowledge can go stale quite suddenly. New knowledge can appear from an academic paper, a different experiment, a competitor, or any of a host of other places. Knowledge WIP, like manufacturing WIP, means that a change in environment can easily change or void the value of that WIP. R&D is especially vulnerable, since any researcher's ability to know what *everyone* in the field is doing is severely limited. It is easy to get caught out while your experiments are running.

Almost as bad, batching tends to decouple the researcher from the purpose of the experiment as designed. Unless a researcher is incredibly diligent in explicitly describing experimental purpose, large batches and their long lead times make it very difficult for the researcher to remember just what was expected of any given experiment in a series. Once lost, the whole learning structure of the scientific method is lost.

For these reasons, the pharmaceutical industry is dismantling its experiment to gain efficiency through batching and automation in the "discovery" processes, an experiment that reduced significantly the cost of producing a single compound, but increased dramatically the time and overall system cost it took to do so. In turn, the damaging effects of batching simultaneously degraded and obscured the effectiveness of pharmaceutical discovery.

Section 4 Summary

As with prior sections, a good learning plan sets the A3 author up for success. By assuming that some elements will fail, the author demonstrates humility and determination in the face of risk. By adopting the principle of one-piece flow, the author ensures a fast route to success. By setting plan measures (time and output expectations or goals), the author ensures at every step that the combined scale of his output will match the overall goals of the A3, reducing unintended underdelivery against goals. At any time, a review or reflection can demonstrate flaws in thinking that can lead to unexpected opportunity, future improvement, or wider engagement of others. By building a plan with different levels of specificity (very specific activities over the next two–three weeks, medium specificity for the next two months, and strategic-level activities over the remainder of the plan), the author satisfies several needs:

1. Provides comfort to managers and others engaged in the A3 that the author will deliver on time with an effective answer
2. Eliminates time spent planning the "unknowable," hence unplannable
3. Provides for the "living" aspect of the A3, by designing activities to support analysis, countermeasure testing, implementation, and so on

SECTION 5: RESULTS AND FUTURE CONSIDERATIONS

This final section is devoted to three things:

1. Enshrining the current state of knowledge about the problem (successful countermeasures, critical intermediate learning during the living development of the A3, and so on), which ensures that the value represented in answering the critical question is captured

2. Ensuring that future researchers can benefit from insights, potential issues, and follow-on implications that the original researcher sensed or observed while answering the question
3. Preserving the future implications of the work left by the current state of the A3

Not ironically, the A3 can be used in partial fulfillment of our original example A3 problem. Importantly, future problem solvers will have access not just to the *results* of an A3 project, but also to the thinking process that went into it.

As most of us learned in graduate school, a research project is never fully completed. There are always several additional experiments that would further inform the problem, improve its outcomes and support a broader understanding or implementation, but there are more important things to pursue, and the research project is eventually abandoned at some acceptable level of quality, which again points to setting a good goal at the outset of the project. This section reflects the thinking process of the A3 owner at the time it is archived.

PULLING IT TOGETHER TO GET THE MOST FROM THE A3

A3 is wonderfully complex in its simplicity. Although it takes years to master, a novice user can gain insights on a problem almost immediately, just by struggling to fill out the form. On even brief reflection, the A3 will highlight flaws in thinking, problem structure, and scientific method. It will enable the researcher to sit longer with a problem before diving into solution state, increasing the likelihood of the problem "speaking to" the researcher and whispering a "eureka" into her ear. It is also a wonderful tool for mentorship and communication, reducing hidden agendas, and opening conversation. It has proved invaluable for sharing information across functions and, importantly, in bringing new team members up to speed. Moreover, since the document is so concise, team members will actually spend the few minutes needed to absorb their contents, where they might resist wading through 40-page research reports.

Finally, at the end of a project, whether functional or product-based, the A3 can be used to memorialize aspects of the project to seed ideas for future project generations. It has been noted that most companies use very little of the prior art they have invested in over the years. Reportedly, Toyota utilizes some 80–90 percent of its prior research through the use of the A3, checklists, and other simple approaches. I have no way to verify this figure, but imagine even a 50 percent leveraging of past work, and the time, energy, and resources it would save. In my travels, I have heard of very few companies that have significantly impacted this area, despite, in some cases, having spent hundreds of millions on databases and knowledge management software. Something is missing in our thought process if Toyota was able to do this for most of its history on large sheets of paper.

6

The Lean R&D Manager

The Lean manager's responsibility is to create environments in which people can flourish. That may not be much of a job description, but it is enough. If a team is struggling with bureaucracy, clearly the bureaucracy barrier is something the manager can work to remove, and a Lean research and development (R&D) manager will go about doing just that. If a team's biases are limiting its ability to see new ways to innovate in an area crucial to the company, the Lean manager will help the team expose their mental barriers. When researchers are struggling with communication issues, the Lean manager will coach them and provide opportunities for them to grow, and shield them as they work through their skill-building process. If her team is having difficulty getting the right information from another area of the company, or operating smoothly with it in some other way, the manager will apply herself to opening doors and building bridges to unblock the flow of work. Within the community, she will hold tension against individuals (and the community) who are thinking poorly, shirking responsibility, or acting inappropriately, while easing the way to collaborative, supportive, and communicative behavior.

Her job, ultimately, is tending to the nonwork systems that surround, infiltrate, and support the community in the pursuit of its common goals. If she can increase those systems' support of learning and collaboration and reduce the bureaucratic or restrictive burdens, she will prove successful. Thereafter, it is the responsibility of each person and the community as a whole to find their own paths to growth.

Not surprisingly, from my viewpoint, every person in a Lean environment is a manager, irrespective of whether or not the company has an explicit managerial function. Each colleague has the opportunity, hence the responsibility, to identify systemic barriers in the environment. Each colleague has the opportunity and responsibility to identify and help expose barriers holding individuals back. This responsibility comes from the *be* state of the Lean person. People who are Lean assume responsibility for themselves, for the community, and for themselves as members of that community, and serve both with equal enthusiasm.

In this way, the Strategic Prosecution of Targets (SPOT) team at Pfizer, which had professional managers, found that it could create and manage its own strategic direction; build its own infrastructure, communication, and collaboration tools; develop immediate prioritization and experimental design norms; and operate virtually independently. Managers explicitly stopped defining work, experimental design and direction, and strategy and priorities. Fully 50 percent of their work time was freed up for the far more valuable task of coaching and removing barriers to growth within the organization.

SKILLS A LEAN MANAGER MUST POSSESS

The basic skills of a Lean manager include the ability to see, without prejudice, group and system dynamics, individual and group thought, and creative and innovative processes. She must be able to see physical, mental, and emotional barriers to innovation within the environment created by those groups and systems. She must be able to reframe the assumptions within the innovation environment and, in so doing, to design individual and group experiences to improve those dynamics as projects progress, ensuring that the growth of individuals, teams, and knowledge all expand as much as possible. She must also have the technical skill to manage knowledge projects, which means she will have to be able to see knowledge growth, an intangible but critical element of R&D delivery.

SEEING EXERCISES

- Observing group and system dynamics in an external setting
- Letting the environment tell you (listening in the internal environment)
- Observing the internal environment (walking the gemba)
- Mapping

Skill-Building Exercise 1: Seeing Group and System Dynamics in an External Setting

These seeing exercises for the Lean manager, like those for the Lean team member, can be done anywhere. The best places to start may be in areas unconnected to your work and personal life. This reduces the likelihood that your mental models will intrude and increases the likelihood of seeing dispassionately, without defensiveness, prejudice or barrier. As you improve your ability to see dispassionately things that are unrelated to you, the chances of your seeing dispassionately in areas closer emotionally to you (home and work) will increase accordingly.

In this exercise, sit in a public place and watch how people interact. Look for patterns of interaction, because those patterns tell you a great deal about the mental models and beliefs held by those people. While you are doing that, consider causes and effects of those patterns. How do those patterns ease interactions? How do they hinder interactions? How do specific, nonpatterned actions and interactions affect others? Do they make others happier, sadder, more anxious, more enthusiastic?

With these questions and answers in mind, since we can almost always see ways in which actions can be made worse (but not always how to make them better), imagine the different ways the people you observe shift their mental models, hence their actions, to make their environment worse. In what ways could they think that could improve their environment? Where do you see the same kinds of mental models, actions, and interactions in your work environments? What experiments could you run to test different mental models and actions to improve those environments?

Skill-Building Exercise 2: Letting the Environment Tell You Its Problems

An absolutely infallible way to see barriers in the workplace, especially systemic and mental model barriers, is to let people describe those barriers themselves. You don't need to set up this exercise; just be there when something unexpected or unhappy occurs. Whenever an experiment goes awry, or when a deadline is missed, individuals and teams will tell you, straightaway, what they believe the barriers to their success are.

Paying attention to what they say gives you an immediate and valuable path to insight, not necessarily into the problems themselves, but, into the mental models of those reporting the issue. It is literally impossible to report issues from a staged viewpoint. People can lie to you, but that immediately tells you their view on honesty as it applies to you. People can shift blame to someone or something else. This reveals one of many things, depending on the accuracy of their assessment:

1. They may be displaying a belief in their own helplessness in addressing problems.
2. They may be displaying frustration with an interface gone awry.
3. They may merely be presenting facts without bias.
4. They may be covering up their own issues, which, again, points to their mental models around punishment, honesty, fear, and so on.

People also can do amazingly positive things, such as showing you how the problem arose, how they thought it through, and what they will do next time. Issue descriptions are an immediate and valuable window into the mental models of those providing the information.

As you can see, it is clear that the first report rarely gives you enough context to act with any real understanding. All you know is that there is a problem and that it is perceived in a certain way by the people reporting it. This leaves you with a valuable set of options for both learning more and for setting yourself up for greater success, both in terms of immediate work progression and improving the environment.

By taking Fujio Cho's[*] advice—"Go see, ask why, show respect"— the manager can gain incredible insight into barriers at the individual employee level, in the immediate work area, and in the system as a whole. In physical work environments, like manufacturing, "show me how it happened" is an excellent next step, but in R&D, it is often not in the physical realm where things go awry. Instead, in the R&D environment, it is more effective to ask the team, for example, what they thought through, tested, and implemented to correct the problem. This provides the team with the immediate feedback that you believe their report to be their correct belief in what happened (showing respect), that you believe that the employees have the ability to have solved the problem (again showing respect), and the expectation that they would have already solved the problem (showing respect and creating positive tension at the same time).

---

[*] Fujio Cho was the chairman of Toyota Motor Company famous for developing a softer style of Lean than Taiichi Ohno.

What such probing questions do not do, however, is indicate that the report is the final word on the problem, or that there is no additional value to be gained by searching further. Such probing questions, when answered, lead both the manager and the employee into a positive cycle of learning about the problem, the mental models of those associated with the problem, and the respective thought processes needed to solve the problem at the same time as manager and employee engage in positive steps to improve trust, the work environment, and problem-solving skills. Each answer gives insight into their thought process and provides a wonderful jumping-off point for identifying and beginning to remove barriers.

If the team members are lying (rare in my experience, but it does happen), then steps must be taken to improve trust. If the team members are blaming others incorrectly, then something must be done to identify and remove barriers to understanding (and trust) that exist between those people or work groups. If the team is reporting that the science just didn't work out, then there is an opportunity to learn what barriers in thinking led to reliance on one experiment when other faster, easier, or better experiments were needed to succeed on time.

Skill-Building Exercise 3: Observing the Internal Environment (Walking the *Gemba*)

Genchi gembutsu, or *gemba*, is the Japanese phrase for "the real place," the place where work actually occurs. There is literally no better and, arguably, no other place where you can understand the environment of the workplace, and yet I made this the third exercise because of its potential emotional closeness to the observer, and the subtlety of the gemba in R&D, compared with manufacturing. This is due entirely to the nature of the gemba in R&D. R&D work happens in the laboratory, but it also happens in the offices of the scientists. It happens when the scientists are spending time with family or friends and, as the famous eureka story goes, it happens in the minds of scientists when they are in the bath. In other words, the workplace for those doing research and development is everyplace.

Unlike manufacturing environments, where the manager can take a walk around the plant, the fact that R&D work can and does occur anywhere, complicates observing the workplace quite a bit, since obviously you cannot be in all of these places. That said, walking the work space gives insight into the social and systemic interactions that cannot be obtained in any other way. You can feel anger, tension, calm, enthusiasm, disillusionment, and determination just by being there.

Another thing that complicates observations in the gemba is that emotional analysis of the workplace is the most subtle and the most easily misinterpreted, and is likely the most valuable of all. In an environment characterized by significant dysfunctional behavior, people will endeavor to act as if there is no dysfunction. But if that can be observed and the barriers causing dysfunction removed, then the gemba will be a much more innovative place.

In this way, I believe that emotional observation should begin in the gemba at the earliest possible time, but before you begin, it is very helpful, for example, to have spent time removing any physical, process or analytical thinking barriers that existed in the workplace (as in Exercise 2) before striking out to find the more subtle barriers that eventually will prove to be your stock-in-trade in creating an innovative environment. This exercise is designed to give you the practice and skill a manager needs to interpret those observations.

Now to the exercise itself: It is valuable to begin by getting a feel for the language and tenor of the conversations and interactions in the gemba. Getting a feel for the environment takes time. You have to be in it for a sufficient time and with sufficient regularity that you can sense changes and sense the truth of things. Once a month won't cut it, so take your time and be present.

Some things to ask yourself while you are there might be questions about the conversations and actions you observe.

Do they feel strained?
Do they feel honest and open?
Do people approach you or turn away?
Do they engage in eye contact or shy away?
Is there banter or debate in the workplace?
Do people challenge other people? If so, how do they do it?
Do you feel comfortable there?

There are an infinite number of similar questions that you can ask yourself. The trick is to be open to those questions, and rather than react to them on their surface, we can begin to look upstream to the mental, emotional, and physical barriers that might inform the activities that answer those questions.

Skill-Building Exercise 4: Seeing and Reframing through Mapping

Value stream maps,* which show all of the activities a team believes it will have to perform in order to deliver its innovation, or Critical Question Maps^SM,† which show the questions that the team will have to answer in delivering its innovation, are the best two methods we have used to identify systemic issues in the work system.

The first value of mapping is that the map itself will show the complexity of the workplace. What functions must be performed (better, what knowledge needs to be gained), by when, by whom, at what level of quality, and for what other group of people to be able to progress smoothly to a successful product? It is absolutely astonishing to most teams to see the work laid out in its entirety in front of them. Without a map, the interconnectivity of work and knowledge transfer required is virtually impossible to grasp.

Second, the map will reveal an incredible amount of workplace bias, unstated assumptions, and uncritical thinking. I cannot tell you how many times people who had previously thought another group's work was easy or unimportant saw things completely differently after a mapping session. It is difficult to describe how often people in the room really had no idea who else was on the team, or how intimately their work affected those other people. It is just as amazing to note the dawning realization within people who had worked feverishly to improve their own work areas that their improvements had significantly and unexpectedly damaged the work of others within the system. In our experience, maps expose barriers to thinking, acting, and communicating, all of which are systems issues that point back to our workplace management mental models (hence designs and activities) and our functional silos, and their effects. Maps are, if built by the scientists who do the work, surprisingly unbiased as well, and reveal obvious problems not just to managers who will be naturally looking for such issues, but to the scientists themselves, who have suffered under false assumptions, often for years.

---

* For a detailed discussion on value stream mapping, see Chapter 9.

† For a detailed discussion on critical question mapping, see Chapter 8.

The difference between a value stream map and a Critical Question Map is also valuable. Often, the value stream map will show work activities that do not answer any critical question. In other circumstances, a value stream map will have no work supporting scientific, organizational, or other questions that are crucial for the success of a project. By pairing the two, tremendous insight into barriers hindering the work environment can be gleaned.

Of caution to the manager, a map is not a gemba walk. Just because it is on paper does not make its circumstances clear, nor will a map reveal the full extent and cause of an exposed issue. For this, digging, dialogue, and experimentation are required.

REFRAMING EXERCISES

Reframing for the manager is the same as for the individual, except the focus will be on systems and community. Once the manager can see the mental models that manage or affect community performance, she can reframe them so that those mental models that inhibit community activity and growth no longer hold sway.

This requires the manager to trace the mental models back to their core operating principle; thus, a dysfunctional activity can be traced back to a mental model, which, itself, can be traced to a controlling belief. Explore alternative beliefs, and you will have reframed the management question.

A classic problem involves functional silos that do not get along. A company always needs both functions to operate, and the interface between them should be so thin as to be transparent. When teams do not play well across the interface, there are usually several mental models operating. "I must control my budget, my employees, material, machinery (etc.) to be successful"; "We must control demand so that we are not overloaded"; or "We are the only people who know how to do this work," and so on. If you can articulate the causes, the feelings, or the beliefs that created or hardened the functional barrier, reframing is often just a matter of changing the verbs, like *control, do,* and *worry*. What if you did not worry about other people taking your work? What if you did not need to control output, input, or budget? If the company grows and you stay static, you will become overloaded, so, if not now, when? How were you planning to handle that eventuality, and why won't that work on a shorter time frame?

We should often remind ourselves of the four main managerial modes of solving problems (hire new people, reorganize or downsize, merge with or acquire another entity, and sell or spin out) and ask ourselves what the immediate and long-term effects any of these will have on the rate and quality of knowledge generation. Compare that to the immediate and long-term effects of increasing the trust and alignment within project teams. Which is faster to instill? Which is least disruptive? Which will have the longest-lasting benefits?

Skill-Building Exercise 5: Disbelieving Your Own Beliefs

When you identify a community issue—be it lack of trust, silos between functions, or any other problem—and have identified the mental model barrier, sit with the problem for a while and think about just flat not believing the truth behind those mental models. If managers are designing work for others, there must be a mental model somewhere that says, "We believe managers must be better at designing work." Sit for a while and try to believe that a manager is *not* better than his reports at designing work. Once you really can see that another belief is possible, you can do two other exercises:

1. Think up as many other beliefs as you can.
2. Think of ways that those other beliefs would be modeled or experienced in your workplace.

Skill-Building Exercise 6: Identifying Other Possible Beliefs

My premise, of course, is that all beliefs, no matter how useful, are also flawed because they limit our vision. But that said, a limitless number of beliefs may be substituted to stand in for the ones you just held. Using our example of "the manager is more able to design work than his charges," we might imagine the following:

- No one is better than anyone else at designing work.
- Consultants are better at designing work.
- Management committees are better at designing work.

- Teams are better at designing work.
- The person doing the work is better at designing work.
- Human resources is better at designing work.
- The Lean implementation team is better at designing work.

What immediately becomes apparent is that all of these are ridiculous. There is no single best solution to the design of work or anything else. At times, a team will be best; at times, the person doing the work and, in some instances, a manager will prove to be better positioned. It is important to recognize that the belief that you use most regularly determines many things about your community. How will a community grow differently if managers, consultants, the Lean team, or the workers themselves design their work?

EXPERIENCE

Once you are in a different frame or, indeed, frameless, you will immediately see other options for the community and ways to implement those options. Your next step is merely designing experiments and seeing their effects within the community. The thing to remember about experience is that what you learn is significantly affected by what you see. Did you observe your experiment with open eyes? Did you allow it to teach you all that it had to offer? If so, your next experiment will be far more effective and, along the way, you will have grown.

Skill-Building Exercise 7: Small-Scale/ High-Velocity Experimentation

A leader I worked with noted that her direct reports looked to her to design and interpret their experiments. This is an obvious barrier to the quick and effective development of science, but just as importantly, it indicates that inexperience (many of her staff were quite junior) or emotional barriers stand in the way of her scientists' ability to innovate. She began by first reflecting their question, "What should I do?" by answering, "Well, what do you think you ought to do?" She then followed them as they described their logic train, asking questions until they had developed a solid experimental design. She did similar experiments in the area of experimental interpretation. Once these skills of experimental design and interpretation were in place, she expanded her push downward to include skills on sharing data and seeking input from others. Importantly, she kept at it until the scientists were fully capable of designing, interpreting, and sharing sophisticated scientific experimentation without help. These scientists, in turn, helped others develop their skills in the same way.

Having identified issues in the gemba and reframed them such that a new outcome (scientific excellence) would result, she was able to identify experiments (mentoring questions, follow-up, and so on) to change the gemba. Using daily practice offered by her normal interactions with the scientists, she was able to gain and transfer experience in improving innovation through her team. Her team proved that capability by transferring their newfound experience to others through their own experimentation.

If you followed the skill-building exercises around seeing and reframing, you will be able, as she did, to find experiments to perform in the gemba that remove physical, emotional, experiential, or other barriers to innovative progress. Jim Luckman, when he was leading the Rochester Technology Center, had his employees create a living list of issues they experienced in the gemba. Each week, the management team would identify one of those issues on Monday. By the end of the day, they would have created a plan to address that issue by the end of the week, and they shared that plan with the workforce. They would then run the plan during the week and share the results with the workforce at the plan's conclusion on Friday.

This process gave the leadership team experience in improving the innovative environment at a reasonably rapid pace. By picking weekly projects, they were able to tackle problems small enough that real and regular progress was assured, but large enough so that meaningful, visible improvement could be seen by all. Imagine how powerful 50 meaningful improvements might be in accelerating work in the innovation environment.

The key, in my view, is to build *regular* experimentation cycles to rapidly improve your ability to create an environment in which scientists can flourish. More than any other, the scientific manager is in position to—and responsible for—creating, maintaining, and improving that environment.

The primary experimental difficulty for the manager is that the experiments a manager runs are primarily concerned with changing assumptions and beliefs, changing behaviors and norms and, in their own way, changing the hearts and minds of scientists with respect to their science and the innovation environment around them. Such experimentation can require very different approaches for different people. Some people respond well and are open to certain phrases and demeanors. Other people, presented with the same phrases or demeanors, will shut down completely.

As an example, note how often companies use euphemisms for their less savory activities. How many different names can you come up with for *layoffs*? Popular terms include *downsizing, right sizing,* and *headcount reductions.* But companies have specific programs, like *transformation, performance management,* and *streamlining.* Likewise, *mentoring, counseling,* and *coaching* have been used to describe activities that companies use to fire people. Obviously, if your company has used euphemisms, you know which words have toxic effects, and if you ever did try the experiment, you quickly learned not to use those words in other contexts. The important point is that we also hold within ourselves much subtler triggers that make us warm or cool to new ideas and approaches. These triggers are not shared equally by all, so the manager is continually developing her experimental approach, in real time, to most effectively engage others in the improvement of the innovation environment.

GROWTH

Growth is of particular importance to the role of the scientific manager. In support of growth, the "performance to plan" metric cannot be overstated. When my friend was experimenting to improve her team, she had two endpoints in mind: First, her team would be capable of designing and interpreting their own experiments that would serve the company's scientific need. Second, her team would gain this experience over an extended period of time. These two goals enabled her to keep, at least at the top of her mind, some key experimental and tracking principles in mind. First, she had a capability assessment, which was the team's ability to independently succeed in experimental design and interpretation. For her to succeed, she had to actually *assess* the growth of the team. She could not just try an experiment and assume it would work.

Second, she had time. No single one of her experiments (or those of her reports) had to succeed, but the package of experiments that she and her scientists tried must eventually yield results. This meant that she could try a method and stick to it for a while. A fast failure did not imply long-term failure (remember, people take time to learn), but at the same time, she could not just repeat the same failed experiment forever. She tracked this with a second experimental parameter, an experiment to see how long it would take for a given experimental course to succeed. She also had a fail-safe point, beyond which she would stop a failing approach and try another.

Taken together, these goals gave our manager a robust set of principles that she used to experiment in her gemba, develop her people, and deliver a more capable innovation environment. To practice growing your organization, you will have to establish and assess progress against these same two elements: First, you will need to define (and assess against that definition) the performance of your innovation environment (or the element of that environment you are trying to improve); and second, you will need to have a time frame in mind to reach that level of performance, and assess yourself against that. Absent the first element, management will lack rigor about when to stop (and shift to a new area of improvement). Usually, this will take the form of slow or no progress, but in other cases will result in unbalanced progress against elements of the system that are well ahead of the rest of the environment. This means exceptional but narrow capability, rather than balanced capability across the whole innovation area. Lacking a time frame, management often takes a "set and forget" attitude toward change. That is, if you do not assess progress with time, you are likely to design an improvement, tell others to implement it, but fail to learn whether it really works with the fullness of time. Quickly, you find that organizations pursuing this form of management train their researchers to not even implement new improvement designs. After a short while, those companies lose even the understanding of how to plan and execute any form of implementation.

Skill-Building Exercise 8: Setting Targets

When you have seen and reframed and decided on a set of experiments, practice setting three other things simultaneously: First, set a performance target—what do you believe the experiment will deliver? Second, set a timing target—when do you believe the experiment will deliver? Finally, set an assessment or reflection cadence or point. If you do an experiment in the lab, you always assess the results. It should be no different when trying to change a system, change a mindset, or change a set of beliefs. How will you assess performance? When will you assess performance? How will you ensure performance is maintained?

Skill-Building Exercise 9: Assessing Performance and Reflecting on Results

Get in the habit of assessing your experiments. Write them down if you have to, but ensure that you go back and assess whether your experiment met expectations. An experiment that meets expectations is the least interesting, because we learn nothing new. We do not even get to say that our assumptions are correct (testing can usually only disprove a hypothesis, testing that does not invalidate a hypothesis is far from proof of its correctness). It does make us feel good, however. What is interesting, is what happens when your predictions did not come out exactly correct. In this case, you know something: Your mental models about that change were incorrect. When your mental models are incorrect, you have an opportunity to theorize and test why. If your organization moved faster than expected, why did it do so? If you can understand this better, your next improvement should be easier and more effective. If your organization moved slower than expected, why did it do so? If you can understand this, you can identify and remediate issues in your thinking as well as issues in your execution style, capability, or follow-through.

PULLING IT TOGETHER

The manager in the Lean R&D environment is most closely linked to improvement of the innovation environment as a whole. She has the same tools—seeing, reframing, experiencing, and growing—that any researcher has, but her realm is completely that of the system as a whole. Her practice should target improving her ability to understand and move that system easily, elegantly, and in a direction that makes it possible for greater numbers of people to flourish to a greater extent.

7

Removing Barriers within the R&D Community

Communities are groups of people that work together toward a common purpose. Their ability to do so, of course, depends on how strongly they see their common purpose, and how effectively they can coordinate their resources against that common purpose. In more than 100 improvement projects within corporate research and development (R&D), some things have emerged in the study of groups in their ability to overcome technical and scientific hurdles over years of effort that, if we are lucky, will yield a new pharmaceutical treatment.

The first is that the majority (sometimes the _vast_ majority) of work that a research community performs is _not_ directed toward achievement of its goals. Instead, a large amount of the time researchers, managers, and support staff spend are in support of the _system_ under which the community operates. Colleagues do work required of them by computers, forms, and facilities. Colleagues do work required to satisfy interfaces between functions, and colleagues do work required by management systems, ranging from project reviews to planning efforts to human resources activities. Even a casual observer will note the amount of time that a project team spends serving the broader system, rather than the scientific work of creation and integration of new knowledge, is quite large. So, let's break down a few examples and show how it looks.

NONINNOVATION WORK

Supporting Basic Work Requirements

In R&D, a basic requirement of every scientist is to document his or her work. She designs an experiment, runs the experiment, checks results against her hypothesis, and then enters it into some sort of record-keeping device. These can be as simple as log books or as complicated as "electronic notebook" systems that substitute for log books, but store information electronically.

In the course of work, materials must often be purchased. In order to do so, the scientist must fill out a form or enter data into a computer system, which then is processed and, at some point in the future, is converted into delivered materials to begin work. In other instances, materials must be machined, and an order must go to a machine shop to perform the work.

These are obvious work requirements, but we can make these activities easy or onerous, and the activities, in themselves, serve nothing but the underlying systems that use or store their data. Forms can be easy or difficult to fill out, and it may even prove that no form is necessary at all, but in the end, minutes and hours every day are spent serving these activities.

Supporting Interfaces

One vice president suggested that 80 percent of all knowledge is lost as soon as it crosses an interface to another group. I cannot even begin to know if that number is right, but consider that there are people who develop formulations, recipes if you will, for the making of something. In the chemical industry, there are formulas for glue, for plastic parts, for explosives and drilling slurries. In the pharmaceutical industry, there are formulas for ointments, creams, tablets, and so on. Each of these is created by someone *steeped* in the understanding of ingredients and their combinations. The person who actually *compounds* the materials together, that is, the person who mixes the ingredients and puts them through an extruder, a mixing tank, a tablet press or what have you, are typically *unskilled* in the understanding of formulation. Their job is to make the stuff, not to design what stuff it is to be made.

The work of a formulator, then, is to condense his science into words, pictures, descriptions, and sequences of steps that the compounder can follow, so that the formulation is made correctly and delivers the desired results. The ability to adequately service that interface—both on the side of the formulator to make the compounding directions clear, and on the compounder's side to understand and implement the intent of the formulator—is vitally important. Now imagine what an 80 percent loss of information might do to the success of that product. The transmission of the knowledge across the barrier is a nontrivial task, and takes a substantial part of our thinking and work effort within R&D. Sometimes all it takes for the transfer to go well is the filling out of a form, while other times require the formulator actually working with the compounder, so that tacit knowledge is transmitted from one person directly to the other through experience.

The transfer processes at handoffs are often overspecified, that is, the sender of materials across the boundary is asked to deliver far more information than is used by the receiver. These processes are just as often underspecified, meaning that the sender of materials does not send nearly enough information for the receiver to do subsequent work correctly. In the former case, extra work is done up front. In the latter case, rework or failed work results.

The total work here should not be understated. There are often many different functions and many more researchers assigned to a given project. At each interaction, an interface between these researchers exists. These can be easy, with low personal and knowledge barriers, or they can literally be walls over which nothing valuable seems to be able to pass. Not uncommonly, people describe the transfer of knowledge at organizational interfaces using the phrase "throwing it over the wall." This is not typically a sign of a well-functioning interface.

Supporting Management Systems

Work systems absorb tremendous amounts of work, and so too do management systems. Everyone knows the effort that goes to support the human resource management systems. The development of yearly goals and the filing of that work into the appropriate forms on the right computer system; the production of quarterly, midyear, and annual evaluations; and finally the analysis and normalization of all of that data so that ranking and promoting and punishing and the like can go on: These activities do not support the growth of knowledge needed to solve a set of biological problems, develop new chemistries, or understand the toxicity and other safety issues surrounding an emerging therapy. I pick on these not because they are useless to a company, but because they stick out as being *not of the scientific work* of the team.

A different example of work spent serving the management system includes project reviews. These reviews are conducted of R&D projects by senior management, with the purpose of understanding the work of R&D, understanding the progress of that work, and then to make decisions about what to do in future evolution of that work. Management can decide that the work should remain on track and keep it headed in the same direction with planned resources. Management could also decide that the work is progressing better (or worse) than expected and that additional resources should be added to (or removed from) the project. Management could decide that emerging circumstances dictate that a new direction should be set for the work. Management could also decide for any number of reasons to terminate the project entirely.

It would be difficult to argue against the validity of any of those choices or the need for assessment. We all want the work to be relevant to the purpose of the company and the company's ultimate success. Reviews, however, constitute work on the part of R&D managers and scientists alike, and a typical work breakdown for a quarterly review might be as follows:

1. Scientists spend three days reviewing their scientific work, summarizing its progress, and preparing thought around its implications, especially as regards future work and the overall success of a project.
2. Scientists spend two days writing up their summaries and preparing PowerPoint presentations for the quarterly review.
3. First-line managers typically spend two to four hours with each scientist learning about scientific progress, considering the presentation materials, and making suggestions to improve the scientific presentations. This typically occurs a week before the quarterly review meeting.
4. Reviews of meetings take upwards of two days, culminating in directional changes to R&D projects that support the strategic needs of the company.

5. Scientists engage line managers in postreview discussions to define tactics to support the new strategic project direction. Subsequent replanning efforts may consume another day.

Formulated like this, the entire quarterly review process takes around two to three weeks and consumes approximately eight scientist working days (about 12 percent of available time). But the big impact is not in the consumption of the scientist's time for meetings or even meeting preparation. It is the redirect itself that causes the greatest impact to the R&D function as a whole.

If we assume that there is a strategic need to redirect a project, then an obvious question is: "When is it most advantageous to redirect the project?" If all scientists are to be engaged 100 percent of the time on work that supports the strategic direction (relevant work) of the company, then it follows that the project must change direction the *instant* either the project work shifts away from established strategic direction, or if the strategic direction itself changes, then the project should change. Any work beyond the instant a strategic shift could be known is wasted work.

And how much wasted work might that be? The amount of wasted work could easily be zero. The project might always remain on track, and no new information might come in to suggest a shift in strategy. However, as our model review is quarterly, the project could conceivably go in the wrong direction for three months, and it could easily go in the wrong direction for as many as two months. These are days, weeks, and months that scientists could have spent working in support of the company, but instead were spent uselessly. Moreover, I believe that you could imagine five or ten different ways of ensuring that the *purpose* of the review is served without either the overhead work involved or the multimonth delay.

Of course, the two examples cited represent only a small portion of the vast, complex noninnovation work that goes on in a team. The amount of time that scientists spend ordering materials, specifying equipment, writing reports, getting information from our libraries (hard copy or electronic), and wrestling with the myriad computer systems of the R&D environment of a company is usually staggering.

Seeing the Noninnovation Work

The previous descriptions of where the work goes is meant to draw attention to the fact that our researchers spend a massive amount of time performing activities that do not strictly increase our levels of knowledge and deliver our innovation. What is more, the work that happens in these and other areas compounds itself. A poor interface slows work on an annual review, which then causes a late handoff, which makes it impossible to order materials before the holiday season, which delays start of work and pushes the project timeline enough that a competitor project appears to leapfrog our technology. Management review then cancels the project and reapplies the work elsewhere. Waste begets waste in R&D as much as it does in manufacturing, and soon, an opportunity is lost due to the literally incalculable interactions of small pieces of work throughout the division, all of which impact other small pieces of work in unexpected and nonlinear ways. The butterfly flapping its wings in our Australian operation causes us to lose a contract six months later in Tennessee.

It is our job, then, to see the work not merely of one person, but of the *system as a whole*, so that it can be made smooth, easy, fast, and relentless in its creation of innovative knowledge. This is not a trivial task, but it is far easier than one might otherwise imagine. After all, organizations are large communities of people and, as a result, have a certain sort of intelligence of their own. If we can see, reframe, and experience better approaches in our own work, our organizations can be brought to see, reframe, and experience improvements of their own. Teams and organizations just require us to develop appropriately scaled exercises and engage management in the wider task of seeing, reframing, etc.

Creating Purpose

Purpose was something left largely unspoken in our dialogue on the individual, but in the community sense, purpose is such an important commodity that I am singling it out. People join groups because they have an affinity for one or many of its stated or tacit purposes. People join the cancer foundation of this or that sort because it is important to them that the suffering caused by that cancer be eradicated from the human condition. People join churches, synagogues, temples, and mosques to align with other members of their faith and share support-ing the values of that faith. People join companies to make cars, to insure others against disaster, to help others invest, to help others treat patients, and so on. Some people join companies for the money, of course, and it is good for these people that companies are a source of wealth that can provide that purpose.

Conversely, people leave organizations when the purposes of those organizations no longer align with their personal beliefs. Churches that offend their parishioners soon have no parish. Companies that have no other purpose than making money often fail in their mission, as there is no other aligning function to direct their strategies, rally their employ-ees, or craft compelling messages to customers. Importantly, it is not the *espoused* purpose of the organization that is important in either draw-ing or losing adherents. It is the effective purpose, and the capability with which that organization fulfills its purpose, that determines how force-fully people are compelled. While most companies have reasonably loyal employees and customers who are regular buyers, there are certain com-panies that have had fiercely loyal employees, and other companies with fiercely loyal customers (think, for a moment, about the implications of people who purchase stickers of their favorite company to place on their car). This loyalty is not generated by a company's love of profits but, rather, by the company's ability to deliver a vision that aligns so closely with peo-ple's sense of being that they carry objects and advertisements from that company to show that they share the same values.

Distilling the company purpose into a message that people can under-stand and relate to should not prove difficult. Think, for example, about how we converted actions into questions. The same thing is true of objects. What question, for example, does an automobile answer? What questions could it answer? What questions could be answered by a toaster oven or a refrigerator? Refrigerators are appliances. They are also displays of wealth, displays of technology, fashion statements, and architectural accents. These are answers to very different questions than "What can I use to pre-serve my food?"

Functions and teams can have defined, passionately held purposes as well. A friend of mine, who was a sales manager in a high-end retail estab-lishment, imbued her direct reports, and through them the company's customers, with the company's purpose of "changing people's lives." The company engaged its customers as if their purpose in coming to the store was to have their lives changed, if only for a few moments, and only in a small way. An Alzheimer's team I had the pleasure of working with had the most powerful unstated purpose of any team I have known. The best way I can think to describe it is that the existence of that group spelled the end for that disease. When you walked down the hall, you knew something big was happening.

SEEING WITHOUT PREJUDICE

In exactly the same way as the individual, the ability to see without prejudice is valuable to a group, just on a grander scale. The first difficulty is in finding ways for the group to see *approximately* the same thing at the same time, and the second is in identifying *what* the group should see without prejudice. The first is handled by using group "intervention" or facilitated activities. The second is a matter for consideration. I have personally mapped communications, work activities, and innovation knowledge gaps. I am quite certain that it is possible to map assumptions, but I have not yet found the right way to facilitate such an exercise.

Group Exercise 1: Seeing without Prejudice, the Current-State Value Stream Map

There are many exercises that enable teams to see, but one of the best is an extended value stream mapping (VSM) exercise in which the team is brought together to map, from inception to completion, each member's activities in doing the work that the team prosecutes (see Chapter 9). By getting all of the activities, along with a few basic metrics, up on a wall with step-by-step flow, the incredible complexity of the work suddenly appears, and it proves invariably more complex and more difficult than any one person could hold in his head. The team, on seeing this, drops an unbelievable amount of pretense about who does what or how hard anyone's work is, and begins to see clearly the interactive effects of working well and collaboratively as opposed to the alternative. Team dynamics improve from just that one activity.

A value stream map shows all the streams of activities that a group takes to create something of value. Just about any work process, either physical, mental, or combinations of both, can be mapped without great difficulty. A group can create a value stream map by placing a description of each activity that they perform in a value stream on a sticky note, and placing those sticky notes in order on a large blank wall (often papered with butcher-block paper or its equivalent). Value stream maps can easily be made on notebook paper, of course, but 20 people applying sticky notes to a wall generates maps of very complicated processes in very short periods of time, perhaps an hour or two.

What results is invariably astonishing to everyone involved. The work, when mapped, leads people to the easy understanding of how much of their work supports the system, and how little of it supports innovation. The map shows just how hard it is for anyone to get anything done because of the complexity of steps required for even simple tasks. The map shows just how hard everyone is working, and this is an invaluable realization for the team as a whole. Perhaps half or more of the teams we have supported contain members who imagine that other groups, functions, or individuals do very little work, while they toil long hours at difficult tasks. There are a few deflated self-images, and occasionally, a few team members see that their work has actively contributed to the suffering of others within the system.

The fact of their common work laid out in front of them has another interesting benefit. It brings them back to their sense of community in solving a *common* problem. When the work is on the board, building toward a goal—say, the clinical testing of a drug candidate or the launch of a new product—everyone on the team suddenly realizes that their work is part of something much larger, and that they are together in the work. The community not only sees its work laid out, it also sees the ties that do, or should, bind them together in a common fight. They externalize whatever enmity they may have felt and begin, again, to see their shared destiny for success or failure.

People are always astonished when the current state emerges, as many of their mental models disintegrate in front of their eyes. For example:

- The biggest single source of work is not my boss or my science, it is *feeding the system*: reports that go nowhere, approvals that add no value, delays because of too much planning, a lack of planning or planning in the wrong places, delays because of finding things, coordinating things, and delays that result from an insufficiently robust process to ensure quality, capability, or speed.

- The belief that the work of the team is easily understood gives way to a clear vision that we work in environments of tremendous complexity, making it nearly impossible for anyone to know with any precision what goes where, by when, by what method, and in what quantity, hence...
- Other people on the team have difficult jobs. In fact, everyone on the team has a difficult job.
- Work is intimately and distantly connected across the entire system. One person's work impacts the work of *many* others.
- Much of what people do negatively impacts the work of others.
- Much of people's work product is built to the wrong level of quality—too much quality in some places (overdelivery) and too little in others (underdelivery), which leads to delay, to rework, and to headaches for everyone.

In seeing these and other things, people suddenly see that they belong to a community, not so much a functional group, and that their poor or confused behavior in the community significantly degrades the performance of the whole. They also see immediately the small things that they can do to improve the system, and that these small things are easy and can have large downstream effects. Seeing, in this case, simultaneously reveals big opportunities for work improvement and brings a community together.

Issues in Value Stream Mapping in R&D

There are two main problems with VSM in the R&D space. First, the whole point of R&D is to create something new. That being the case, there must be some significant changes in either the R&D process or the content of R&D work within that process in order to generate unique value. We must be careful, in other words, to make processes that innovate smoothly and quickly, not processes that just repeat activities that proved successful in the past.

It often happens that the delivered innovation is largely similar to existing products or is an adaptation of an existing design (the next version of our appliance). VSM works exceptionally well in this case. It also can happen that the intended innovation is truly new and has not been attempted anywhere, at least not in our company. As a result, there is no current value stream to map, so VSM will not work. Much of early-stage research falls into this category, as do radically new pathways to similar outputs. (Think for a moment about our polycarbonate example. You cannot use the same processing infrastructure for the large-scale solvent manufacturing process and the customer-based extruder process.) Absent a current state to map, the team will have to devise another route to seeing together. In this case, Critical Question Mapping(SM) (see Chapter 8 and Group Exercise 3 in this chapter) allows you to map a path to the result without any current process to use as a guide.

The second problem is that building a current-state map sometimes results in locking in existing assumptions about how work is or should be done. An unexpected consequence of seeing the system as it is, absent other understanding, is that it influences and reinforces our mental models to see what we already do as "correct." A surprising observation that we had in VSM exercises is that a team that easily maps their current state often has difficulty reframing and designing a new future state. In especially difficult cases, the current-state map can become a full-blown barrier to new thought.

Group Exercise 2: Seeing Team Assumptions

I have honestly had spotty luck with this because, in asking teams to map their assumptions, you are asking people to look at something they had never thought to examine before. It is even difficult to describe what "underlying assumptions" might mean with any great clarity of understanding.* You are, in effect, trying to get others to break through very difficult barriers of perception, to try to do something new and entirely unexpected, which is like asking someone to use a hula hoop for the first time, except that with a hula hoop, you get to see the thing you are trying to do.

In any event, a good place to try this exercise is as part of the monthly reviews in a VSM project. The exercise really begins when a subteam misses a key deliverable and the facilitator begins questioning the team. The questioning begins with the facts. The circumstances and so on are discussed, but once that line of questioning is well covered, you should

---

* I have to confess that it took me several times to see what this concept meant, and I had the advantage of months between exposures to think about it. A team may, in a facilitated session, have as much as a few hours, but usually only tens of minutes to perhaps an hour, to figure it out before moving onto another exercise, so perhaps it is not a surprise that teams struggle with the concept.

begin a second line of questioning around the thought process that went into the plan. What assumptions were required for your original plan to work? Assumptions about the availability of people's time, about how people behave, about governance, about the support or undermining that might come from a dialogue with leadership, about the way in which people interact in the community, about people's motivations, and so on, should be covered until a solid set of questionable assumptions arises. For example, a good facilitator will ask how the team knows that leadership will not allow a test to be run, or will not allow the team to operate in the way that they propose. She will ask the team what evidence it has that people do not want to make a proposed change, or why the team believed that the organization would just accept their proposals without demonstrable improvement data showing its value.

A team that is open to new ideas and new thinking will catch on to the thread of the questioning quite quickly. Pretty soon, they will be asking themselves and their peers the same questions, and the mentoring role of the facilitator will have begun to shift to the team itself.

Just keep in mind that it takes a while for people to understand what you are talking about when you describe hidden or underlying assumptions. It helps immensely to talk about this in one-on-one conversations, to point out your own assumptions at regular intervals, to bring up assumptions that you find exposed in the VSM or other workshop, and so on. With repetition, people will begin to see what you are talking about, and if they begin to practice it themselves, they will soon begin to understand the depth of opportunity that exposing and removing those assumptions will have. This takes time and energy, and the ability to create and hold tension, not letting the team backslide, but instead holding them to task until they develop the skill of seeing assumptions on their own.

Group Exercise 3: Bypass Assumptions Entirely—Critical Question Mapping

People seem to be able to pose questions required to create, do, or deliver almost anything. Interestingly, these questions, to a great degree, seem to bypass people's current thinking and past experience. As a result, if asked to create a map of all of the questions needed to deliver an innovation (a Critical Question Map), a team will bypass the whole assumption question entirely and focus directly on the outstanding technical and business questions facing the team. It is possible, through Critical Question Mapping, to develop a map that is resistant to the creation and holding of mental models in the first place. Over a significant period of time, if the project is built with and managed through the Critical Question Map, there will be no need for the assessment of assumptions. It is my belief, without much supporting data, that this method actually teaches people to see assumptions without them actually having to be explicit about the definition and impact of assumptions in the first place.

I recommend getting as much of the group as possible together at the outset of a project, and have them map the critical questions that must be answered for the successful completion of the project. When this has been accomplished, individual scientists can then develop learning plans, experiments, and the like, to answer the questions. This provides the community with a self-created and yet minimally biased aligning structure for all of their work, a simple and easily constructed "true North" for developing their experiments. By having it laid out, team members also can see who might have similar technical questions to answer—a platform for collaboration and for questions that precede or succeed their own; a platform for establishing standards and goals and for handling questions that are not clearly covered by one function or another; a platform for ensuring that issues do not fall through cracks. Finally, the CQM provides flexibility for elements of the team, i.e., those who get ahead of or behind the overall plan, to rethink how their work filters along many axes, so that the ultimate team goals are met on time and under budget.

REFRAMING EXERCISES

Reframing for a team is a matter of the larger systemic items that they identify from analysis of a current-state map coming together in the minds of everyone on the team, such that the team can then create a common vision of another way of doing things. Future-state mapping serves to codify the results and enables a team to consciously agree on what to change and how to change it. It also serves to stimulate additional reframing, but the reframing itself occurs only within the individual and, hopefully, within the collective mind of the group.

Absent the "seeing" value of the current-state mapping exercise, teams will find it difficult to make explicit trade-offs to improve the work of others. After seeing their own and their coworkers' efforts in a map, researchers find it much easier to make such switches. But before this can happen, they have to make internal switches in their underlying thinking. They have to believe that the system is changeable, that they will have support, and that they are in it together. Their time together in the workshop helps them begin to make these implicit switches when their personal bonds are sufficiently close and the individual scientists recognize each other's capabilities sufficiently well to gel into a new performance state. In these cases, the entire organization will realize together that a change must be made. Often this happens all at once, without realizing that a decision to change has actually taken place. Most high-performing teams gel at some point. In the oft-cited *storming, norming, performing* progression of teams, transitions between these stages are not explicitly agreed to, but occur implicitly without thinking.

So too is the acceptance by a team of Lean. When we support a team, we set goals that cannot be reached by merely doing the same thing "only better." The team cannot succeed by working overtime. If the team is to succeed, its members will have to think and act differently. As long as we hold the team to its goals and continue reinforcing the seeing, reframing, and experiencing exercises, a few members will begin to understand the philosophy. If the tension is held (and holding a team against backsliding into its old ways can be difficult), a point will come where the whole team suddenly crystallizes in a Lean *be state*. People on sports teams or in the military know how to do this, and its application in Lean or other work environments is just as valid. Again, holding sufficient tension within a team while removing enough other distractions will eventually cause the switch to a *be state*. As described, this exercise is one that may be difficult for those not in leadership positions to initiate, but managers should be able to do such things if they have strong intent and perseverance.

The best exercise for helping groups reframe their thought processes, however, is the Critical Question Map. The team can revisit the map and consider different frames to answer those questions every hour of every day for a year, and never consume all of the options. As a result, a well-developed Critical Question Map facilitates reframing while taking very little time or effort to build, and the only tension that would ever need to be built is to ensure the continued use of the map. This is easily effected by merely using the CQM as a project management and tracking tool. In this use, its newness to teams diminishes rapidly, as we are almost all familiar with activity-based tracking and planning tools, and this is only a slight twist on that basic approach.

BUILDING GROUP EXPERIENCE

Group experience is never difficult to build. People interact constantly: At work, the people you most interact with are those who sit near you and those with whom you share common work. These two factors actually tend to align. People who work on common problems tend to be located near one another and vice versa. Although globalization and telecommuting are impacting this somewhat, the phenomenon still holds.

In either case, the important thing is to build common, *positive* experiences within the team and, to the extent possible, to remove opportunity to engage in negative or failing experiences between and among team members. External experiences may be positive or negative without creating significant damage to a team, but internal strife will fracture a team and can make it impossible for the team to succeed. As an example, we worked with a team composed of employees from four different companies working to pull off a large multinational project. The project got off to a poor start, and by the time we were called in to help, the project was two years behind schedule. As the project deteriorated, the team began to fracture along company lines.

To rebuild the team and engage its members in long-term success, we began with a four-day mapping workshop. In the workshop, the maps showed clearly that everyone on the team was working incredible hours, largely doing work to assign or remove blame rather than advance the progress of the project. The workshop—through the visual display of work and the time spent together creating the maps, future states, and plans—solidified enough internal team cohesion that it could begin to function again. It began to distance itself sufficiently from the intercompany wrangling and was able to reimagine its work and its working approach. That team went from a multiyear delay to being on track within six months, despite repeated setbacks to its original plan. The gelling experience of the workshop followed by progress against the main purpose of the team enabled them to build a rapidly improving positive spiral of performance.

PULLING IT TOGETHER TO REMOVE BARRIERS

The key exercise in getting a team to increase its performance is for the members to work together for a significant time against a common problem or, better, a series of problems or, even better, a series of increasingly difficult problems under significant time pressure. This will help them see with a common vision, provide practice in solving problems of increasing difficulty over short time periods, and learn how to quickly improve their performance.

If the company does not have sufficient resources to engage in a multiday intervention, the company could just as easily create a series of smaller but similar situations within the work environment itself. It merely takes reframing on the part of the company and testing some approaches to see which ones move teams and which ones do not. Lean is, after all, an experimental science.

8

Critical Question Mapping

THE EMERGENCE OF CRITICAL QUESTION MAPPING

Value stream mapping (VSM) has been invaluable in getting large research and development (R&D) groups to *see*. It creates a common, visual representation of the work and the basic metrics around how, and how well, that work is performed. But in running VSM workshops in R&D, three problems emerged. The first is that VSM activities do not represent elements of value within R&D.

The second is that, in R&D, we often run into research problems for which there is no precedent. We have no value stream to map, since the value stream has never been designed or executed. This can occur in areas like strategy development, the design and start-up of a new business, the creation and execution of a new type or branch of science, or the development of a new type of product. A recurring case in pharmaceutical R&D is the development of different biological approaches to drug therapies, which require vastly different development and testing approaches than other biologics, let alone the small chemical molecules traditional to the pharmaceutical industry.

The third, and most important, problem is not so much the VSM tool's inability to help people *see*, but rather its inability to help people *reframe*. Our experience is that a value stream map that a team finds easy to develop proves a very powerful mental frame that the team finds difficult to break through. While the logjam is nearly always overcome, this inability to reframe proves very frustrating for teams.

In the course of our early work, we came across value streams that had poor precedent, but we always managed to map something akin to the value stream that the team needed to (re)design. About two years in, we came across a project with no precedent whatever in our company, and we had to try something new. Our design issues were that the team, who had never worked together before, needed to do three main things. First, they needed some way to *see* with a common viewpoint. Second, they needed to be able to convert that common viewpoint into an actionable plan, if not a future state. Finally, they needed to build the trust needed to operate collaboratively across a wide number of functional and organizational boundaries. With this combination, they would be able to progress rapidly against their goals. In other words, they needed the values of the VSM workshop that provided structure to their problem and social context for success, without having the benefit of the structural alignment that a current-state map would provide.

Some of our initial thoughts included group development of A3s and the development of a different paradigm (a different sort of map) to power the VSM workshop. We dismissed the A3 concept on three grounds: First, in our prior work, we had attempted to develop A3s as a group activity. The A3 builds we had done worked well with some teams and not so well with others. When they did not go well, the team would grow frustrated and lose the growing social connection of a VSM workshop.

Second, our experience showed that these efforts, successful or not, were invariably clunky. I initially attributed this to our newness with using and facilitating them, but later found that experienced, outside facilitators had similar issues, and we wanted to support our team with something higher than a 30 to 50 percent success rate. Third, while A3s are fabulous for transmitting information on complex issues in short periods of time, they are not as visual as a map. Somehow, in our culture, visual tools seem to be a big positive for teams. We wanted the visual win.

Meanwhile, we came up against thorny scientific issues in other workshops that the scientists needed to work through. In breakout sessions with these subgroups, we had them develop lists of scientific questions that needed to be resolved. In contrast with our A3 work, these exercises proved smooth and easy to execute. The subteams were always able to describe and develop frameworks and plans for solving these problems without much additional assistance. Importantly, these subteams often developed significant technical innovations as unexpected outcomes of these exercises. Why not, we reasoned, try to build a *mapping* exercise around this concept?

The potential benefits of such a mapping exercise were enormous. While the accurate mapping of a sequence of *activities* required to accomplish a goal requires actually having run that process, if a team could accurately identify the *questions* needed to define a successful process, then we would have a way to create robust *new* projects from scratch. Second, when a person answers a question, she has gained new knowledge, which means that management of a set of questions is the same as management of the build of knowledge. We noted earlier that the completion of activities does not, a priori, get you closer to successfully developing the knowledge required to deliver an R&D output. The answer to a critical scientific question, however, most certainly does move you toward a successful R&D deliverable. It stands to reason that if we have a map of questions required to achieve a scientific or product development goal, we should also have a way to track and manage the growth of knowledge in a scientific or research program. We will know, in effect, how to track and manage R&D value.

Another important observation was that the teams seemed to experience less contentious dialogue when considering questions. While the psychology is not clear, the effect is dramatic. People appear to engage their egos when they interact with statements. For whatever reason, people engage in debating the "correctness" of statements. "We need to get a structure of this protein" may not set off a holy war, but it could easily derail a team into a 30-minute conversation about whether the time and energy of such a path is a wise trade-off compared to its knowledge. By contrast, the identical concept framed as a question, e.g., "How will we understand the protein's structure?" will go completely unchallenged.

Finally, another observation that we really liked was that people can almost always identify new ways to answer a question, but they often cannot come up with alternative activities to accomplish the same task. For some reason, people, when presented with statements or activities, seem to lock their orientation as to what might be possible. These same people, when presented with questions, not only do not display orientation lock, but the opposite happens. Their orientation seems to *open up* to other possibilities. Although we did not know it at the time, a Critical Question Mapping[SM] (CQM[SM]) value has proven itself as an unparalleled reframing tool. It was our thought, going into this project, that we could get the team to define the questions they needed to answer their strategic problem (creating their new business unit or research approach), which they could then order on a board in a flow scheme exactly as a current-state mapping project does with activities. This question map, we reasoned, could then be converted into a future-state map and implementation plan in exactly the same way as a traditional VSM project would. This prediction turned out to be only partially true, and slightly problematic. We did not really know how to describe the mapping process at that time, or how to crisply define what a *critical question* might be, and there was a bit of confusion, but once the team started rolling, it turned out that three unexpectedly valuable things appeared.

First, teams can quite easily define the questions that need to be answered for virtually any project to be successfully delivered, whether or not the team is experienced in running or designing a similar project. This means the CQM concept worked not only for its intended purpose in R&D, but it was also valuable in growth strategy development, organizational structure definition, and many other "fuzzy" areas within a company.*

The second value resulted from something I had initially thought was a problem. We have observed repeatedly that teams building CQMs could not easily create a logical, step-by-step flow by which their critical questions should be answered. This seemed problematic from a project management point of view, but I have since concluded that this shines a beneficial light on the nature of R&D projects. There is *no single, logical way* to flow questions for a multifaceted problem. Some questions are causally linked, of course, but most are not.

A quick example may suffice. The 1968 Dodge Dart automobile was unusual, in that it was a small car for its day, but it accepted *every engine in Chrysler's lineup.* Chrysler put its largest V8, the massive "hemi" power plant, in it. They also installed their workhorse small engine, the "slant 6." Each engine answers the question "how will I power this car?" Clearly, engine development can progress independently of body shell development in automobile design. You could conceivably start engine development 10 years ahead of the body shell, or six months after the initial sketches and still deliver a successful car.

Headlight design can progress independently of dashboard design, stereos independent of electrical system design, and so forth. Some elements become interrelated, of course. It is good to know how much power a stereo

---

* As an interesting aside, most project plans are vulnerable to the appearance of *unknown unknowns*. Teams that develop Critical Question Maps do not seem to have that type of problem. Of course, unknown unknowns do appear, but they are associated with *activities and their output*, not so much with the questions that must be answered. Unknown unknowns appear to be *path dependent* and not linked to the critical question structure. This may not be a general observation, but it has so far held within the problems that we have structured using CQM.

will draw, and how many wires it will require in order to complete the final electrical system design, but as long as the interface is known, the two can operate almost completely independently.

While a precise flow for answering questions is rarely apparent, there are always logical groupings to the questions; in fact, these prove so self-evident that CQMs invariably define subteam project structures without additional work. In any case, there are a lot more questions that can be answered in virtually any order as the project progresses than are causally linked.

Scientists can therefore productively progress any of these questions in whatever order delivers the fastest rate against the retirement of the map as a whole. This means that the CQM is the *most flexible* approach to moving an R&D project ahead. It has the *minimum* structure needed to progress smoothly to the project's logical conclusion. Within the context of what real structure must remain, scientists making breakthroughs in one area, or having epiphanies in another, can quickly jump to those questions without worry about detriment to the overall project progression. This maximizes the team's ability to capitalize on the eureka moment and still stay within the overall integrated projection of project success.

The third value is the alignment of scientists and their work against the project's goals. Great scientists have a tendency to follow up on interesting science, which can pull them, and a project, off course. In projects with large numbers of scientists, there can develop a significant amount of "Brownian motion"—scientific activity directed toward interesting but ultimately not project-progressing objectives. But with R&D teams that develop CQMs, the need to spend effort realigning efforts drops dramatically because there is no real limit on where in that project the scientist can provide value; therefore, a scientist's natural tendency to find something attractive to work on is always immediately at hand *in support of the project's success.* As long as there is an open question, scientists flocking to and answering that question are serving the greater goals of the team directly and unequivocally. The second reason is that there are no *a priori* limits on *how* a question or set of questions are answered. A scientist finding a blind alley can go back to the question and propose one or many other approaches to learning the same thing, and begin again from a different direction. When things get *really* tough, scientists can get really creative. If the team comes back to the map and spends some quality thinking and brainstorming time, they can almost always find another question or set of questions that *obviate* the need to answer the question they were struggling with.

An example of such thinking can be seen in GE R&D's pursuit of new polycarbonate manufacturing methods. Polycarbonate is an engineering plastic made in billion-pound-per-year scale. It serves markets as diverse as automotive parts and optical storage for computers. This is a substantial volume of material, and it was a big moneymaker for General Electric, but the plants required to make it were expensive; the manufacturing method used phosgene (a toxic gas used in WWI); and making modifications to it to serve different markets was tricky.

GE scientists made a breakthrough with a new polycarbonate manufacturing method that used much smaller amounts of phosgene, thereby improving dramatically the safety risks at the plant. GE then licensed and substantially improved a "melt" process that did not use phosgene at all. This process enabled different properties to be built into the plastic, opening up different markets. The next change came when one of these scientists created a new melt process that was even more flexible in delivering product properties, but importantly, this process would work in a plastic extruder, removing completely the need to even *have* a polycarbonate manufacturing plant, a move that could save hundreds of millions of dollars in capital expenditures.

By answering fundamentally different chemical questions, GE scientists changed the basic assumptions about how polycarbonate manufacture could proceed. As a result, GE was able to find ways to reduce and eliminate a key safety risk, and then to eliminate one of the key cost drivers of manufacturing for polycarbonate plastic.

In fact, this is the final value of the CQM. The CQM, *especially when problems occur*, drives the team to *breakthrough innovation*, which is easily accomplished by finding questions that obviate entire sections of the map, or answers those questions that are well established using fundamentally different approaches. The CQM for automobile lighting is not much different now than it was when Henry Ford was rolling out the Model T. That is, the strategic question, "How can I see to drive at night?" has remained with us throughout the history of the car. But this (and its subquestions around styling, visibility, power consumption, and so on) are answered quite differently by the oil lamp, the incandescent bulb, the halogen lamp, the projector beam, and the LED. Pretty powerful stuff.

The reason for this is pretty straightforward, and is linked to our observations about how people are affected by statements and questions. People's orientation tends to lock when they come across statements. Objects, statements, and solutions are fundamentally the same thing. They are answers to questions, and those answers actually hide the underlying questions that might be answered differently. Questions, by contrast, have no predetermined answers; hence, people's imaginations run free to find new ways to answer them. Faster ways, better ways, easier ways, more stylish ways, and, for the 10-year-old child in all of us, cooler ways. A CQM does not seem to lock a scientist's orientations to one or another path; in fact, it tends to open them up to other, more valuable approaches. We predicted this to a certain extent, but the power of it was not clear until projects had progressed, both in speed and in innovative context, well beyond their future-state expectation. It turns out that the CQM is the most powerful reframing tool we have come across in our wanderings.

DEVELOPING CRITICAL QUESTION MAPS

Critical Question Mapping is a five-step process (Figure 8.1):

1. Define a strategic problem or question for a team to resolve or answer.
2. The team brainstorms all of the questions they can think of that need to be answered to resolve the problem or question.
3. The team arranges the questions on a large map, where possible in causal order or flow, and elsewhere in affinity groups of aligned questions.
4. The team reviews the completed map, removing overlaps and identifying gaps.
5. The team iterates steps 2–4 until the map is robust.

Step 1: Defining a Strategic Problem

Critical Question Mapping is just a *seeing* or *framing* approach. Being content neutral, a CQM can be built to help frame literally any problem, but just like value stream mapping, CQM makes its value acutely visible

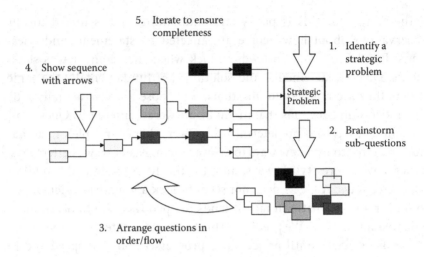

FIGURE 8.1
Critical Question Mapping is a five-step process.

when framing the sort of complex problems that face communities. When things reach a certain level of complexity, it is no longer possible to see them in their entirety, and a visual representation of the problem then becomes quite valuable. That problem could be something as difficult as "find a cure for Alzheimer's Disease (AD)" or as straightforward as "plan and execute next year's chemistry symposium." We have used CQM to address problems from organizational redesign to the creation of business plans and the creation of new businesses themselves. We have mapped the questions necessary to discover the causes of disease and used other maps to overcome the barriers to enrolling patients in large, multinational drug trials. We have helped people map the difficulty that a global conglomerate had in promoting ex-U.S. scientists, and we have used CQM to help another company redesign the development of new medical devices. We have used it to create continuous improvement strategies and build plans to address them.

Once you have picked your problem, identify a team of people who will be working on solving that problem. That group could be the entire community for a strategy development project or just a few individuals, but the group should ideally contain every member of the team that will solve the problem as well as representatives of suppliers and customers that that team will call on or deliver to in the course of its work. It should, at minimum, represent every *function* of the group that will be called on to solve the problem, along with representatives who can speak for suppliers and customers.

Next, develop a goal. The goal may be contained in the problem statement or not, but it is best if the problem statement and the goal are separated.* The goal should be something like a performance measure or definition. What, for example, does *cure* mean for an AD patient? For some it might be that the progression of the disease stops. Perhaps a little memory loss remains, but the patient gets no worse. For others, it may mean the complete reversal of the disease to a fully restored state of health. In this case, our goal would have some desired level of performance for whatever "cure" is developed. As for our symposium, it may be OK to get the scientists together with an agenda in a nice geographic location and otherwise let them fend for themselves, or it may be the goal of the team to expand membership or scientist satisfaction with the event. Whatever the performance level is, its attainment should be impossible using existing thought processes. Different goals generate different questions, which demand different types of innovation to answer them. Therefore, define what you really want up front so that the questions, when answered, yield the level of innovation and performance you'd like for your community.

Step 2: Brainstorming

Get the team *physically* together in the same room. This can hardly be stressed enough. Mapping is a visual thing that cannot be phoned in. This part is obvious but, in addition, the team dynamic created in the mapping process will prove critical to the community come innovation time. This dynamic happens when people put questions on the board, sparking thoughts and ideas in other people. Those people create new questions that reinvigorate thinking on the part of the first group. A rapid, positive spiral of learning, questioning, and common discovery results, delivering two key elements needed for implementation: First, the team builds trust from working with others in a positive, engaging environment. Second, the team as a whole begins to see

---

* As there is with A3 development, there is often great difficulty here in creating problem statements that do not already contain answers (i.e., the company does not have an <answer> to do *x*). Such answers are the result of our mental models prematurely defining paths we think will prove successful. The point of a CQM, however, is to provide problem-solving structure without intrusion of our mental models.

the problem or strategic question and its complexity and nuance in the same way. Absent this alignment, integration of learning and innovation is difficult.

In terms of facilitation, we ask the team to discuss both the strategic problem or question and the goal of the project, and ask the team to put both the problem and goal into their own words. Rewording is important psychologically in shifting problem ownership from the person who proposed the problem to the community itself. Once the team's language has been settled on, the problem is no longer someone else's to solve, but is now linked to them personally. The last step is to ask the team to brainstorm all of the questions they can think of that are required to answer the question at the level of the goal.

The team is then given a definition of a *critical question*, that is, a question whose answer is required if the strategic problem is to be solved. They are asked to brainstorm such questions against the problem they just redefined and to write each question on a sticky note.* There is only one rule for the brainstorming session: All sticky notes must be worded in the form of a question. No statements are allowed, not even as shorthand, because, as we've demonstrated, people do not react as well to statements as they do to questions.

Step 3: Arranging the Questions and Flow

The next step is to arrange the questions on a map.† Logistically, any large-sized, vertical place where the sticky notes can attach will do, including walls, butcher paper, a whiteboard—whatever works. Size dictates the level of specificity of the questions. We find that 5 feet × 12 feet (1.5 meters × 4 meters) usually gives the right level of strategic perspective. Too much less, and important details are lost; too much more, and the team can get stuck on minutiae. We arrange the problem in chronological order, where such is possible, and then add arrows to show causal linkage between questions or groups of questions that must be answered in sequence.

---

* We use 4-inch × 4-inch sticky notes (e.g., Post-It® note paper) to provide enough space. We have also found that the visual effect of mapping functional areas using color-coded sticky notes provides valuable insight.

† Concurrent brainstorming and placement of sticky notes often proves more effective than a step-by-step approach.

Steps 4 and 5: Review and Iteration

Review is quite simple. The team reads through and discusses the questions on the board. Redundant questions are removed; missing questions are either captured and inserted immediately or saved for another iteration of brainstorming. We use the latter case in three instances:

1. Where there are large sections of questions that have not been considered
2. Where there are large sections of questions that have insufficient detail
3. Cases where teams are very large and dynamic interplay may not be possible

MANAGING CREATIVE AND R&D PROJECTS USING CRITICAL QUESTIONS

A very detailed critical question map will represent the entire body of knowledge required to successfully deliver a project. In the case of R&D, a detailed CQM will define the body of knowledge needed to deliver a new product, including its capabilities (for marketing to describe and for sales to sell) and its manufacturing methods and needs. For products that rely on the same types of technology for all iterations, many of the critical questions will have plug-in answers that already meet the community's performance needs for that project. The rest of the questions will have no answers, or they will have insufficiently mature answers to meet customer or market performance requirements. This set of questions represents, quite clearly and effectively, the knowledge that R&D must accrete for the project to succeed. It is a *knowledge or learning gap* map! Managing the critical question map is equivalent to managing learning.

There are three main activities that the community engages in while managing a critical question map.

1. Managing and tracking the flow of knowledge accretion
2. Managing learning cadence
3. Improving the environment (generally by identifying and removing barrier mental models as they become apparent)

The first two are quite straightforward, almost box-checking exercises, comparing performance to plan. Are the questions answered on time with the desired level of knowledge? Of course, answering each question can prove easier and faster than predicted, exactly as predicted, or more arduous and time consuming than predicted. In normal project management, the idea is to shift resources from questions that are easily answered to those that are proving less tractable, thus staying on time and budget; or when the team as a whole is ahead, the team can deliver more quickly to launch, to build more features and content into the current development project, or to shift resources to another project entirely. When the team is behind, it can create its success in one of two ways: first through typical Lean R&D measures, that is, by reducing the scale and increasing the cadence of learning, or by engaging in the rapid, holistic improvement of the environment in which the community currently operates. The only way to do this is by identifying and removing those mental barriers that separate the team from its success.

The second way is by returning to the Critical Question Map and asking a *different set* of questions. If there is a problem in building a manufacturing plant, the team could succeed by answering, "How can we find a way to *not* have a manufacturing plant?" GE polycarbonate scientists were able to do just that. If there is a problem in making something last the life of the underlying product, as there was with photocopier parts, answering the question, "How can we make those parts cheap and easily replaced?" can resolve the issue. Canon did just that with the toner/fuser cartridge, upending (or perhaps redefining) the photocopier and laser printer business.

My initial forays into managing R&D projects using value stream or Critical Question Maps relied heavily on mechanical approaches. These were based on tiered *learning reviews*, with large, structured reviews every 30 days to cover the entire project; shorter, weekly reviews focusing on problems; and daily (15-minute) reviews to describe the purpose of the day's activities and the experiments to support them. These reviews were, respectively, full-project Plan-Do-Check-Act (PDCA) checks, weekly PDCA checks, and daily PD checks, all using A3s to simplify, condense, and inform the discussions. What happened at these reviews was that the team could, as a group, again *see* the larger picture, *see* the hurdles in the science being discussed, and work together to reframe the project with the subteams so that it remained on track or, in fact, moved forward at a much higher level of innovation and speed. These reviews build or rebuild trust; they maintain alignment within the community; and they enable team members to once again step forward and lead their own approaches to answering questions.

As stated, these reviews are a *mechanical* approach to enforce the use of learning cycles and a fast cadence of learning. For teams just starting out, these reviews are invaluable, and, in fact, the monthly reviews are crucial. When we talk about managers holding the tension, it is in the 30-day review that this becomes most obvious. Typically, teams that have not had discipline in designing and executing their own science let things slide, work on other aspects of their jobs, find something interesting to work on, or worse, see the whole exercise as an *addition* to their current workload (rather than the entirety of their workload).

At the 30-day review, a good half of the teams we have worked with are barely further along than the day they designed their future states and experiments to get there. At the 30-day review, when the subteams are asked, one at a time, why they did not begin or complete the experiments they designed for that period, the tension ratchets up dramatically. There are always many reasons why they have not achieved their own goals or followed their own plans, and these are legitimate but, more important, they provide fodder for the next set of questions.

In offering their reasons, these teams are telling you precisely what the barriers are that exist within themselves and within the environment. Quick follow-up questions shift the thought process quite a ways *if management is willing to hold the tension!* Follow-up questions might include

If you did not have enough time, what experiments did you do to reduce the workload so that enough time was available?

If the materials were not available, in what other ways could you have answered that question?

If you are waiting for equipment, what other questions can you tackle while waiting?

These questions immediately engage the team's thinking on a different level. They *assume* the reasons for failure against plan were legitimate. They *assume* that the scientists could have thought about the problem and come up with a different approach and succeeded. In other words, they build on a belief that problems are real and that the scientists themselves are fully capable of solving them, and doing so in the time allotted. These questions create tension within the team members to step up to their own capability, and serve to showcase the community's need for their very best work.

The mechanical approach is not a requirement. The Strategic Prosecution of Targets (SPOT) team at Pfizer did a dynamic review. The daily conversations shifted from describing achievements to describing problems, and the discussions shifted to developing multiple options for overcoming those problems. They did go too far between full team meetings at one point, and the science began to diverge from the purpose, but the full meeting quickly brought the team back on point.

As a result of this, I strongly recommend that management, rather than looking for a cookbook on managing Lean, take a different approach: Experiment with an approach that you think may work. Identify its problems in use. Redesign it to remove those problems and repeat. In other words, pursue management as a scientific research project.

CQM IN THE REAL WORLD

Critical Question Maps turn out to solve some very important problems in creating, managing, and succeeding in R&D projects. From a strictly business perspective, questions represent a proxy for valuable knowledge, the only valuable output of R&D. By engaging people visually, people can quickly see gaps and overlaps in the map, helping to ensure project robustness from its outset. By answering adequately the questions posed in a robust map, a project will successfully deliver against its goals. By managing the progress of question answering, a management team can often bring projects in ahead of time and under budget, just by continually coming back to the question format and engaging scientists in answering questions differently, more easily, more quickly, and more cheaply.

From a social perspective, engaging people through questions helps reduce interpersonal barriers to work and immediately begins aligning people through a common purpose. By allowing freedom to engage in problems across the map, scientists will naturally engage each other, irrespective of status or specialty, establishing and strengthening interpersonal bonds and strengthening the social fabric of the team. Critical Question Mapping is a powerful tool for the development, management, and ultimate success of a Lean R&D organization.

9

Value Stream Mapping in the R&D Space

I am no fan of tools because they can very easily begin to substitute for good thinking. However, there are three tools I discuss in some depth, and for very specific reasons:

A3 format
Critical Question Mapping[SM] (CQM[SM])
Value stream mapping (VSM)

The A3 format is important because it embodies the entire Lean (a.k.a. scientific) thinking process, and its use promotes practice in, and the quality of, good thinking.

I promote CQM for two reasons: First, CQM removes people from their current way of thinking and almost simultaneously enables them to see and reframe their thinking. This has all kinds of positive effects, from merely opening people's orientation to establishing a structure to intentionally and *effectively* design breakthrough products and ideas. In a nutshell, it is an invaluable tool for creating innovative platforms within your research and development (R&D) teams. Second, CQM is an incredibly valuable tool for managing knowledge growth. With a good CQM, a team can actively and successfully manage a changing learning and timeline landscape, bringing in projects on time despite dramatic changes in the R&D environment. Researchers, seeing the required technical direction so clearly in their minds, focus all of their creativity in alignment with their peers. This decreases time spent on interesting but ultimately unused science, and it does so without appreciably narrowing the creative space so highly valued by researchers.

VSM is the third of these important tools. Like A3 and CQM, VSM is not a requirement for successfully becoming Lean, but as an implementation device, it is invaluable on many levels. First, it provides the design and implementation team with unbiased understanding of the work they currently perform—a clear vision of their required performance that delivers clarity for design. Second, it builds team unity and direction in a well-structured environment. Finally, and most important in my view, it serves as a platform to enable entire *communities* to experience and adopt Lean simultaneously. This may not be its obvious, or even intended purpose, but it is perhaps its most important one. People coming to Lean must leave much of their earlier ways of thinking behind. They must abandon their old paradigms, and as Thomas Kuhn suggests in his wonderful history of scientific revolutions,* people who abandon one paradigm must simultaneously substitute a new one.

I would argue that the Lean philosophy takes the position that all paradigms are useful in limited context. Similarly, they are all incorrect when more knowledge is gained or a broader/narrower scope is considered. This is quite a difficult leap to make and sustain on your own when your whole life—as well as that of everyone around you—has been focused on finding and implementing *the correct* way to view things, do things, and think about things. As I have found in my own life, and as several of our teams have demonstrated, it is far easier to make that same leap with a group of friends and teammates. People making the same leap talk about the leap and its implications, challenge each other when their thoughts drift away, and support each other in learning how to exist within this new thought process.† Support makes taking the leap much easier to do and to sustain.

The purpose of the VSM projects that we run at Pfizer is to shift the technical, social, management, and learning performance of a given R&D community. Technical performance is simply the community's performance in terms of speed, quality, and integration of the work activities that the

---

* Thomas Kuhn, *The Structure of Scientific Revolutions*, 3rd ed. (Chicago: University of Chicago Press, 1996).
† One group insisted that we include *all* team members in our design workshop. This exceeded our normal workshop size by almost a factor of two, but in my view, this proved to be better in the end because all team members were included, engaged, and transforming their Lean thoughts together.

community performs. Social performance is the level and intensity of social barriers or synergies between people, including such things as trust, communication, and so on. Social performance sets *informal* (unseen) limits on the adjustment speed of the system. Management performance includes the management systems (e.g., prioritization, resource allocation, funding, and governance) and the mental models that establish and propagate such systems. Management systems place both informal and *formal* limits on the adjustment speed of the system. Learning performance encompasses the speed and breadth of an individual's, a subteam's, or a community's ability to rapidly see, reframe, experience, and grow. Learning performance puts unseen but formal limits on the rate and scale of innovation.

Our VSM projects have three phases: scoping, design, and implementation.

Scoping is a discussion with the leadership of the community that defines the performance needs of the community. Scoping establishes leadership's role in the achievement of that new performance level. Scoping determines the participants from the wider community who will be charged with designing how the community will achieve that envisioned performance level. Scoping also lays out the restrictions that the design team will have in getting to that envisioned level of performance. In other words, the leaders will define the performance level their R&D system must deliver, who will design and implement the new R&D systems, and the design limits in terms of things like staffing and investment levels, organizational structure, and so on.

Design is the actual mapping workshop that we hold with the team. Although we use other variants, a very effective format, for a variety of reasons, is the three-day VSM workshop, which includes an introduction to mapping and current-state (and/or critical question) mapping on the first day; system analysis, reframing, and future-state mapping on the second day; and the building of experiments in the form of, for example, A3s and synthesizing those experiments into a learning project plan on the third day.

Implementation is simply a cadenced execution (hence practice) of the learning plan using fast learning cycle structures (e.g., See-Reframe-Experience-Grow, Plan-Do-Check-Act, or Observe-Orient-Decide-Act). It is important to note that we *expect* aspects of our design to fail.

During implementation, the team is trained to look for places where the implementation of the future state, or the future-state process itself, is failing, so that they can see the barriers to the success of their future-state vision, reframe their mental models, design and execute new experiences, and grow through their eventual achievement.

One major difference between learning plans and regular implementation plans is what happens when something fails. In a normal process, there is no explicit mechanism to adapt to failure. As a result, even a few well-placed failures can cause the whole project to collapse. In Lean, we recognize that—like in any good research project—a complex, system-wide change will encounter issues large and small. Our mental models cannot reliably predict the future. Failure of some sort, then, is almost assured. Since we cannot avoid failure, we embrace failure of elements of the change. We seek them out as platforms for additional learning and use them to engage the next level of seeing, reframing, and experiencing, so that the project can grow its value faster and farther than its original design. In a Lean implementation, failure should actually improve the outcome of the implementation in terms of both speed and value.*

This approach quickly enables shifts in management mental models and management systems. If leadership (a) sets the performance vision, (b) allows the team to design the future state that embodies that vision, and (c) lets the team define its own path to that vision, leadership will establish an implicit bond of trust. If, during implementation, the researchers on the team work through the problems that surface in testing their future-state system, and prevail in achieving the community's performance goals, the team will establish a level of trust with leadership. Once established, leadership need no longer hold the mental model that it must design the work of the researchers. It can then apply its time to more strategic pursuits.

The key here is one of holding tension. For the project to succeed, leadership must insist that the team achieve its goals despite setbacks. Moreover, leadership *must not* step in and design or dictate implementation when the team is struggling. To do so shifts the responsibility back to leadership

---

* Nassim Nicholas Taleb calls this sort of improvement from failure or abuse "antifragile," which he describes in an interview for *The Economist* (http://www.economist.com/blogs/multimedia/2010/11/nassim_taleb_antifragility). In his formulation, antifragile objects actually improve when they experience failure are ill treated, and are thus the opposite of fragile objects. Most learning systems are, to a greater or lesser degree, antifragile.

and away from the place where the work is clearest and the need most acute. Leadership may mentor, for example, by asking questions of the team, by probing whether thought is sufficiently robust, or by looking into whether planned actions are likely to deliver against project goals. But importantly, management cannot dictate situations or thinking processes. It is *extremely* difficult for a manager, especially a caring manager, to stand back when the team is struggling the most and simply insist that they think the problem through to a successful conclusion. The tension can be unbearable, but if you can hold out, when the breakthrough comes, the organization will have entered a new realm of ability.

This breakthrough is accompanied by very important shifts in the team's management systems and social systems. The management system can change immediately. Since managers need no longer define and design work for researchers, they can apply their time to more strategic pursuits. Researchers can design and implement their own work, given a framework of performance and time to envision appropriate paths to achieve it. At the same time, the social system will have changed. Scientists will have hard evidence that their ideas, in all types of work areas, are valued at all levels of the community. Trust within the community will leap, no matter how strong it was prior to the project. This increases confidence, provides experience in problem solving away from the bench, and reduces those mental models that inhibit honest dialogue between researchers and managers. Managers, in turn, have their own barriers reduced—gaining trust in their scientists' creativity and ability to work in "management" space while increasing their own ability to step back and apply their skills to more valuable problems.

A VSM workshop brings other social aspects into play. Like training or boot camps, a VSM workshop is an immersion event, holding a team's total focus for several days on solving a community problem. Because researchers spend considerable time exclusively on the *common* problem in front of everyone, the barriers that may exist between people dissolve to a significant extent. In large companies, it is astonishing to note how many people who work on the same team have never met. This happens in cross-company projects and in other circumstances where many people from different functions, sites, organizations, or even different countries may work on the same team. For these teams, immersion brings people together long enough against a shared purpose to build a sense of community where none may previously have existed. This helps researchers understand who is on the team, their expertise and role in doing the community's work, and how each person's work connects to the whole. This removes such basic barriers to human interaction as knowing whom to call when something goes unexpectedly well, when something breaks, or when unique advice is required, and it enables people to support innovation, pitching in with unexpected talents.

In fact, this social aspect of the VSM project can be measured quite readily using what are called *social network maps*. Chapter 11 details a case example of a Lean R&D transformation in which changes can be seen through their before-and-after social network maps. Figure 11.1a shows the social network of a team before a project. In this figure, you can see the organizational structure reflected in the connections between people. Everyone is linked, but not directly. Only the managers are truly cross-functionally connected. In Figure 11.1b, created at the end of the project, nearly everyone on the team knows what each member of the team does and communicates with them directly rather than through an intermediary, like a manager. This map implies knowledge, familiarity, and collaborations impossible in the preworkshop network. Consider, for a moment, how much faster knowledge can build if an individual need not call a meeting with a manager to set up a meeting with another manager's direct report. In the team shown, the broad team communication of emerging, strategically important external knowledge[*] was on the order of 20 minutes. The resulting dialogue and reset of strategy based on that external knowledge was on the order of 2 hours.[†]

SCOPING TO DEFINE DIRECTION AND PERFORMANCE LEVEL

At some point, a community's purpose will change or the community's performance will no longer adequately support its purpose. At that point,

---

[*] Examples of such knowledge would include significant research papers, clinical data, and emerging scientific news.

[†] Times are based on the publication time stamp of a landmark journal article. As a point of comparison, other researchers (outside of the team) were forwarding to the team that same scientific article a full two weeks after this team had already changed strategy.

something must be done to change the direction or level of performance of that community, or the community itself will eventually fail.

What sort of performance shift are we talking about? Toyota product development provides many good examples, the first of which is the development of the Lexus. When the Lexus was designed, the purpose of the R&D community shifted from producing very high-quality low-cost cars to producing very high-quality luxury vehicles. The systems and mental models viable in the low-cost model had to change in order to support the level of performance expected by the luxury car buyer. Importantly, Toyota did not want to be just *any* luxury car manufacturer, but the *leading* luxury car manufacturer. To do this, Toyota had to redesign its product development system, creating research efforts in sound control, power, electrical, and other systems that they would need in order to lead the luxury market. Their performance goal was not simply to develop a competitive luxury model, but to create the top-selling luxury model in the market.

The difference between Toyota changing its R&D, and most other companies changing their R&D, is that Toyota started with a very strong understanding of how it performed its R&D. Toyota had a well-established, well-articulated process for developing automobiles, an R&D system. By understanding which parts of the system would support luxury vehicle development, and which parts needed to be changed or augmented, the lead engineer had an excellent starting place from which to proceed. He also had clear expectations for his product. As a result, when the Lexus debuted as a marque, it quickly became the leading luxury brand, as Toyota had intended.

A second example from Toyota is its R&D cycle time. To ensure its competitive position, Toyota product development knows that its total cycle time, from clean sheet to product launch, must be the shortest in the industry while delivering the highest quality product. Toyota knows that if it does not enjoy a lead in product development cycle time, other companies will learn faster from the market, adjust faster, and always have fresher, more compelling products.* This lesson became most clear during the Honda-Yamaha motorcycle wars of the 1980s.† Yamaha built

---

* Chester W. Richards, in his book, *Certain to Win: The Strategy of John Boyd Applied to Business* (Bloomington, IN: Xlibris, 2004), shows clearly the link between learning speed in R&D and elsewhere as contributors to corporate success, and describes Boyd's fast-learning theories and their implications for success in conflict.

† George Stalk Jr. and Thomas M. Hout, *Competing against Time: How Time-Based Competition Is Reshaping Global Markets* (New York: Free Press, 1990).

a new, high-capacity production facility to produce its bikes at low cost, and then publicly announced that it was going to take the number-one market share position away from Honda. With Honda's existing superiority in product development cycle time, and a strong push to decrease that time further, Honda delivered more than 60 new models in 18 months. Because their product development time was far shorter than 18 months, and knowing Yamaha's goal, Honda was testing the market, revising, and introducing new models during that period. As a result, Honda actually *moved* the market to a new place. Yamaha, reading the same market, shifted its direction as well, but by the time their shifts were brought to the market, Honda had created another shift. Soon, Yamaha's high-capacity plant was pouring out models that no one wanted, and Honda actually extended its marketplace lead. Toyota is not insensitive to this understanding. To maintain its lead in product development cycle time, Toyota has redesigned its product development systems with some regularity.

In the cases in which Toyota wished to leap forward in R&D performance, Toyota has charged the chief engineers of key products to also redesign R&D to operate at the community's new performance expectations. The primary purpose of the scoping meeting is to create, on a smaller scale, the sort of community vision that Toyota creates for its chief engineers as well as the parameters in which chief engineers and their teams can operate. In this way, the scoping session helps leadership define the performance that the new R&D system must deliver and the boundaries within which the team must operate. Often, these boundaries include obvious things, like leaving organizational structures intact or achieving performance without additional capital expenditures or hiring, but typically they also exclude information technology (IT) changes, because new software often takes longer to develop than the 90-day implementation period of the project (and because a good, well-tested business design converts to software far more effectively than devising a software answer when the business design is not robust or already is embedded in the company).

The performance level and boundaries set a strong aligning direction. For very large and complex systems, the scoping session also engages the leadership in identifying representative members of the community to design and realize that new performance level. It is our experience that the more members of the community that are engaged in the design and

realization of the future state, the fewer problems you will have in implementation. This is only natural, as more of the team will have the same
vision of the future and how to get there. It also creates a much more cohesive community, as noted previously; on the other hand, there may be limits to how many people can reasonably be in one room together working
on the same problem. Our current high level is 50 people, but I believe we
can facilitate groups of up to 75. The trade-off is that it is a *lot* easier to
facilitate groups of 20 or fewer than it is groups of 50 or more. I encourage
you to experiment, testing the limits of your best facilitators in engaging
the community.

Who should be in the room is a critical consideration. Important to the
success of the team is the inclusion of representatives of the system being
changed as well as the suppliers and customers of that system. Without
solid understanding of the needs and capabilities of those interfaces, the
future-state performance of the community will be susceptible to unintended consequences impacting people, organizations, and companies
outside of the community. These impacts could undermine most or all of
the value intended in the development of the new systems.

We use many tools in the scoping of projects, none of which is
required, but any one of which could prove useful. To get leadership
groups to see together and define precisely the opportunity they want
to capture, we use things as simple as open discussion, as strange as
neurolinguistic programming (in which we ask the leadership team to
envision themselves on a beach a year from now, celebrating the success of their community, thinking back on what was achieved), and
as structured as abbreviated A3s and Critical Question Mapping.
To structure the boundaries of the system, we use SIPOC (suppliers,
inputs, process, outputs, customers) templates. The tools themselves
are not important. What is important is gaining alignment on the part
of leadership as to the direction and extent of change the community
must undergo. In some cases, this is as simple as a half-hour discussion. In other cases, when leadership teams have been at loggerheads, it
takes four hours just to get alignment on vision, and the nuts and bolts
of who will attend the design meeting is left to individual discussions
held at a later date.

Once direction is set, the team assigned, and the logistics (date and
location of event) are locked in, the community is ready to engage in the
design workshop.

THE DESIGN (VALUE STREAM MAPPING) WORKSHOP

Current-State Mapping (Day 1)

As noted, the workshop flows in three sections, which might be described as our favorite seeing, reframing, and (design for) experiencing sections of our learning cycle. The first day is solely devoted to seeing and aligning the team against our current performance as distinct from our intended or required performance. We initiate the project by showing the team their leadership's output from scoping, which includes things like performance, out-of-scope items, start and end points they think the project should encompass, and so on. The team then redefines these things in their own words before starting. The point of this exercise is to transfer, at the earliest possible moment, ownership of the project and its success from leadership to the team. To paraphrase the Tao, when the leader has been successful, the people will (in this case accurately) say they have done it themselves.*

When the entire team is aligned on goals, we begin a light exercise to train them in VSM. As with every other tool, the training exercise is not a requirement and we do not always do it, but it helps, in particular, to see barriers within the value stream—things like a lack of flow, redundancy, and poor quality as well as possible ways to address and overcome those barriers. It also helps to break the ice, enabling people to actively participate in mapping something, thereby reducing fears before having to actually show the performance of their own work in front of others.

After our exercise, when everyone knows how to map and how to see, we go into VSM of the team's work. This progresses in the following steps:

- Write down on sticky notes the activities that your group performed in the course of a recent project.†
  - Metric 1: Cycle time (the total time it took to perform that activity from notification to handoff)

---

* Lau Tsu, *The Tao Te Ching*, trans. Stephen Aldiss and Stanley Lombardo (Boston: Shambhala, 2007).
† We usually try to map two projects. To show contrast, we map the best of the best projects and the worst of the worst projects. Our experience shows that the best projects do not differ markedly from the worst projects. The same mistakes and issues are involved; however, in the best projects, luck broke for the team, while in the worst projects, the team's luck broke against the team. This is an interesting observation on its own, but one that help get teams to see the value of creating and returning to systemic views of their work.

- Metric 2: Process time—the actual time *people* worked on that activity (full-time equivalent [FTE] hours, minutes, whatever is appropriate)
- Metric 3: Percent complete and accurate (%C/A is the first-pass success of that process step as viewed by the *customer* of the process step)
- Arrange the sticky notes in chronological order from the start of the project to the completion of the project.
- Show dependencies by connecting sticky notes with arrows.
- Review and revise.

These are quite basic steps and, it turns out, very easy for most teams to perform. The level of detail is set arbitrarily, and teams often ask to what level of specificity they should map their activities. It turns out that for reasonably large systems, a 4-foot-high by 12-foot-wide map provides the right "zoom level." When the map is reasonably full of sticky notes, there will be sufficient specificity, in most cases, to provide a doubling of performance across the entire system and, often, a doubling of performance for nearly every function represented in the map.

Another trick we use to help the group visualize the work includes giving different functional groups different-colored sticky notes. That way, when the map comes together, it is very easy to see the flow changing from one part of the project team to another and the issues that (may) arise across handoffs and organizational borders. We are in R&D, where activities have long names, so we use large (4-inch × 4-inch) sticky notes. We insist that people put metrics on the sticky notes when written, because once they are on the wall, the team will never write the metrics down, removing much of their ability to see issues within the workplace. We push the team to be honest in their metrics. Until the map goes up and people see that others have the same trouble they do, there is a fear of embarrassment in putting up honest metrics—no one wants to look bad. In actuality, I have yet to see a team ridicule anyone for their metrics, but people feel responsible and want badly for their work to be seen in a good light. Gentle but insistent tension on this point helps the team immensely. Cycle times are never really as short as process times. Very few process steps deliver 100 percent complete and accurate information on a first-pass basis.

This brings up another point: System metrics roll up in a beautiful but, for the team, disappointing way. Typically, teams that have a better than 4 percent first-pass quality are incredibly rare, as are teams that have process times that are more than 20 percent of cycle time. For the purposes of the community, however, this is *wonderful* news. At minimum, *half of all work is wasted in quality*. Similarly, at least half of your time is soaked up in delays and poor handoffs. Two- to fourfold improvements in performance should be easily achieved without dramatic or wildly upsetting changes.

The only thing that the team must resist on Day 1 is moving into solution space. This is absolutely vital. Scientists are trained to dive into detail, and given the opportunity to begin problem solving, will quickly track themselves out of the purpose of the day. Gently but firmly bring them back.

Finally, everyone in the room is expected to participate. Facilitators and leaders (those, at any rate, who do not do direct work on the project, but only manage) inquire; researchers discuss and map; and all of us learn. The atmosphere is dynamic, often loud, and sometimes cathartic, heated, or euphoric. You can never tell.

Analysis (Day 1)

Time permitting, we spend a bit of time talking about barriers in the current state. What activities, if changed, would greatly improve the operation of the system? Usually, these are quite obvious. Places with very low percent complete and accurate, places where work stops, places where cycle time is very long and process time is very short, and places where a lot of effort is applied to planning are flagged every time. If we have the opportunity, we go around the room asking each team member to identify something that they could change in their own area that would help a different group succeed or operate more easily. Throughout the project, we work to connect people to each other, to realize that their work affects others, and that others' good work affects them.

At the end of the first day, the team leads out to the leadership team. This is a time of reflection on the day's learning and also helps the leadership team learn a few things. First, they learn that the system they lead is far more complex than they had imagined and far different as well. Second, leaders paying attention will see that many of their own actions contribute mightily to the confusion and complexity of the system as it sits. For these leaders, the opportunity to support the improvement of the system is great because, typically, the smallest and most powerful changes can occur at their level.

Analysis (Day 2)

Analysis is really still about seeing. What is *really* there? What kinds of barriers are in the current state? Thinking in solution space short-circuits the ability to see barriers; therefore, we begin the second day without going into solution space. Typically, our first exercise is to break the current state into large actionable sections of work. We look for three or four clear subunits of activity. Interestingly, current states often have a "dog bone" shape, where a lot of activities from several functions come together at one point, and then a single effort, typically the execution of an experiment, is followed by another large group of activities encompassing the interpretation and reporting of different data streams by the originating functions. This breaks easily into planning and prep, operations, and analysis and reporting chunks. No matter your business, you will see patterns in the work. These patterns enable you to break the current state down into natural segments of flow; and by building SIPOCs at the interfaces, the needs of each team will be clearly spelled out for the other teams; and a smooth interface can commence.

Somewhat surprisingly, the biggest wins often come in the planning and prep stage of our work. Planning is usually ad hoc and difficult. The information needs of the operational segment of projects are rarely spelled out, and when they are, they are usually inaccurate. That is, teams believe they need more information in one area than they really do, and less information in another. Timing is usually a mess as well, with teams asking for things weeks or months ahead of their real need, while other teams deliver late at critical coordination points. Smoothing these handoffs and removing mismatches at the interface often means that a three-month process can be condensed into a single, very dense, day.

Once these segments are clear, with their interfaces defined and frozen, the teams have free reign to build future-state processes that take the minimum amount of time and effort to satisfy the knowledge and data quality issues at the interface. By building the segments to meet only those needs with robust, first-pass yields, projects can progress at sometimes three or four times the speed of their original state.

Occasionally, the science gets tricky, in that a given approach may support the project moving forward, or may prove a bust. Allen Ward[*]

---

[*] Allen Ward, *Lean Product and Process Development* (Cambridge, MA: Lean Enterprise Institute, 2007).

suggested that these were places where multiple-option approaches should be taken. The reason is fairly straightforward. If you run a project knowing that one testing cycle to answer a question has only a 50 percent chance of success, running a second experiment with different parameters but the same chances of success will yield a 75 percent chance of success; five iterations will bring success to almost 97 percent but will take five times the time to complete. While we know many projects that have 10 or even 30 percent time buffers, I know of none that have 500 percent time buffers. A different approach is required.

The obvious answer is to run options in parallel. Our five options will yield a first-pass success of 97 percent, but at a cost of a 500 percent larger investment. This is impossible to justify, but this investment level is only required if we pursue our projects with the mental models we used to design our linear system. In a linear system, because of the time it takes to do each pass, we want desperately to never have to return and start over. As a result, we load up our first experiment with all kinds of side experiments so that, just in case our first guess works, we can progress immediately to the next step, and so on. In a parallel world, however, this assumption makes no sense whatever. Since we will be doing that "first pass" experiment on five different options, we want to do the cheapest, fastest, and easiest experiment possible.

When we remove the necessity of doing an overburdened test, we can easily drop the total investment of each pass by two or more, leaving our five-pass learning system delivering at two and a half times the investment of a lucky first shot. This is a vast improvement. We will definitely deliver our project timeline (97 percent chance of success), but the extra investment is still going to be a tough sell to senior management. We need to revisit our assumptions again.

When we decided to do our full-power (but no extras) five-option experiment, we were implicitly looking for the *answer* to the scientific question posed by the project. We could just as easily have asked ourselves to generate options to test that would provide the definitively correct *path* to the answer. That is, what experiments could we do that would, instead of giving us the answer, tell us what method would work, and then as a follow up experiment, we would use that method to deliver the actual answer sought.

It turns out that these second-order questions (usually) require significantly less time, space, resources, and so on. Often, if we spend enough time on options and their implications, we can *think* our way to a much more likely or successful path than if we just set out on the first experiment that came to us. But let us, for the moment, imagine that it will take us 10 percent of the effort and time of a single pass to identify and test each of our five options. We will now know a successful path to complete our science within 97 percent accuracy.

Using this approach, we will find a successful path and then do our full-on research project. Our nominal cost is now 110 percent of a first-pass lucky shot, both in time and treasure, for a 97 percent certain result. Most project plans have contingency timing built in. Often this is 10–20 percent of the total time for the project. So, this part of the project will have 3 percent risk of not meeting its expected time frame, with a 10 percent overage. Moreover, in the event that every one of our five paths proves unsuccessful (3 percent chances still come up), we will know of the failure 10 percent of the way into that learning activity. This gives us a lot of time to fill the impending timeline break before the project itself is put in jeopardy. We will have plenty of time to think of other options.

Still, we should not be happy with our current state of affairs. With our current assumptions, we will use all of our time and resource contingencies. But do our assumptions hold? When we explore options, do we learn nothing of value about the process that we are about to undertake? My belief (and observation in several different systems) is no and that we learn in two ways. First, we learn a lot about how to do our work better just by trying it out first in model systems or even in our minds. This means that our actual answer-generating experiment will not take 100 percent of the time. Our practice will help us in the game. But an even bigger prize awaits. It turns out that, most of the time, our most successful option proves not merely successful, but is far faster, easier, and cheaper than our original estimates would lead us to believe. It turns out that our follow-up experiment takes much less time and effort, often about half of the expected value.

At this point, we have five path-defining experiments that cost 10 percent of our original estimate and take 10 percent of our allotted time. Nearly all (97 percent) of the time, a successful path is identified, which often uses as little as 50 percent of the time and effort of our original estimate. By thinking differently, our new multiple-option design delivers our desired output with 60 percent of the expected resources in 60 percent of the planned time.

Let's follow the logic a bit further. Advantages of the multiple-option approach include the following:

1. Early, and nearly certain, identification of a winning pathway comes at a cost far less than that of the original test.
2. Option value: If many different pathways prove successful, the team can choose the one most advantageous to the community's purpose.
3. Option value: An early, low-cost decision point allows the team to decide on whether to pursue further experimentation in case of widespread failure.
4. Successful options, once they are identified, will progress at lower cost and higher speed.
5. Timeline and cost success is assured in all but the low percent of cases where all paths fail.

Real-life examples bear this out. At Pfizer, the structural biology team employed a parallel approach to developing and analyzing protein crystal structures. In their first four attempts, their cycle times were cut by a factor of four, besting the company record by a factor of three. Meanwhile, their first-pass success rate was three out of four, with no technical improvements required; previously, at least some technical improvement work somewhere in the system was needed. Importantly, it was determined that the single failing project could not be successfully crystallized using current technology, and that project was abandoned.

All of the predictions from the foregoing analysis proved pessimistic. The team's investment per project was actually significantly *less* than a normal project; their timelines were one-third of their prior best; and when failure occurred, the team had actually established that the project could not be completed with currently available scientific techniques.

Future-State Mapping (Day 2)

Future-state mapping is quite simple. The team—having found barriers to flow, quality, learning, and coordination in the current-state map—assesses the impact of those barriers and maps the activities, metrics, and flows of a new, notional system that does not contain those barriers. This is, in essence, a solution without a path, since the team still may not have a solid idea of how to remove those barriers, only that if they do remove them, the new system will appear something like their map.

By focusing on barrier identification and removal, rather than on the community goals set out originally, the team almost always finds that their reduced-barrier future predicts performance that exceeds their original design goals. When the team reviews the notional future state together and sees that the previously unthinkable doubling of performance is not merely possible, but well within their grasp, they gain renewed energy to plan their path to their future state.

Creating the Learning Plan (Day 3)

Planning is the entire focus of the third day. In this exercise, the differences between current and future state are assessed, and experiments are designed to bring the team to the future state. These experiments and activities come in three varieties—activities to develop systems and processes consistent with the future-state performance, experiments to test those systems and processes against performance predictions, and experiments and activities to embed those new systems in the community—so that all future projects utilize the new, improved systems.

Research teams often struggle with planning, and rightly so. Most experiments yield part of the answer that the researcher was hoping to learn. This means that plans based on activities often shift and morph with time. They are not especially predictable. Lacking this predictability, researchers find planning an especially frustrating and value-free proposition, so they have little practice with it and not a lot of positive reinforcement. Of course, in planning systems' changes, they have many more opportunities for success. Their experiments are on things that are more certain and more tractable, and this will provide them good practice for other projects.

In any case, we often spend a great deal of time teaching researchers how to plan, in particular, how to plan in a learning environment. Depending on the project, we use two different methods for planning, both of which have been successful in the R&D space.* The first planning approach is to build A3s for each cluster of changes throughout the system. We are

---

* Again, this section is meant to be exemplary, not prescriptive. The processes described work for us and show that at least two methods are viable, implying that an infinite number are possible. You must define the one that delivers all of the same value for your community.

increasingly using this approach as it maintains context throughout the implementation, and we use A3s in reviews, thus reducing the work that the team needs to do through the implementation process. The second planning approach we have used is a straightforward project planning approach that, at least in our hands, has five elements:

1. The new system element that is to be created
2. A goal or target condition that the change is to bring about; that is, the *performance level* of the new system element that is to be developed to support an aspect of a future state
3. The activities and experiments needed to create the system element, prove its performance level, and implement the successfully tested element throughout the system
4. The expected start and end dates for these activities and experiments
5. The overall owner of the system element and its performance, and the owners of each activity and experiment

To illustrate the goal or target condition, let me provide a typical example we see in the pharma R&D space. It is not unusual, given the scope and complexity of some of our clinical and nonclinical experiments, to have six or more functional groups provide data to properly define the study. To gather these data, the team lead for that study may spend months calling around, socializing information, updating information, and making and revising proposals as team members provide input. Nearly all of this planning and data-gathering activity is wasted effort, and most teams try to design something to remove the headache of this element of the process.

Goals for such a process include a new system element—a single meeting that will be successfully completed in two hours. At that meeting two things will happen:

1. All of the required data needed to design the study will be collated.
2. A 100 percent complete, accurate, and approved study design and a plan for its execution will be produced.

The goal, however, does not suggest to the team *how* the goal will be achieved. It is merely the performance of the new system element.

The second thing that the plan requires is a list of elements that the team feels are needed to achieve that goal, experiments to test those elements, and activities to embed those elements in the community so that all future work uses the new design. In our example, one can immediately imagine several elements needed to make our two-hour meeting go well.

1. Every function that has data needed for the study must be present in the meeting.
2. Those functional representatives must bring complete and accurate data.
3. The requirements of the study design and plan must be well known in advance of the meeting so that data can be plugged in, a design developed, and a plan produced.
4. The work of the meeting must be sufficiently easy that it can all be accomplished in two hours.
5. The team that enters the room must have the power of approval.

If any of these elements are not present or fail, then the meeting cannot achieve its performance objectives.

The activities that the team may be required to perform are the design of work aids, like lists of data (perhaps checklists or templates) to be brought, definition of attendees, definition of meeting outputs, possible templates for studies, and so on. The needed experiments will include things like testing the templates or job aids, running a mock or real meeting, engaging leadership to gain acceptance of a new approval scheme, and so on.

Activities to embed the *successfully tested* design element will have to be developed as well.

- How does your company train and embed new processes?
- How well does that work?
- What should you do differently to ensure that *this* process works in perpetuity (or at least until the community needs a better one)?

Each of the activities on the plan should have two elements of their own: dates by which the activities will be performed (start and end dates) and the name of the owner of each activity. The activity owner need not be the person doing all of the work, but should instead be the person responsible for the thought process by which the activity is to be made successful and for finding, through repeated rethinking, if necessary, a path to ensure that the project element is completed successfully and on time.

MANAGEMENT INTERVENTION DURING DESIGN AND PLANNING

In discussing our approach with people who use other VSM or change processes (e.g., GE Workout) in which nonmanager teams develop solution space, ours seems to be unusual in that teams at other companies develop change recommendations, which are then approved or rejected by leadership teams, whereas we do not allow leaders to adjust the future-state vision or plan once it has been developed.

There are several reasons, both technical and social, for this. First, leadership was not in the room when the system was mapped, analyzed, and redesigned. The small changes that yield big results often hang together as a package. Removal of some of the elements means that overall system performance will suffer. In other words, leadership knows far less, so their instincts are far more likely to be incorrect than the team's instincts. Their redirection of the team is almost certain to diminish the technical performance of the future state.

Second, by transferring selection of change elements from the team to leadership, leadership wrests control over the changes, which shows a lack of respect for researchers' ability to identify and create meaningful change. This destroys trust and reinforces the mental model that some people are capable of designing work and others are not. This, in turn, creates or reinforces a codependent relationship in which researchers, having had their designs judged (some of them judged inadequate), will feel less confident and will be significantly less interested in proposing future changes. Researchers' disengagement in future change efforts leads leadership to doubt their abilities further, resulting in a negative spiral.

Finally, design success and failure lead to crucial learning and skill-building opportunities for the team and leadership alike; many of the team's stranger ideas will prove unexpectedly successful. Other changes will prove dismal failures. By identifying and addressing failures as implementation progresses, the team will learn not only better design skills, but also learn better problem-solving and implementation skills. This will lead to greater confidence and a positive spiral of capability, respect, and learning within the community, and it will, during the course of implementation, achieve the community's goals.

Our position is that leadership's vote essentially ends when the scoping is done. Their part was to set the direction and performance needs of the community. It is the community's job to create the environment that supports the performance.

IMPLEMENTATION AND FAST LEARNING

The three-day workshop is, of course, just a design forum. The real learning occurs when the team begins to engage in changing the system. There is an assumption on our part that the team will succeed in many areas and fail in others, and these successes and failures cannot be predicted. That is why we use a learning loop–based implementation approach. The team is *not* bound to utilize the process they designed in their design session, but they are on the hook to deliver a new system whose performance level supports the community's need (they have to deliver the goals set by leadership).

Successful implementation does not require, but greatly benefits from, the use of a learning process. In my experience, very few implementation programs explicitly consider learning or explicitly acknowledge that some aspect of the implementation will fail. Significantly, no matter how good or bad previous implementation projects might have proven, implementation without learning is anathema to a person who *is* Lean. Such a person could not implement without carefully observing and adjusting (learning) as she went, because any change both creates and destroys at the same time. Without looking for the change's destructive aspects, a Lean person will not be living up to her promise to the improvement of the environment. We refer to our plans as *learning plans* because we believe that the team's success hinges upon its identifying and overcoming barriers to its own thought processes, which were unforeseeable during the design of the future state.

Learning and Review

Implementation of learning plans requires review of some sort to occur throughout the process. These reviews are designed to achieve two things: First, they are designed to realign the team, both on the purposes and goals of the effort, but also on the integration of efforts as well as maintaining team coherence and technical alignment through time. Second, the reviews serve to expose and address deviations in performance or timing from the original plan. This reveals technical barriers in your designs for the new system and in designs to gain acceptance of change by the community. By observing deviation from the plan, you can reformulate your designs in a timely fashion and reassign resources to complete the project on performance, on budget, and on time.

This is still only half the picture. As you progress through implementation, those barriers in design and in the implementation process will point to flaws in your mental models that you can remove to better operate within your environment in the future. For example, the installation and uptake of a new meeting design, for which you had planned a month-long campaign, might take only four days. In that case, you would ask yourself what was wrong with your thinking that you imagined it would take that long, and ask, as well, how you would use that information to implement differently next time. You might find that the design you had for executing Widget A testing yielded only half of the performance expected. You would then have to review the barriers in widget testing, and also review how you originally assessed the barriers within widget testing, and your process of analysis of those barriers, that led you to design a process operating at half of its expected value. Moreover, you would have to do so in a way that would ensure that the improved-performance Widget A testing came online in the originally scheduled implementation window, a secondary problem of significant importance. Failure to do so would mean that the rest of the team would have to wait for Widget A testing improvements, breaking their timelines, and letting down the community.

We schedule monthly team reviews that focus on the following points:

1. What was the expected result of work in the last time period, and how did each segment perform against expectation?
2. What went better than expected, and for those elements, how did you capitalize on them?
3. What went worse than expected and (a) how did you overcome those new problems and (b) how did you engage the team to ensure that the entire project stayed on track?

4. What went so unexpectedly that the team, as a whole, must reconsider approaches to work, so that the overall project can achieve its goals?

5. Finally, subteams are asked to share their detailed learning plan for the next month.

This may sound complicated, but it is, in essence, just a variation on an A3, and we use one-page templates for read-out purposes.

These monthly review cycles are invaluable for social and technical alignment, and serve as a community problem-solving mentorship platform. Unfortunately, these events occur with low frequency, and work must occur at a much higher pace if it is to deliver doubling or more of capability within 90 days. To serve this need, we strongly suggest to teams that they engage in medium-speed (weekly) learning reviews that are far more tactical. Historically, we have suggested that teams engage in very light, but very high-speed (e.g., daily), subteam learning reviews that instill "fast learning" discipline.

Fast Learning and Strategies for Fast Learning

Throughout this book, I have avoided a discussion on an important point of Lean R&D, and that is *fast learning*. Boyd makes the point that the only sure way for a community to succeed is for it to learn faster than the surrounding environment.[*] Luckman[†], Ward[‡], and others make it plain that Lean product development rests on establishing and integrating fast cycles of learning. I agree, but after considerable thought, I am not certain about the implications and the approaches.

Fast learning, it seems to me, is the *result* of good thinking and the instilled imperative of any person who *is* Lean to improve the environment. In what ways would a person who is Lean improve the environment? By working to see and remove any barriers she can identify in the environment. When would a person who is Lean improve the environment? She would improve it immediately upon seeing a barrier.

---

[*] Frans P. B. Osinga, *Science, Strategy and War: The Strategic Theory of John Boyd* (New York: Routledge, 2007).

[†] James Luckman, private correspondence.

[‡] Allen C. Ward, *Lean Product and Process Development* (Cambridge, MA: Lean Enterprise Institute, 2007).

Fast learning discipline can be a very mechanical thing akin to takt time. Takt, you will recall, is the clock speed of production, specifically, the exact operating rate at which work must progress so that daily output matches customer demand. Fast-learning discipline can be set up like takt, in which a learning cycle has a specific duration. That is, if you design, build, and run an experiment every day, your learning cycle will be one day long. Just as takt time creates tension in a manufacturing system, a specified duration for each learning cycle creates the same kind of tension in an R&D environment. You are expected to deliver your work within the cycle time, and, if you do not, this provides the impetus to think through why you were unable to do so, and how you will address the problem in the future. This forces very, very rapid learning at both the bench (executional) level and at the thinking or thought process level. It is therefore highly effective in bringing about and integrating rapid innovation in new product development or research science. It enforces a discipline of reducing scale, thinking critically to enable very small experiments to be designed and run, and so on. It has much to commend it, and, in fact, work at a printer manufacturer shows that in their hands, a fast-cadenced learning (two-day learning cycle) approach could improve the performance of product development by a factor of *seventy*!

A seventyfold improvement in product development capability is nothing to sneeze at; indeed, it is something to celebrate. Based on that performance, I have tried diligently to instill metronomic reviews at a high cadence, daily or every other day, and failed miserably time and again to get teams to even attempt it. Teams resist it not least because it could, in practice, require meetings to occur at a high frequency, reducing time in the laboratory, and because it is quite difficult to design one- or two-day learning cycles in environments where experiments take weeks or months.* They also resist because the idea is fundamentally foreign in an environment where hypotheses are forwarded, designs are made, experiments are run, and data are analyzed. The idea of breaking the subparts sufficiently to generate a learning cycle seems artificial and wasteful. I can differ with that idea all I want, but it is their work.

---

* This, of course, is not the point of cadence. Cadence ensures that the greatest possible learning is achieved in every time period, not that the entire learning cycle of a specific experiment will be completed in one day. This is a somewhat unusual concept that causes understandable resistance.

In any event, my mind changed on this point completely with the progress of the SPOT (Strategic Prosecution of Targets) team discussed in Chapter 11. The SPOT team had weekly learning cycles *as a team* and embraced the *concept* of fast learning, but did not install the daily mechanical learning system favored in the previous discussion. Instead, what they found was that their *integrated* learning was occurring faster than daily. That is, parts of the team would read out new knowledge almost hourly. These readouts occur unpredictably, but, importantly, the team needs to absorb and act on this emerging knowledge. If it does not act, some experiment will continue well past the time when other data will have proved it nonviable or nonuseful. The instant new knowledge indicates a new strategy or failed line of experimentation, any additional work along that experimental path is wasted, and could be more effectively applied elsewhere. For any mechanical cadence, there is built-in delay until the team comes together, shares information, and redirects efforts. This delay is an unnecessary cost to the system.

In recognizing the damage such delays cause, SPOT took a different approach. They developed fast social and electronic means of sharing emerging information. When new data or ideas were discussed, people acted immediately on those data. When new internal data emerged, those data were sent immediately to the people most affected by the new data, and hallway conversations and reprioritization occurred dynamically. In practice, cycle times for prioritization changes that I observed occurred within 15 to 30 minutes, saving a full day of experimental learning time at each prioritization as compared to a mechanically synchronized system operating at a daily clock speed.

External information, for example, absorption of information from newly published scientific journals, often takes a great deal of time. It is not unusual for a team to take two to three weeks to read and absorb new information emerging from the literature. A system that takes a week to process means that an entire week's worth of work could accrue from any given published article. The waste from such a delay caused the team to build methods to extract data from external publications, integrate that data into their current thought models (kept electronically), and publish and share the implications of the emerging knowledge as quickly as possible. Time stamps show that this cycle time for incorporating new external findings and sharing its implications was less than 20 minutes, with strategic shifts based on that emerging knowledge occurring across the team within two hours.

If a team does what SPOT set out to do, it will absorb new observations and react immediately. It is literally *not possible* to operate faster than this in a mechanical sense, which brings us to my next objection: Good thinking (at least in R&D) beats good operations every day. If SPOT also keeps coming back to its critical questions and asks itself two questions, it can accelerate continuously with no additional effort beyond its agreed-to future state.

The first question is: In what *other ways* can I answer each of these questions? By asking that question, the team is bound to see new ways that are harder, easier, more elegant, less elegant, more complete, or less complete than the ways they originally designed. They will, because of their Lean *be state*, select the best experimental path they can imagine at the time work begins, and continue rethinking this choice as the experimentation progresses, ensuring that the questions they originally posed are answered in the shortest, most valuable way possible.

The second question is: Is there another question, or set of questions that, if answered, will obviate the need to answer chunks of this Critical Question Map? In other words, they will press themselves to define newer, better maps that deliver the same or better product value faster and more elegantly than could be done using their current approaches.

If a team does all of these things, it reaches a state I refer to as *organic fast learning*. It operates mechanically as fast as thinking allows. It operates experimentally in the smoothest, most elegant way, and it answers the most valuable and easiest set of questions it can define in order to deliver the required innovation package. I cannot, in my mind, imagine how a mechanical system could compete with such a process, and, in fact, the numbers bear this out. The SPOT team's performance blew past its future-state performance goals within 60 or 70 days. The future state they were trying to install within 90 days was completely outdated in advance of its planned arrival date (talk about missing performance to plan in a happy way!). Within about 150 days, the team was operating at about *two orders of magnitude* higher performance than the future-state design and still accelerating. I have no idea how general this thought process might prove, but for early research, I believe that the SPOT performance increase is available to any team willing to spend the effort to achieve such a harmonized environment.

THE NEXT LEVEL: LINKING THE PROJECT TO LEAN STRATEGY AND THE LEARNING PROCESS

Each project, for better or worse, is a part of the Lean learning and adoption strategy of your community. Done well, Lean embeds itself very deeply into the community's participants and spreads out to their friends. Done poorly, a project will generate antibodies to Lean within that project group and with their group of friends that will be difficult to overcome. This is nothing to be afraid of; it is something to use to your advantage.

Since it will happen anyway, how will you use each project as an explicit part of your Lean learning and adoption strategy? Since your first efforts are likely to be rough, how will you find places, within your organization, where you can learn the fastest to become smooth and capable in Lean implementation? How will you identify places that are both friendly to you and your ideas and hard-working enough to overcome your early failures? How does this project fit into your overall Lean learning and adoption strategy? How will you use this project to identify barriers and mental model issues in your own thought processes? How will you use it to identify barriers in the community's mental models? How will you use it to identify barriers within Lean thinking and presentation that inhibit adoption?

What do you need to learn from this (in fact, for every) project? How will you design parts of your engagement that teach you what you need to learn? What will you do to look for other learning opportunities that may present themselves through the course of the project? How will that learning fit into your overall growth as a Lean person?

10

Implementation Strategy

At this point, we have developed learning theory, in the form of the "See, Reframe, Experience, and Grow" learning loop. This loop describes the innovation experience from the gathering of background knowledge (sensing) through the "eureka!" moment (reframing) and on to the required post-eureka transition to delivery of true innovation.

This learning loop, in turn, allowed us to develop practical paths to build individual and team innovation capability. We developed practice exercises and tools to guide individuals and teams to sense more effectively. These exercises—individuals performing deep observation, teams developing current-state maps, and people and teams building the left half of an A3—provide people a deeper and more holistic understanding of their work and its assumptions. These exercises enable facile "reframing," the "eureka!" moment when vast connected and disconnected bits of knowledge can suddenly crystallize into new configurations with tremendous innovative power.

To enable and capture the eureka moment of reframing, we developed other tools and practices to help individuals and teams break through their current frames of reference and, once through, redefine their innovation performance. Future-state mapping helps a team codify its vision of a breakthrough system of work activities that is no longer constrained by its current working methods, but instead routinely operates at breakthrough performance levels. Meanwhile, we developed Critical Question Mapping^{SM} (CQM^{SM}) to enable both the understanding of what must be innovated and to create a platform to enable a continuous string of effective, breakthrough reframing, eureka events. Finally, we developed learning plans and practices based on A3 thinking, high cadence, and reflection to ensure smooth, effective integration of *proven* innovation as projects progress.

Taking this to a more strategic level, we developed "organic" management thinking centered on creating environments in which people can flourish. Organic management practices can be engaged by anyone in the organization. Engaging in these practices supports the personal growth of the practitioner as well as the growth of everyone around him or her. The business processes improve, but so do the learning processes. As success builds, the emotional processes that support the internal life so important to individual creativity and innovation improve as well.

What we have not yet done is touch on how to approach an entire organization, engage it with Lean thinking, and transform both its performance and capability into a living, growing Lean research and development (R&D) system. The problem is not a small one. Each R&D organization, no matter its size, comes with a portfolio of projects with a breadth (and often a myriad) of functions; with a set of aligned and conflicting goals; and with political agendas, needs, and worries of its people. It also comes with an existing culture with a thought process about what works, what does not work, and how work should progress. Each R&D organization is peopled with individuals of diverse experiences and a spectrum of interest in new ideas of all sorts. Some people will embrace new ways of thinking, while some will reject it in favor of prior methods that have worked for them. Some people will have a lot of experience in "how it is done around here," while others will have little experience or ties to the current way of thinking.

This means that no matter how effective and powerful our philosophies and tools or our mentorship and management thinking, developing a strategy to install a Lean R&D system will never be a straightforward, formulaic exercise. Lean implementation failure stories are not hard to come by, but in fact, strategies for implementing *any* strategic initiative are fraught with peril. Several studies* suggest that strategic change efforts, from general strategy to corporate reengineering and Total Quality Management (TQM), fail significantly more often than they succeed, perhaps as much as 80 percent of the time. Lacking a proven strategy for Lean

---

* P. Senge, *The Dance of Change* (New York: Currency Doubleday, 1999), 5–6; A. Raps, "Implementing Strategy," *Strategic Finance* 85, no. 12 (2004): 49–53; D. Miller, "Successful Change Leaders: What Makes Them? What Do They Do That Is Different?" *Journal of Change Management* 2 no. 4 (2002): 359–68; P. Strebel, "Why Do Employees Resist Change?" *Harvard Business Review* 74 no. 3 (1996): 86–92.

implementation,* we may freely chart our own path, safe in the assurance that we can at least do no worse. Armed with some knowledge about Lean and our own corporate culture, and past failures within our own organization, we can be reasonably certain that our results will surpass the efforts of those who have gone before us.

USING A CRITICAL QUESTION MAP TO DEFINE A STRATEGIC THINKING STRUCTURE

I propose that, rather than begin with the failed experiences of others, we begin along two completely different lines of thinking. I propose that we use Critical Question Mapping, fast learning, and Plan-Do-Check-Act (PDCA) to develop strategies for Lean R&D implementation tailored to our own organization and our own learning environment.

The Critical Question Map will remove the need to worry about how strategic initiatives have been planned and executed, and will focus efforts on what needs to be done for a Lean implementation in a specific environment. At the same time, if you pursue this or a similar route in building your Critical Question Map (I will provide a partial example, but you will need to create one for yourself with your own R&D colleagues), you will necessarily build that CQM within the understanding of your own experience and your company's frame of reference. You won't be applying General Electric's experience or Pfizer's experience; you won't be building your implementation plan from a playbook run by a consulting firm; you will be developing it from the stuff of your own company's experiences, history, diversity, and future. You will immediately bypass one critical mode of failure: aggravating your people with an ill-tailored, not-invented-here initiative.

Of course, to build a Critical Question Map, we need a strategic problem to solve or a question to answer. As with an A3, defining the right problem can be tricky. It cannot have an answer embedded but, rather,

---

* This is not exactly true. Toyota has a very strong track record in training their suppliers in Lean. However, Toyota is especially patient and generous in its efforts. It is willing to send its own trainers to work for years at a supplier's facilities. Patience, perhaps, is the one sure method to instilling Lean into a culture, but unfortunately, we do not always have the patience of Toyota, and must imagine other ways to achieve the same or similar ends.

must embody the right problem. It is enough to describe a lack of performance, as long as that performance gap will lead to an ever-improving environment. The good thing is that there are virtually an infinite number of problems that will serve to develop a Lean implementation strategy.

I propose that we use one of three different problem statements:

1. Our R&D system cannot predictably create the speed and quantity of innovation required to satisfy corporate growth goals.
2. R&D lacks a systemic capability to improve its own performance along any desired axis (e.g., cost, speed, innovation, colleague growth, etc.).*
3. R&D lacks the ability to remove barriers within its environment that affect colleagues' and the organization's ability to thrive.†

Selecting randomly, let's build a CQM on statement 3, starting with the object of our map: What questions, if answered, will give R&D the ability to remove barriers to its thriving? Some general questions that would seem to be needed include

- What sorts of barriers exist in our environment?
- Who would remove them?
- What abilities would that person have?
- Would it be possible for one person to remove large barriers alone?
- How would large barriers be removed?
- How would we define a large (vs. small) barrier?
- Who would remove large barriers?
- Does this person/group differ from small-barrier removers?
- How would removers know what barriers to prioritize?
- Do they know how to remove barriers?
- What would they have to learn in order to be able to remove specific types of barriers?
- Can someone learn to remove any types of barriers?

---

* This statement is dangerously close to having an embedded solution, "a systemic capability," but I feel that "systemic capability" is sufficiently broad that it constitutes a performance gap, rather than an embedded solution. You may feel differently, in which case, try a different thought process.
† Anticipating a potential criticism, it is impossible to imagine that R&D employees or an R&D organization could thrive unless it was delivering exceptional business value at a rapid pace. That is, any barrier to successful innovation is also a barrier to people and the organization thriving.

- If so, what would that person's abilities include?
- Which barriers impede our current R&D purpose?
- Which barriers are biggest?
- Which barriers are easiest to remove?
- Which barriers were the most important to remove first?
- How much of our time do we devote to barrier removal?
- How do we ensure barriers are removed and not merely "treated"?
- If we do not have "barrier removal" capability in our organization, how do we develop it?
- Where do we start?
- What are the attributes of a good first point of intervention?
- What are the attributes of the first intervention itself?
- Do we need to protect that first innovation?
- How do we protect it so that it can grow and establish a positive first example?
- How do we spread that first intervention to a second one?
- How do we spread those first few interventions into a vector, a divisionally accepted philosophy?
- What did we learn from that first (second, third, etc.) intervention?
- What does it imply that we need to learn in the second intervention to improve its success?
- When do we stop "intervening"?
- How do we link this to business need?
- How do we link this to culture?
- How do we define the most effective/easiest path to spreading successful ideas?
- How do we modify or eliminate unsuccessful ideas?
- At what point do we link our intervention efforts to business performance?
- How much time do we sequester for our initial efforts?
- How do we create tolerance for failure or partial early successes?

This list is not, by any means, a complete critical-question brainstorm, but it serves as a start. From this list, we can categorize and, in some cases, develop timing in answering some of these critical questions. The first list of questions is often not complete. To see what we have, in a more coherent state, we rearrange the questions in order to see patterns emerge, identify (where possible) flows between questions, and from there, begin to understand how those flows and groupings create a framework that will lead us to a successful strategy. For this exercise, I actually put the previously listed strategy questions onto sticky notes and put them onto a wall. Sure enough, when I began to arrange the sticky notes, several things emerged: First, I could see that there was a flow to many of the questions (see Figure 10.1), a flow that represented a learning loop for the growth and control of the implementation itself. Second, I could see that there were gaps in the questions. These gaps were places where the flow was poorly or wholly unsupported by enough knowledge to function smoothly. These were places where I would need to ask other questions to make sense of the whole, and many new questions emerged to fill out my list. Finally, I noted that there was a whole section built around barrier removal. This section appears critical to the success of the learning flow, but is separate. It might even prove to be another learning loop if we dig a little more.

So, let's dive in a bit deeper and see what the map showed us.

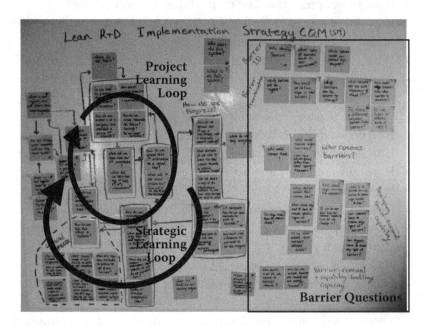

FIGURE 10.1

A Critical Question Map of Lean implementation strategy. Note the structure that emerged on mapping yielded three sections: a project-level learning loop; a strategic learning loop, covering the learning process needed for successful company-wide implementation of Lean; and a section on barrier questions and how to address them. This map took less than 2 hours to develop, arrange, and observe the emergent elements.

Flow and Learning Loops

As I noted previously, I was able to see a flow in many of the questions (see Figure 10.1). Without my intending for it to happen, that flow turned out to define learning loops. For the Lean implementation to succeed, I would have to select and begin the first intervention, let it grow, learn from it, and use those learnings to develop new projects and ultimately transform our culture. Before making that first project selection, I asked some basic questions that would enable me to make a well-informed decision about where that first intervention would be and what it would look like. These questions included basic and often difficult-to-define questions about culture and about how this project would link to our business. These questions formed the start of the flow.

- Where do we start?
- What are the attributes of a good first point of intervention?
- Who will run this project?
- What will he/she need to be able to do to be successful?
- What is our biggest lever to short-term experimentation?
- What is our biggest lever to long-term success?
    - Culture?
    - Performance?
    - Line workers?
    - Managers?
- If there is a gap (between long-term and short-term levers), how do we bridge it?
- How do we link Lean interventions to business need?
- How do we link this effort to culture?

Once we identified a starting point, we would want to have an idea of how to ensure the cultural and operational success of that first project. Would we need to protect it, so that people would not kill the initiative while we were learning? How much time would project team members need to set aside from their normal work so that the project would have the capacity needed for success? Is our culture already tolerant of failure, or would we need to do something special within this project to ensure that the inevitable failures that occur while learning do not sink the project prematurely? These questions formed a middle section around operational aspects of an individual project:

- Do we need to protect the first (or any other) intervention?
- How do we protect it so it can grow and establish a positive example?
- How much time and resources are needed for this intervention?
- How do we create tolerance for failure (and experimentation)?
  - Within and for this project?
  - Generally within our culture?

After a project started, we would have the opportunity to answer a set of questions geared toward expanding that project onto a wider stage.

- What would we want to learn from this initial project?
  - To help understand our operational processes?
  - To help understand our managerial processes?
  - To help understand our culture?
  - To help us align the lessons from this project to help future projects succeed?
- What did we learn from this intervention?
- What would we do differently in our next project and why?
- What did we learn about where to initiate the next project?

These questions led into a second, strategy-level learning loop. While the first loop continues to support the success of individual projects, this second loop supports the creation of a successful path to move the entire organization through the Lean initiative.

- How would we convert that (first project-specific) learning into a positive path forward, not just for the next project, but for Lean as a whole?
- What methods do we use to direct the total project toward a coherent complete change?
- Can we make a map of the organization and portfolio to see how interventions can build to 100 percent engagement of R&D?
- Can our path be emergent?
- If emergent, how do we steer the path to success?
- At what point do we link our intervention efforts to business performance?
- How much time and resources do we need to do the initiative?

This second loop feeds back in two ways. First, the knowledge generated—both at a high strategic level and in the tactical, project level—will be codified somewhere, so that we build rather than just forget the knowledge that we just created. Second, this knowledge is fed back into our decision-making loops—where to go next, with what project, using what approaches, addressing what set of employees—so that we have a coherent, upward-spiraling development of knowledge and progress. Examples of second-loop questions include

- How do we incorporate that learning into our future work?
- What does it imply that we need to learn in successive interventions?
- How do we remember these lessons so we do not reinvent them?
- How do we modify or eliminate unsuccessful ideas?
- What is/should be our learning cadence? This reflects how fast we need to start new projects, adjust our methods, or improve our approaches to ensure that the overall strategy delivers on or ahead of target.

The learning from these projects and from the second (strategic) learning loop inform our understanding of culture, R&D process and capability, and the next places to begin projects. Emerging questions about culture include

- What do our people love and embrace?
- What aspects of Lean R&D align with our culture?
- How do you use these to grow lean?
- What attributes of culture are common between our current culture and new (Lean) culture?
- What are key new attributes of culture to add to our division?
- What (projects, people, ideas) do people accept/reject as indicators of value, success, or reality? These are things scientists use to drive their cultural decisions about what to adopt and why.
- What causes people in our division to balk or get uncomfortable (with new ideas, processes, and so on)? These are resistance triggers to avoid, where possible, in future Lean work.
- Who is trusted and respected?
- Who is watched to see which way to form opinions?

The answers to many of these questions will change through time. As Lean gains adoption, the potential for resistance *should* decrease dramatically. People should be learning faster, getting more products out, solving problems they had trouble solving in the past, and making progress on a daily basis. The ratio of bureaucratic work to valuable innovation should decrease dramatically. The collaboration between individual scientists and even between departments should improve, reducing headaches and further improving overall performance. With time, Lean should be viewed increasingly as an opportunity rather than a second burden on top of the daily grind. These changes will affect how these cultural questions, in particular, are answered and their resulting answers feed forward into decision making.

Our second learning loop is closed out by a single question: When do we stop? The answer to this question could easily be: when the company closes its doors for the last time. It could be that we would stop with active interventions of various types when certain criteria were met. But there are many other possible ways to interpret that question. One could easily see interpreting it not just as "When do we stop?" Lean, but perhaps more specifically, "When do we stop a given type of intervention?" Once everyone's work processes are changed, and people know how to operate them smoothly, we *might* need never do another current-state value stream map. We should, after all, have current value stream maps of all of our work processes, so that we need not build another one from scratch. We might stop working on *activity-based* interventions and move toward knowledge-based interventions. We might find better interventions than outlined in this book and move entirely to those. We may decide that interventions, at least on a system scale, are not as valuable in our culture as individual mentorship of employees.

The answer to this question is also expected to change with time. When we start out, we might imagine our stopping point to be a specific point in time or a specific cultural milestone. However, this will almost assuredly change as our company changes, and where it comes out probably cannot be predicted in advance.

Filling Gaps in the Questions

In the first section of this chapter, I presented an admittedly incomplete list of questions that just got me started in building a CQM. Quick analysis revealed significant gaps—unasked questions that would prove critical in any reasonable strategic framework. Questions that would help me define where best to start my company's Lean transformation. Another set of questions emerged about the politics of corporate culture, and how to protect nascent ideas, knowledge and cultural elements to flourish in what might prove, at least initially, a hostile environment. In all, gaps covering six major strategic areas appeared, and were filled, by small, detailed sets of supporting questions. Such analysis helps deepen our understanding of the strategic landscape, helps build our ideas for implementation, and helps us anticipate areas of danger, such as selecting projects for short-term wins that might deliver long-term failures or focusing on business transformation and ignoring competing imperatives in cultural transformation.

The emergence of these questions shows the importance of the learning process that Critical Question Mapping starts. Perhaps more importantly, mapping exposes an interesting concept that might otherwise remain hidden. First, once a flow starts to emerge, it becomes quite clear that a *learning strategy* would work for implementation. That is, we do not need to design the entire implementation at inception. We could begin with a project somewhere in our organization, nurture and learn from that project, and then use those learnings to select and pursue another project or projects. With the benefit of having fresh learning incorporated into our implementation process, the second set of projects should be easier and more effective than our first project. The learning obtained from the second set of projects should drive an even better third set of projects, and so on. As we progress, we improve; as we improve, we gain support; as we gain support, we build momentum. The goal is to develop an implementation strategy, and a vision of Lean, that effectively transforms itself by its very act of implementation.[*]

Although I have used just such a learning strategy in the past, the Critical Question Map did not demand it. It was not, in fact, an expected result. One could easily imagine that we could answer, in advance, the questions we would need for a fairly robust initial design, but we ended

---

[*] Interestingly, Toyota was having a difficult time reaching younger buyers in the 1990s. In order to improve its chances, it used a learning strategy in the marketing of the Scion brand. Rather than launch simultaneously across the United States, it launched Scion in one region of the country, used the successes (and failures) from that launch to design its second regional launch, and so on. By creating a plan that could adjust as it went, Toyota avoided an "all or nothing" gamble on one potentially flawed initial plan.

on a different route than we had originally set out to explore. Maps of these sort often expose hidden meaning and thinking elements that, once visible, can lead to better science, better strategy, and at least clearer thinking for individuals and teams alike. Mapping here also showed critical gaps in my thinking that, upon reflection, could be filled in and supported without significant difficulty,* but in hindsight, it was surprising that these gaps had not been addressed originally. "What is an R&D system?" "Who owns the R&D system?" "What does success look like?" and so on. These seem like the sorts of thing you would want to have asked up front but that only became glaringly obvious when mapped on the wall.

Methodology/Philosophy (Barrier Removal) Section of the Map

When I began to categorize the questions, I noted that two linked learning cycles appeared, but questions that dealt with barrier removal often did not immediately fit in with the learning cycles. These questions range everywhere, from "What is a barrier?" to "Who removes it and how?" In a sense, these are mostly methodological questions, revolving around how we identify and remove barriers, but they also contain philosophical inquiries. The answers are telling, exposing much about how we think about people. Imagine how different two cultures would be if one culture believes that managers are the only employees allowed to identify barriers and design barrier reductions, while a second culture assumes that everyone in the company is expected to identify and remove the barriers they find in their work and surrounding environments. Which culture has the greater respect for people? Which one has the greater chance of finding and overcoming small issues before they grow into large unwieldy ones? Which is likely to be faster and more dynamic?

The questions around barriers also contain personal and organizational development questions. What are the attributes of a person who removes barriers? What do we do if we do not have a barrier-removal capacity within our company? What if elements of barrier removal are not present (management support and other problem-solving behaviors, for example)? How much time do we set aside for barrier removal? The answers to these questions require us to consider our training, coaching,

---

* I think that the total time to build this map was less than 90 minutes.

and learning skills—at the individual level, at the organizational level, and everywhere in between.

One final note on how these questions were developed leads to another insight about mindset. When I began brainstorming questions, I did them free flowing in a word processing program (see the first bulleted list). My thoughts went from one to the next, and I built the questions by typing in one line after another. You can easily see several related questions building from an initial question. You can then see me shift to another question that creates its own cascade. This is especially true within the cluster of questions (nearly half of them!) on barrier removal. Of course, I began with the strategic question that included barrier removal, but the extent to which these ideas played and cascaded down from starting ideas was a bit startling when analyzed.

What this shows, I believe, is our propensity for bias. The first question, which may in fact beg many other questions, nevertheless becomes a point of familiarity and a rallying center for our minds to cling to. The breadth of questions I was hoping to see with my first brainstorm was notably absent. Moreover, seeing these questions in a list hides their repetition and narrowness, while putting them together on a wall highlights this issue immediately.

I am reasonably certain that it is not possible to be unbiased, and Critical Question Mapping will not eliminate bias any more than any other technique. The great thing about Critical Question Mapping, however, especially compared to the listing method I began with, is that it is visual. The visual element somehow exposes biases very quickly as we progress, so that we are more aware of and can adjust for the more obvious biases in our thought processes.

Converting the Critical Questions into a Strategy

A Critical Question Map is a strategic framework, but it is not yet a strategy. With our reasonably complete set of critical questions, we can create our implementation strategy by answering some of the more important questions on the map. We can also develop individual tactics by answering the more detailed questions, sometimes repeatedly over time, as our strategic implementation gets under way.

Let's start with the most obvious first questions: "What is a system?" and "What does success look like?" I would define a Lean R&D system in the following way. Everyone in the R&D division could tell you how we identify customer need; how we convert that into innovation problems; and how we understand and apply our internal and the current external state of knowledge as a basis to resolve those innovation problems and deliver valuable goods and services. Everyone would further know the performance of that system and its weaknesses, and they would be involved, at some level, in removing those weaknesses. Moreover, leaders would be primarily focused on managing the *system,* mentoring problem solving, and engaging in strategic change based on emerging opportunities and threats. This, in theory, is what normal management practice attempts to do, but it does so in the absence of a clear understanding of all of the work elements of our company and how those work elements interact. Lacking a clear vision of the interacting elements, managers often focus on fixing the *parts* of the system. This piecemeal approach makes it difficult to create meaningful change that is not offset, in part, by unintended effects elsewhere in the company. When managing at the systems level, the interactions are explicitly taken into account, so that changes have fewer, and generally positive, side effects.

Culturally,* a Lean implementation could be deemed successful when everyone in the company, both individually and collectively, actively identifies and removes, through structured problem-solving methods, barriers preventing people from thriving in their environment. Key words here include *actively identifies, everyone, removes,* and *structured.*

- *Actively identifies* means that people are actively looking for problems hindering their success. They do not overlook issues in the workplace, nor do they "put up with" issues once an issue has been identified. Instead, they begin immediately working to remove them. Most people, on hearing about a plan to work on every problem, will imagine that there would be a resource problem. There are, after all,

---

* I focused almost entirely on cultural answers to this question, largely because I do not have a specific business and its performance to guide my answers. Focusing on culture *is* reasonable in the abstract, since Lean is a philosophical and cultural transformation more than anything else, but companies always have their own business situations, which can sometimes be quite dire. Importantly, Lean is famous for its ability to deliver dramatic business performance improvements, and this is no different in R&D than it is elsewhere in a company, so if you find yourself in such straits, answer these questions with a focus on *your business need.* In all cases, there should be focus on both business transformation goals as well as cultural aspects, but your emphasis will be determined from your business context.

an infinite number of problems and a finite amount of people and time to resolve them. However, two things work in your favor in this regard. The first is that, as problems are fully removed and their root causes *eliminated* so that they cannot recur, the remaining problems become far more subtle and take more time to see. This is the secret of those Japanese production lines that have "andon cords" that line workers pull when they identify a problem. When the line first starts up, it can move slowly as many small plant and process start-up problems appear. But after those initial problems are resolved, it moves faster. As the line moves faster, more problems are found and removed, and the line moves even faster. As time progresses, the line speed exceeds that of a line where problems were allowed to continue. The second mitigating factor is that if you combine a low tolerance for problems with high enthusiasm for problem removal, people will strike the right balance.

- *Everyone* means that literally everyone in the division—from the division president to the newest contractor and summer intern—is involved in identifying and removing barriers using common approaches. If the people at the top do not use the same methods and thought processes expected of those at the bottom, this expectation will soon disappear, as those at the bottom seek to model and be promoted for the behavior seen at the top.

- *Removes* means to *fully eliminate* the root causes of barriers from the workplace so that the barriers cannot reappear. This has all kinds of benefits, but the one most overlooked is that root-cause elimination removes one key element of bureaucratic creep: When a new problem is observed, rather than blanketing everyone and everything in the organization with a new process, root-cause removal surgically attacks the one thing that is causing the problem. Countermeasures are therefore targeted tightly; hence, these countermeasures affect fewer people and deliver better results.

- *Structured* means that the utilized problem-solving methods will be robust and systematic. People will not solve problems using random methods, but will solve them in a way that others can understand, share, learn from, and apply themselves. This is important in manufacturing, of course, where the environment is typically quite structured. It is far more important in R&D, where the environment and its activities are inherently less structured. In such unstructured environments, new people in particular find it difficult to understand how to engage and become a part of the unfolding success of the R&D enterprise. By using structured problem-solving methods, like A3, people can immediately see how to engage their talents on the problems around them, including problems other people are already in the process of solving. Finally, the use of structured problem solving provides the basis for long-term organizational learning by providing ongoing, easily retrieved documentation on problems that have been eliminated in the past.

With that in mind, intervention projects must begin and build coherently so that, within some defined amount of time, two things happen: First, the *system*—our coherent understanding of how work starts and progresses—must emerge for the whole division; and second, the entire organization must become engaged in the process of removing barriers using structured methods. In my view, the first aspect will very likely happen on its own. As people understand how their work interacts with others, develop maps and improvement plans, and begin sharing their knowledge, this will take care of itself. The cultural piece, however, will take a bit more thought.

For very small organizations, this might require only one or two interventions. For large organizations, this may require dozens of interventions progressed over years of effort. The end goals in mind suggest that progress toward full implementation could be designed with reasonable accuracy. If the number of people and the R&D projects are known, and if the type and scale of each Lean intervention is known, then an approximate number of Lean interventions required to cover the entire organization will be known. If a time is set for full implementation, then an approximate cadence of new projects can be developed, and its progress can be tracked using a map that represents the organization and its workload. Figure 10.2 shows one type of map containing the number of employees and the number of R&D projects run at each of three sites. The extent of the organization covered by Lean interventions is shown in gray. Interesting insights can emerge from such maps. No projects have been initiated at Site 2, which may be deliberate (Site 3 was a good test bed for some reason, while Site 2 is our first site to "scale up" our learning), or it could be some other reason. All of the projects at Site 3, for

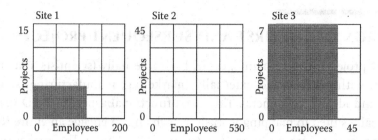

FIGURE 10.2
An example analysis of Lean penetration at three R&D locations. Many different types of analyses could be used. This one tracks adoption/penetration by number of employees and number of projects.

example, have been affected, but a significant (25 percent) of the employees have not. That suggests further review to see if there is a class (managers, perhaps, or segments of first-line workers or some other slice) of employees who were not exposed to Lean.

This brings up an interesting aspect of Lean improvement project design. If our ideal is that every person in the entire organization be engaged in Lean, then it stands to reason that each improvement project should engage a breadth of people affected by the work being improved. Even if we are just focused on improving bench-level science, that science is affected by the managers, maintenance crews, stockroom personnel, and administrative assistants who interact with the bench scientist. A holistic *system* of work would be difficult to design without some level of input from everyone who contributes to or gains from the output of that system. Ideally, then, each project should include participants that represent every aspect of the local system of operation. If a normal R&D project has two managers, six scientists, a secretary, and someone from maintenance, then a project to improve R&D projects should have managers, scientists, secretaries, and maintenance people in representative proportion. By pursuing this principle, the effort should remain fairly balanced across the organization as projects progress. There is much to be learned by having visual depictions like these handy. If you are a Lean practitioner engaging the organization, these are great conversation starters with management and, of course, great tools for tracking progress against our plan of engaging all projects and employees in whatever our definition of Lean might be, within a certain amount of time.

DESIGN OF THE FIRST AND SUBSEQUENT PROJECTS

R&D projects involve many people, both internally (scientists and engineers within R&D) and externally (marketing, manufacturing, suppliers, and ideally, customers). This cross-functional aspect of R&D makes it ideally suited to mapping workshops, which can engage an entire R&D project at one time, as outlined in Chapters 7, 8, and 9. This makes mapping workshops very effective at creating simultaneous cultural change down through an organizational hierarchy and horizontally along the portfolio progression path. Done well, it can anchor Lean in a new area of the division or bolster it in areas where Lean has already established a foothold. Mapping workshops also quickly establish new levels of performance, which generates enthusiasm in leadership and research colleagues. Although it is by no means the only approach to begin Lean, the mapping workshops prove quite effective in R&D and provide a solid design approach to begin a cultural transformation.

Other types of Lean intervention are possible and, in many cases, preferable. With leadership teams, A3 mentorship may work very well where current-state mapping of the work would be, in some cases, impossible. Critical Question Mapping might prove even more powerful, especially when combined with A3 problem solving to answer complex but crucial strategic questions.

Selecting Lean Practitioners

A question that will bias the initial path of your Lean implementation is "Who will run these projects?" This is really two questions: The first one concerns the type and training of the person or people you will have supporting your Lean implementation effort. The second one revolves around the number of Lean practitioners supporting your implementation. There are many options here. You could lead it yourself, and there is a strong case to be made for a senior manager doing just that. You can hire consultants to support your effort, in which case you need to develop a separation plan early in your efforts so that your organization does not become permanently dependent on them. You can select someone internally to do this work. (There are often people with experience in Lean, and there are always people with interest and capability to be great Lean coaches within every organization.) The difficulty is finding the right ones and exposing them to Lean in a way that makes this work. The last option is that you can hire someone or several people from outside your organization.

Each of these options for selecting Lean practitioners has advantages and disadvantages. Internal people have intimate knowledge of the organization, but they won't have a lot of experience. They will also come with baggage of their past successes and failures, and it may be difficult for people to see them as catalysts for change. Importantly, these people will have to learn a great deal, but all of their learning will be specific to your company. External people will come with little or no knowledge of your organization. They won't have internal baggage, but they will have prior beliefs stemming from their prior training and Lean experiences. In my view, the best way to resolve this is by experimentation and keeping your options open until the right path presents itself.

The quantity of Lean practitioners is another question you will need to wrestle with at some point. The number can be zero, that is, particularly in a small company, the "Lean practitioner role" could easily be taken part time. In a large R&D division, part-time support is less likely to deliver a successful implementation, as the number of interventions required to move thousands of employees into a coherent R&D system could be quite high. As a point of reference, our Lean effort started as a part-time effort by a highly interested person who attended a few classes, read voraciously, and tried a few experiments. Within eight months, it had grown to encompass 4½ people. With that effort, we supported more than 80 projects and transformed the work of more than 2,000 employees in less than three years.

Was our number the right number? For us, at the level of thinking we had at the time, I think it was just about right. In fact, we had no alternative. This was the number we were allowed, and at one point, I complained about not having enough bandwidth for the projects we were running. My mentor was characteristically unsympathetic, "How are you going to solve that problem?" he asked. This single question spawned a lot of thinking on our part, and developed a lot of the practices that we adopted that led to our successful work with such a small team. Our Lean practitioners coached and mentored colleagues, facilitated workshops, developed and tested new Lean thinking, and engaged senior and middle management in Lean design and execution. We did not, however, do the work of the teams; we did not fill out forms; and we did not run the projects themselves. We felt that that was the normal work of the teams and, as such, should remain with them.

What turned out to be a provocative question actually got us to think about what we were trying to teach people and how to teach those lessons. If we allow our teams to shift the burden of redesigning their work onto us, then they will not learn how to redesign their work. If we allow teams to shift their project management tasks to us, they will not learn how to manage their projects. In this latter case, had we taken responsibility for those project management tasks, we would not have observed the emergence of "organic" project management, and we would have lost valuable learning on just how effective teams could be. In any event, our model was highly leveraged. In the end, there is no magic employee-to-practitioner ratio; you will have to find your own ideal level.

Identifying That First Project

Moving from the grand strategic level to the very tactical, we need to define what project we initiate first. There are a number of questions that, if answered, will support a fairly robust and successful selection of a first project. These questions are really about finding a project that matches the organization's entry (and exit) points for new ideas.

- What project/nonproject areas does your company believe to be important and represent the normal work of its R&D organization?
- What project/nonproject areas does your company believe are unimportant and whose improvement through Lean may be discounted?
- Who in your organization is a thought leader, a person who, if he or she adopts some new approach, will shed positive light on that idea?
- Who is seen as unreliable, weird, or toxic within your organization, and whose endorsement actually stigmatizes an idea?
- Who is "in pain" (under significant performance stress) and really needs (and is looking for) help?
- Who is in an area that is so important that he gets everything he wants?
- What projects are connected to lots of other projects?
- What projects, though small, affect the lives of many people (shared services often have these attributes)?

- How risk averse is your company? (If high, don't start projects that affect the company jewels!)
- What triggers your company's "immune response" to reject new ideas?
- What triggers your company's "receptive response" to *embrace* new ideas?
- How are successful (and still active!) ideas identified and spread in your company?
- Where did these projects start?
- Who championed them?
- What was the trajectory of an initiative that did not succeed (or limped endlessly)?
  - Where did it start?
  - Who designed it?
  - Who championed it?
  - Where did it begin to fail?
  - What killed it?

By answering your critical questions, you can easily plan a path to find a low risk, highly enthusiastic, culturally accepted place to begin. In my experience, there are three likely places where people are willing to engage a first or early project. The first is a relatively highly placed manager who is struggling to meet his or her objectives. That manager will almost always welcome your help, and will usually engage in supportive work to ensure the project's success. These managers will be exceptional at getting the business value out of the project and spreading the word about the value that can be gained.

The second place is managers who also happen to be early adopters. These folks are open to new ideas generally, and often supply insight and help you think through new experiments to try to get more value within their departments than you have been able to get elsewhere. These people often prove very capable in supporting cultural transformation, and will often give you the best learning opportunities.

The third way to find valuable projects is through the friends and associates of managers who have gained from your work in the past. It is not unusual for these people to seek your services, but in the case that is not forthcoming, a brief dialogue with your prior project leaders often uncovers other areas where Lean might find a welcome home.

Spreading Lean through Fast Learning: The Wildfire Strategy

This "soft strategy" of spreading Lean through the social networks of early engagements is well precedented in all sorts of environments, from viral videos on the World Wide Web to warfare, from evolutionary biology to epidemic infection. Fundamentally, all that needs to happen for a video to "go viral" is for one person to find a video that really resonates with his or her psyche. He or she will invariably share it with a few friends, and no matter how isolated that person is, one of his or her friends is bound to have several friends, who will also find that video interesting. These people will share it with their group of friends, and so on. It is easy to see how networks of friends overlap and how those overlapping networks could easily support exponential or faster spread of a really fascinating video. The same thing is true of people who experience value from a method that helps their careers, their business objectives, their personal purpose, or their quality of life. Not everyone will share that experience, but those who do will find new friends for you to engage.

When we proved successful in helping those managers, they used their personal networks to open doors for us (see Figure 10.3). At times, this was more successful than we had capacity to support. At other times, we had to work these networks ourselves, reaching out to people through our managerial and our own personal contacts. The success rate of this method that we called the "wildfire strategy" was such that at least half of our engagements resulted from customer pull.

While there is a whole area of sociology devoted to it, the important thing is that social networks can help spread Lean for you. We often talk about cultural or personal resistance to change. The idea is that people dislike change and that change must be overcome. The "soft strategy" assumes the opposite: Most people love change that they think is good; they just don't like change that is forced on them by someone who might not have their best interests or underlying beliefs at heart. We can succeed as long as we engage people in change they desire, and change like this is often triggered by recommendations from friends. If you take advantage of the ability of social networks to create "customer pull," you may find a much easier path to changing culture than if you attempt to force change and engage people in their natural resistance to things forced upon them.

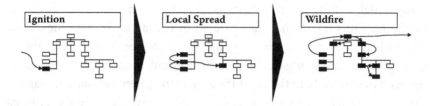

FIGURE 10.3

A graphic depiction of the "wildfire" implementation strategy used successfully to spread Lean through an R&D community and on to successive R&D communities. On the left, the first project or engagement of Lean is initiated within an organization. When that proves successful, participants within the first project talk to their friends and colleagues in other areas about the success of their work. This leads to "pull" for more Lean from other teams and functional organizations within the community (center), and eventually leads to "pull" for Lean from people and organizations outside of the local organization. This process can happen very quickly and produces very little resistance. As described, "wildfire" is a strategy that uses neither top-down nor bottom-up approaches. Rather, it uses the natural learning and social networks that exist within a company to engage new people, teams, and communities in the use of Lean. Critical to its functioning, the "wildfire" approach requires that Lean projects successfully support the missions, cultures, and goals of stakeholders throughout an R&D community. For it to work successfully, a Lean approach requires careful matching of language, approach, and implementation to existing cultural structures and beliefs.

There are ways to accelerate and hinder this process. As with a video, for Lean to go viral, it must connect, somehow, to the psyche of those who spread those ideas. In this respect, we have some questions concerning social acceptability of Lean within our company. If you are in the pharmaceutical business, stories about Toyota are likely to have little positive resonance with your colleagues in R&D. In fact, stories about Toyota are likely to get you branded as a nutcase and dramatically inhibit your cause. By contrast, if you build your Lean language and examples around things that are important to the researchers in your company, you will likely have a sympathetic ear. For example, the word *Lean* is often linked inextricably to the word *mean*. If this is true in your company, then *change the name!* Nobody cares. I found out that my company *hated* the name Lean for this exact reason. So, I called our effort Agile R&D[SM], which was not merely innocent sounding, but actually sounded like something you would want your R&D to be. From that day forward, we never had any more barriers because of the name.

Similarly, if you can connect Lean to the progress of innovation, or to culturally adored aspects of your company, you will do well. People, researchers in particular, join pharmaceutical companies for the opportunity to

conquer debilitating disease. If people perceive Lean as a power for eliminating bureaucracy so that they can get in the lab and create those new
treatments, Lean will be their friend. If people see in Lean the ability
to help them think innovatively, to bridge and broker innovative ideas
between people, to help them get those new treatments to patients earlier,
they will embrace Lean wholeheartedly. If, however, people see Lean as
creating and enforcing *process*, especially at the expense of creativity, they
will see it getting in the way of new medicines, and your ideas will find a
cold welcome and your initiative a short life.

These cultural aspects are not unique to pharmaceutical companies.
Engineers join car companies because they love cars, motorcycle makers because they love everything with two wheels, tractor manufacturers
because they love farms, and software makers because they want to be a
part of exciting technologies. Yes, people do join companies to earn a living, but their selection process is not completely random, at least for most
people, so connect with the spirit of the company and let it help you in
your efforts.

To this point, we have identified the number and cadence of projects
needed to make our implementation timeline. We have identified a good
first project and the Lean facilitator for that project, and perhaps we have
thought about who would lead additional projects as our effort continues. We identified ways to think about what works well in our company
and what our company rejects out of hand in order to adapt Lean language, and perhaps the philosophy of Lean, to the underlying culture of
our company.

But once our project is joined and in motion, a tactical question or two
could spell the difference between strategic success and failure. If our
company is intolerant of failure, even a minor setback, which can easily
occur early in any new intervention, could cause our company to reject
the idea out of hand. We build in, at the operational point, consideration
about how to protect the project, if needed, from just such a possibility.

LEARNING AS ITS OWN STRATEGY

Once a Lean project is joined, we will get a regular stream of learning
about the project itself, about our company and division culture, about

our colleagues' and team's problem-solving skills, and about our skills as facilitators and mentors. Before even starting our project, we want to ask ourselves several questions that will identify ways to improve our effort even as it progresses. What is going better than expected? What is not going as well as expected? In both cases, why do we believe that progress is not tracking to the plan? For portions of the project that are exceeding the plan, how do we capitalize on them? For portions of the plan that are falling behind, what can we do to bring them back onto the plan? What does the first project tell us about our selection process? Did we find a good place to start or not, and how can we use that to find or prepare a better place next time? We modified our approach to Lean with the idea that these modifications would enable a close cultural match. Which parts matched? Which parts did not? What does that tell us about how we should change our Lean approach? What does it tell us about things we need to change in our culture?

These are critical questions required by our strategy in order to increase acceptance, increase value, and accelerate uptake of Lean in the company. We will have new knowledge from our first (and also second, third, and *n*th project) about how well certain types of projects progress, how we accept or reject them, and how effective they are in moving the performance of the business, culture, personal growth, and so on. We can use this knowledge to improve both the company and our capability to change the company. When we synthesize all of this project-generated learning, we can develop and grow our own methodology and philosophy for changing R&D. New projects will benefit from improvements in methodology to make our interventions more effective, faster, and easier to accomplish. This emerging method and philosophy will be tailored specifically to our R&D division, with its cultures and quirks. It will be unique to us and uniquely powerful in our setting. We can, with such an emerging knowledge base, forget entirely about what someone else did at some big name conglomerate or at some small tool-and-die manufacturer in another part of the country. We will no longer be chasing what our competitors are doing but, instead, will be concentrating on ever more rapid ways to remove barriers to our own internal change. By learning about ourselves with each succeeding project, we set ourselves on a course to diverge, happily and in the right direction, from everyone else, and at an alarming rate of speed.

This second, strategic level of learning, if continued beyond the original Lean implementation effort, will set us apart from almost every other company in the world. Taken together, from project and method development to new project and method selection, this cycle represents one turn of a learning spiral required to take an R&D division from zero to full Lean. Figure 10.4 shows the entire strategic overview on one map.

One final question completes that upward spiral, "When do we stop intervening?" The answer to the question of when do we stop intervening depends on a few things. If we interpret *intervention* to mean large mapping exercises, then the answer will be very different than if we describe *intervention* to encompass any designed change to remove barriers or improve the nature of the R&D environment. In the former case, the number of big interventions should fall dramatically once everyone in the division knows how their innovation work could or should flow smoothly from its inception. With CQM, my belief is that small interventions should be occurring on a regular basis as teams face new hurdles in

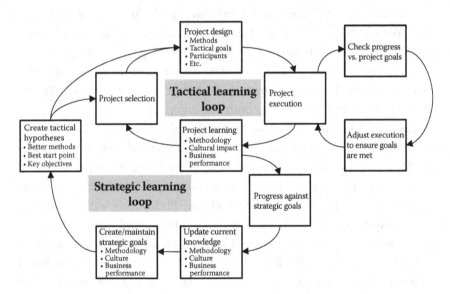

FIGURE 10.4

The learning processes emanating from the example Critical Question Map for Lean implementation strategy. This process shows that each project is adapted to support the overall Lean implementation. Each project generates both project learning and learning about how to implement Lean. This higher level learning loop is then used to store and analyze learning, adapt Lean methodology, and design new Lean experiments for future implementation projects.

their product innovation cycles, but that large, multiday mapping exercises should probably only occur when a very large change in overall divisional performance is warranted. Such redesigns are nearly unheard of in R&D units, which often have no conscious design for project progression.*

Larger mapping exercises may be required for very long-cycle projects or projects involving large numbers of people, even if a well-worn path is already known. This might be true of pharmaceutical R&D, where projects can take as much as a decade, involve upwards of 50 to 100 people, and contain unique challenges compared to prior R&D. That said, I can easily envision a team where this proves unnecessary or redundant. Product development of durable goods, items with significant knowledge carry-over from one product iteration to the next, could easily begin with a standard CQM and proceed to improve on the basis of its current knowledge.

Nevertheless, companies decide to quit using Lean quite frequently. Sometimes this happens quite unconsciously. Senior management may move its attention to other things, like an impending merger, an emerging business situation, or a change in management. Sometimes, the decision is quite deliberate. Senior management may become frustrated with the pace of change or with the implications of change. The first intervention could go quite poorly, and management, or even the rank and file, could reject it wholesale. But by having an explicit question around when to stop, we put on the table that an end could happen, and we can begin to marshal arguments for and against such a decision, conscious or otherwise, and begin to take countermeasures.

The Implications of a Learning Strategy

What emerged from my map was a learning process that both implements Lean and learns to improve the implementation of Lean at the same time. Very little is required to begin: a few hypotheses about the organization, a few experiments to define a likely place to start, and some methodology to try within the walls of the first project. With that small bit of information, the first project will generate tremendous amounts of knowledge about the

---

* Many R&D units do have "stage gate" processes, which describe the steps of work in the R&D division. Often, because the nature of a project changes so much from one to the next, the steps are very strategic and do not describe the daily or even monthly work required at the bench level. As a result, many stage-gate processes serve more as governance structures than as detailed designs for project progression.

organization. It will tell us a lot about flaws and cracks in our cultural and business hypotheses. It will expose gaps in our understanding of methodology, philosophy, and theory of Lean R&D. It will provide substantive benefits that we can build on. It will enthuse some people, who can then be called on to champion our efforts in the future. It will annoy others, whom we can call on to help us learn what not to do in the future, or what we can do to make our next project easier and more effective. In the end, it is self-sustaining and self-controlling, scalable, and relatively straightforward to accomplish on limited resources.

Many other strategies are possible. This one emerged from a Critical Question Map that I developed. Your own map would have different questions and might very well suggest a different approach. Even armed with the same questions, you may arrange them differently or answer them in a sufficiently different way that your strategy would look completely unlike the one described here. The one thing that I do believe is that, given enough time and an absence of corporate upheavals, the strategy I outlined will work and that it cannot help but create a new, custom-tailored Lean developed entirely on the basis of, and in service for, your company.

With that in mind, I would again like to consider the studies of strategic implementation failure rates. Why do you suppose Lean initiatives fail? It is hard to tell, but we can ask a few questions:

- Was the design bespoke to the implementing company, or was it "borrowed" or adapted from a "best case" company?
    - If it was adapted, what elements did they consider in adapting it? Did they consider the financial differences between the companies? Did they consider size differences? Did they take into account cultural differences between the companies? If so, which aspects did they adapt? What aspects were not accounted for?
- Was the design a "big batch" effort, in which the entire roll out was developed ahead of time?" If so:
    - What happened with failures? Were they kept hidden for political purposes? Were people punished for failures? Were failures in areas dear to company morale? Were there efforts to resolve issues caused by the Lean initiative in order to stem the natural spread of bad news?
    - What happened with successes? Did they celebrate them? Did they allow and encourage the natural excitement of a win to

spread and build engagement naturally within others in the organization?

- Did anyone notice the dissonance between big-batch design and implementation and the principles of Lean?
- Were there active learning mechanisms built into the strategy?
  - How quickly were problems identified?
  - Once identified, how quickly were they solved and new approaches tested? Immediately? After a number had built up? Never?
  - Where new approaches were attempted, did they address the root cause of the issues that had been identified? Was there a concerted effort to share and implement findings broadly?
  - Were the employees that designed or received new work problems engaged in their resolution, or were their concerns and issues ignored in order to maintain speed or momentum of the project?
  - Did people notice a dissonance between Lean's call for "respect for people" and the initiative's treatment of people as doers, not thinkers?
- Who did the problem solving/changing of work processes and practices?
  - Were "experts" designing all of the new work? Were managers designing the new work? Were the efforts and ideas of those closest to the work the ones used to create the change? Were these ideas and creations even taken into consideration?
- Was the effort linked to headcount reductions?
- Were people punished for their successes by loading them up with more work?
- Was the effort linked to business drivers?
  - If so, did the projects also engage cultural drivers, or were the projects linked only to numbers and business success?
  - Did the early efforts target projects of such high importance to the company that employees and managers were too afraid of failure to learn and engage a new way of thinking?
  - Conversely, did initial efforts target areas nobody cared about? Could the rest of the company write off the project because that area of the company is "unimportant" or "stupid" or "incapable" or "just a mess anyway," etc.?

- Was the effort a throwaway?
    - Did the Lean initiative start because "everyone else is doing it" or because some board member decided it should be so, but the leaders of the initiative did not believe in Lean to begin with? (Employees can always tell when your heart is somewhere else, and they will act accordingly.)
    - Did it fail by improving things that nobody cared about?

There are, no doubt, a hundred more such questions that could be asked. Each of these questions may peek into a single corner of a veritable maze of possible issues that might crop up during implementation, and this brings us to one important finer point. You can do a relatively quick analysis of your last three strategic implementations to find practices that work very well in your organization and others that work poorly. Using this as an overlay to development and answering of your critical questions, you can easily develop a coherent, successful implementation strategy for your own Lean transformation.

IMPLEMENTATION STRATEGY SUMMARY

History and academic research suggest that implementation strategy is a poorly understood, if not failed, art. Lean, by contrast, is a philosophy for improving systems, processes, and thinking. With that in mind, it stands to reason that Lean, long known for its ability to create transformative change in short periods of time, might provide the philosophy and tools necessary to improve implementation art, delivering successes where others have failed.

I have taken you through one approach, based on Lean R&D thinking, to design and develop a company-specific Lean implementation strategy for your company. Based on Critical Question Mapping and management of learning, this approach will be tailor-made to your company, its people and culture, its business needs, and its future direction. It would, I believe, be just as valid to value stream map the implementation of one (or hopefully several) of your company's prior strategic initiatives. With the "current state" of how your company designs and executes implementation, you will be able to identify weak points in the process, dead ends, poor decisions, knowledge gaps, and other barriers to your smooth and easy success. You should be able to improve your implementation process dramatically and create a solid success for your Lean initiative.

It intrigues me that, despite all of the strategic failures that appear to go back to the same hypotheses about why initiatives fail, the lack of sponsorship or leadership from the top is often cited as the primary problem. I will grant that senior management can have an enormous impact on the success of any project, but Toyota's Lean transformation was not led (certainly not from the outset) from the chairman's office. It was led by Taiichi Ohno, the manager of a machine shop who had strong ideas about experimentation and how things ought to work. I will be willing to bet that you can find two or three examples from your company's past where people with drive and passion have changed the fundamental nature of the company without (or even despite) the CEO's blessing.

Another stumbling block people cite in the failure of strategy is a lack of knowledge within a company around the change that is being implemented. It is, one might argue, difficult to create a Lean company without deep knowledge of Lean. Knowledge is good, but of course, Lean itself was not a fully developed set of ideas in 1950. It is not a fully developed set of ideas now. Successful implementation cannot, then, be pinned on knowledge; it must arise from something deeper.

My belief is that learning and vision are the keys to the successful implementation of any strategic vision. We cannot know before we start exactly what areas of the company will be enthusiastic and which ones will prove tepid. We can only find that out through experimentation and intentional learning. Lean provides several platforms for such learning, from CQM to value stream mapping and on to A3 thinking and beyond. What baffles me is that we often do not see what is right before our eyes. We have an exceptional platform for creating success; we merely need to apply it—thoughtfully, patiently, and relentlessly—until we succeed. In the end, the transformation of the company does not come about because we changed the *company*, but because we changed ourselves.

11

The Formation of Lean R&D Communities: A Case Example

Einstein once famously remarked that his work rested "on the shoulders of giants," namely the scientists and philosophers who had gone before him. The contributions of these giants, and their less significant colleagues, shaped for scientists in that community both the extent of known and accepted physics as well as the body of problems whose answers remained unknown but of interest to the community. They defined the perspectives that physicists should hold about their science as well as the problems that physicists should spend their energies in solving. In this respect, the scientific community had a very strong effect in *aligning* Einstein's thinking and scientific inquiry. By contributing to the body of knowledge of this community, and gaining acceptance of this body for his work, Einstein was able to contribute an entirely new paradigm of thought to the community's worldview and usher in a renaissance in physics that extends to this day.

We have spent a great deal of time discussing the fact that science is, at its heart, a social activity in which researchers come together in a community to share in and progress against a higher purpose. In the case of Einstein, as is the case of all creators, inventors, and researchers, the community they select to align with creates an environment, a context, and expectations for that creativity, including expectations about what is valuable, a reflection of their higher purpose, what proofs will suffice to show valuable contributions toward that purpose, and so on. By their absence, those things on which the community has not agreed form a set of contributions and proofs that are not yet (and may never be) valued by that community. In return for commitment to this community, the community synthesizes the valuable contributions of its members into a growing body of knowledge, which it carries with it. It recognizes those contributions and carries a place for contributors in its legacy.

Of course, some communities function better and more smoothly than others, even communities of the same type. Some communities thrive and grow, their members becoming increasingly satisfied and committed to the enterprise over time, and these tendencies attract still more people to the group, people who might share their same sense of purpose. This does not preclude the odd fight; in fact, the history of science is filled with conflict, yet, despite this, the community continues to thrive.

Contrariwise, dysfunctional communities limp along, losing membership and drive over time; in extreme cases, they cease to function entirely. In dysfunctional communities, valuable output, even (perhaps especially) by the reckoning of the group itself, is inadequate to serve the community's purpose, and over time, people begin to disconnect as a result of such unfulfilled purpose. Even those communities with *stated* purposes sufficiently compelling to attract new members will lose those members and eventually fail if their purpose is inadequately supported by community members.

In other cases, communities lose members if the daily operations and output of the community are at odds with the stated purpose of the community, that is, if the actions that the community or its membership undertake are "corrupt" in comparison with the stated purpose of the group. In such cases, the moral dissonance between the two cannot be tolerated by the group, and it splits apart. History is littered with examples. Thomas Jefferson wrote these words to describe one of the most famous of political splits in the Declaration of Independence: "Governments are instituted among men, deriving their just powers from the consent of the governed. That whenever any form of government becomes destructive to these ends, it is the right of the people to alter or to abolish it, and to institute new government." Thus, a long-standing community with close ties of brotherhood and ancestry fractured and became two communities solely as the result of leadership dissonance with the expectations and mores of a part of that community.

Corporations are communities within the wider community of a municipality, state, nation, or the world, and the best companies acknowledge and build on that understanding. Companies each have their purposes.

Some purposes, like Toyota's of providing individual transportation (cars) or Pfizer's of alleviating disease through pharmaceutical treatment, are easily recognizable. Others, like General Electric's, are less apparent, since their many business units serve many purposes. Such companies have fostered other aligning purposes, like GE's, which is a community tied together by a common, highly competitive business culture. Companies like GE go to great lengths to support these aligning elements to ensure that their communities grow and remain strong through time.

Within these wider purposes, narrower purposes exist. Manufacturing and sales functions affect the purpose of the company, and they bring that purpose to others. The research and development (R&D) function improves and sometimes expands the purpose of the company within the wider community by creating valuable packages of knowledge that embody the purpose of the company in the form of new products, services, or processes.

Around the narrower purpose of R&D, a research community forms to further its aims. Going deeper, a project team is a community that has been formed around the purpose of creating a specific, valuable package of knowledge that will serve the higher purpose of R&D and, in turn, the higher purpose of the company. These purposes are crucial elements of community building in companies. People's connection to purpose can be so weak that they rotate companies and functions almost at whim, or it can be so strong that they will abandon otherwise productive careers to join a more aligned community. As an example, it is common among cancer researchers to be so committed to their community's purpose that, rather than be reassigned within their company to fight another disease, they will quit their company, even damage their active research careers, to join another organization fighting cancer.

Aligning purpose can be powerful, affecting not only the fervor of those committing to the community, but also the mental models in which those people engage in their work. NASA's great race to the moon is a clear example of a massive organization with a single-minded purpose and an incredible *be state*. They were, quite literally, the best and the brightest. They did not *aspire* to the best and brightest, they just *were* by force of outlook and vision. They did not need to *have things* as much as they needed their best mental efforts in order to *create* things and knowledge of value.

Like people, organizations can operate from *be* or *have* mindsets. In the glory days of corporate R&D, the Bell, General Electric, and IBM corporate research laboratories, to name but a few, competed in a serious battle to prove their supremacy as the best scientific research lab. Each employed Nobel laureates, conducted basic and applied research, and fought amongst themselves and with academic and government research centers for the best and brightest. Each thought its research exemplified its corporate image, and spent significant amounts of money inventing amazing things, but *having* was not their hallmark. *Creating* was their stock in trade.

By contrast, I am certain that you can easily find researchers (even in those places and at those times) who, in order to pursue great science, believe that they must *have* certain equipment and surround themselves with certain other scientists, and so on. The *be state* of this type of culture is markedly different, and so, too, is the value of their output.

As noted, R&D is not so much a game of completing activities; it is an enterprise in which good thinking reigns supreme. This is not merely true of the individual researcher; it is just as, or perhaps more, true of the community as a whole, since in any large research project, many—perhaps dozens or hundreds of researchers—must create and integrate their communal knowledge into a coherent, usable whole. A well-functioning community can act in concert, almost as a single organism, or it can act as a loose collection, fractured into subgroups and hampered in its communication. Unsurprisingly, the difference in performance of these two models—a community that "thinks well" and purposefully versus one that entertains fractious thinking—is tremendous. The community that thinks well will forward its stated purpose far further and more quickly than one that does not.

CASE STUDY: FORMATION OF A LEAN COMMUNITY

The project to support the Strategic Prosecution of Targets (SPOT) team culminated a lot of the Lean R&D practice we had developed over the first two years of our work. We had run value stream mapping workshops for the entire tenure of our work, but usually we limited the size of these workshops to 20 people. SPOT leadership wanted to have everyone involved, so this workshop involved 45 people. We had just invented and deployed the Critical Question Mapping[SM] (CQM[SM]) approach for the first time on a project, and had identified new opportunities for it in research. Finally, we had recently begun working with teams, and particularly managers and "chunk captains,"* on using A3 for management and problem solving.

Given the size of the project and the enthusiasm of the team's senior manager, we wanted to see how the entire system, engaged all at once over an entire community of researchers, would play out. The experiments were critical to improving our strategy for Lean implementation, for while we had regularly achieved two- to fourfold improvements, those improvements stayed within the teams. We did not see growth of those principles in groups that supported or were adjacent to our project teams. Moreover, although project teams would continue to apply their improvement designs, it was the rare individuals who applied the Lean principles gained in the group setting to their immediate bench work. What we saw most often was that we could create quite large scale but punctuated improvements, but we did not see the spark of sustained, continuous improvement begin to take hold. Obviously, we were anxious to learn how, within our R&D organization, we could begin to change our work from large, one-time gains, to large and continuing gains within groups that would spread their newfound successes to others in the company.

Our design, then, was fourfold: first, begin mentoring leadership in A3 mentorship. Importantly, in this experiment, we made a strict effort to do our A3 mentorship in a Socratic style. We did not *tell* anyone how to do things, and tried very hard to not even make suggestions. Instead, when we saw issues, we would note the discrepancy and have the team or team member work through the discrepancy themselves. We purposely strove to do no thought work for the team, but to support them in learning to create their own.

Our second design principle was, since the SPOT team had not existed prior to our work, to facilitate a workshop beginning with a Critical Question Map to create a full understanding of the innovation problems facing the community. In turn, the CQM would be converted into a value stream map of activities, so that people could see the handoffs and linkages needed to collectively deliver their innovation. The final step of the workshop was to develop a learning plan to achieve the future state and ensure that the knowledge gaps were adequately supported.

---

* Leaders of subsegments of our R&D value streams.

Our third project design element was to engage team members both one on one and in small groups on A3 problem solving to answer the critical questions emerging from the workshop. This was a separate effort from the management team that was designed to deliver Lean thinking all of the way to the bench level and to support it on a regular basis so that continuous improvement would take hold at all levels of the team. The fourth and final design element was that we would follow the project proactively through its lifetime rather than transition off at a predetermined time point as we had in projects past.

The experiment, in terms of its insight into Lean, provided a lot of new insight into our future work. It succeeded in building Lean all of the way through the organization. It was less successful initially in expanding its influence outside of the team, but eventually this hurdle was overcome without any specific design or implementation effort. Finally, the effort threw off several new tools ("good-better-best" and "organic fast learning," to name two) and created a new paradigm for Lean community.

THE SPOT PROJECT

The SPOT team was created at Pfizer to identify new, valuable targets to address a horrible degenerative disease with no really effective treatments then on the market. Significant literature and research effort across many companies, institutions, and universities had not, to that point, made much of a dent in understanding the cause of the disease, let alone come up with viable approaches for treatment.

Every member of the team was committed to this purpose in a very personal way, although SPOT was formed by bolting together several different existing laboratory groups. Each group had its own history and was devoted to a single scientific discipline or function that would now be a part of this larger group (community). None of these groups had ever been connected or operated completely together.

At its inception, SPOT was an idea, not a working, interacting community. Within five months, SPOT became a harmonious, undivided community with effectively no functional boundaries, minimal hierarchy, and a dramatic sense of being. Individual team members had committed not merely to the community's purpose, but to the community itself, its norms, and the other individual members. There was, within this team, the palpable sense that this team *was* the doom of this disease, an inevitable and irresistible force that would overcome the biology of the disease and the suffering that it caused. In *becoming* SPOT, members shifted all kinds of operating norms and expectations, including their understanding of who should define and assign innovative work and the type and extent of innovative contributions that could be expected from members.

In many environments, managers design and direct the activities of the team. In R&D, this model is only randomly the case, since innovative contribution is the reason for hiring great researchers. That said, in many cases, the manager-design model lives. Making matters worse, in most PhD-centric organizations (and pharmaceutical research is nothing if not PhD-centric), non-PhDs often have difficulty offering, being recognized for, and making their best innovative contributions. Instead, their function is to often act as an extension of the ideas and creative contributions of a PhD, who designs their work and interprets their work product when it is completed.

In SPOT, these hierarchical tendencies diminished dramatically. Managers no longer decided what people should work on—people decided that for themselves. PhDs did not generally dictate the innovation work non-PhDs performed; instead, researchers contributed their efforts in the best way that they could to the most important scientific questions. Communications went from "through-channel" to "direct," or as Southwest Airlines might describe it, from a hub-and-spoke model to a point-to-point model of communication.

The following set of figures illustrates the change from a social perspective. Figure 11.1a shows a picture of communication across the team, which existed in independent silos *before* SPOT's formation. Each line represents a communication channel that is used at least weekly. Figure 11.1b shows how communication was conducted *after* SPOT's formation. In Figure 11.1a, it is easy to see who are managers and who are scientists, whereas in Figure 11.1b, it is impossible, without a key, to distinguish the reporting hierarchy.

Figure 11.1c is an innovation network map. Each line indicates a member seeking innovation advice from another member at least once a week. The figure clearly demonstrates that every single member's innovation advice is requested on at least a weekly basis. For readers not accustomed to the hierarchical nature of research, it should be noted that, in most

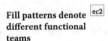

Fill patterns denote
different functional
teams

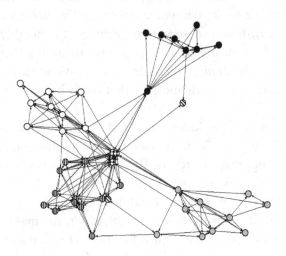

FIGURE 11.1A

A social network map of weekly communication patterns within a team. Each circle represents a person on the team. Each arrow represents one person reaching out to another person on at least a weekly basis (self-reported data). The pattern seen here is typical of a hierarchical, siloed organization. Almost all communication occurs through the intercession of a manager (hence managers are easily identified in the map).

R&D organizations, innovation advice across educational boundaries (PhD to MS or BS) is one-way or nearly one-way. PhD scientists, by dint of their education and experience, are expected to design the work of their non-PhD coworkers. Moreover, they are trained in graduate school to design and execute their own research, independently from others within the group. It is unusual to have as high a level of interaction across a group of PhDs. It is downright rare to have non-PhD researchers as innovation hubs as can be seen in Figure 11.1c. It borders on the shocking that every single member of the team, including a college graduate who joined the company literally on the day of the kickoff workshop, is engaged in providing innovative advice to others on the team.

Other evidence of SPOT coming together as an open, highly integrated community included shifts in norms and behavior. Figure 11.2 summarizes SPOT team norms. Team members no longer tolerated in themselves, the missing of deadlines—too many other people depended on each individual delivering work on time. In the same way, the need for speed

**Fill patterns denote
functional teams**

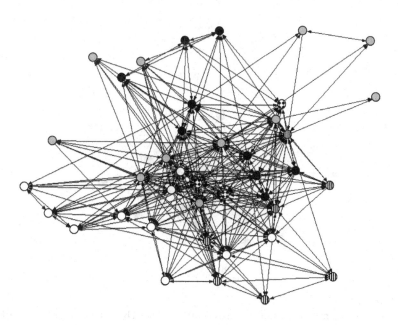

FIGURE 11.1B
The weekly communication social network map of the same team as Figure 11.1a taken several months after a Lean value stream and Critical Question Mapping project was initiated. The density of interaction has changed dramatically, and the "point to point" communication style is clearly evident. Managers and groups can no longer be clearly identified by interaction alone. (Note, there are some personnel and group alignment changes that occurred during the course of the project. These would be expected to have some limited impact on the outcome of the map.)

demanded that everyone bring 100 percent complete and accurate data to the others, which eliminated the need for double-checking, an operational feature that works only in an atmosphere of implicit trust. Lack of connectedness to the others' research became intolerable for team members. When a team member was called away or absent from a meeting, another team member had to be able to immediately step in and handle whatever presentation was required. Managers stopped speaking for the team, and team members began representing their own work. Team members stopped asking permission and, instead, decided together what needed to be done and what constituted success.

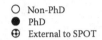

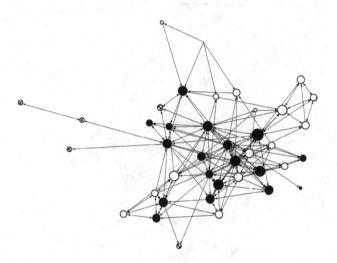

FIGURE 11.1C

A social network map of the same team as Figures 11.1a and b. Each line represents weekly or more frequent outreach from one person to another to gain innovation advice or input (self-reported data). This map shows an unusually high level of engagement across academic levels, a key outcome of Lean projects, especially those using Critical Question Mapping and A3.

Figure 11.3 shows how the team managed as an organic, emergent operation. The center oval is where the team, as a whole or in subgroups, defined immediate next steps, which they did by knowing precisely the knowledge needs of the project (the top oval), the current state of knowledge (the right oval), and the current disposition of team members, including workload, interests, capabilities, and availability. SPOT's response time in adjusting strategy or operations due to emergent circumstance in any of the outer ovals was on the order of minutes, and, it is important to note, the center oval was a dynamic place. Managers *did not* and, given the size and breadth of decision making required, *could not* actively manage the center oval. Aside from large-scale reviews typically run off-site, the team as a whole did not manage the center oval either. Instead, it was managed dynamically by small elements of the team coming together as events warranted.

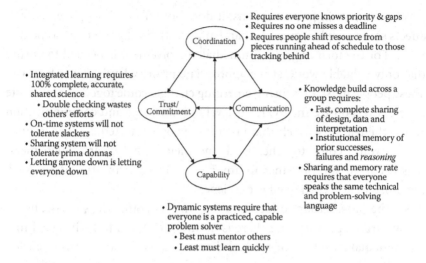

FIGURE 11.2
Cultural elements of Lean R&D as exemplified by the SPOT team.

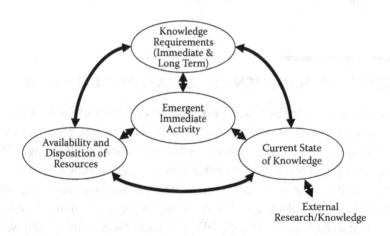

FIGURE 11.3
A visual depiction of "organic fast learning" project management of an R&D team. In the SPOT team, activity was designed and engaged on an "emergent" basis determined from available resources (human, material, equipment, and so on) and existing knowledge gaps. Emergent operation ensures that the team takes fullest and most immediate advantage of all new learning across the team and from external sources as well.

When something new happens, it does not affect all people equally. It affects some people a great deal and affects others slightly or at some distance. For the former group, immediate involvement is needed to ensure that only valuable work, at the appropriate priority level, moves forward. These people must, on sensing emerging change, come together and create coherent responses. In SPOT, the level of knowledge and communication across the team was such that just those people affected by new circumstance would come together to define their path forward. Such meetings occurred several times in any given day, ensuring that daily work remained on the cutting edge of science.

For the latter group, understanding what is going on is useful but is not an urgent priority, and there is no need for them to be inserted into an immediate strategy or tactical discussion. With fast learning cycles, enough is happening in a given week that everyone must at times be involved in these sidebars, so it is crucial that only those sidebars directly affecting one's own work be attended. Nevertheless, the rest of the team needs to remain connected and aligned with the higher purpose. Update e-mails, updates to team Wiki pages, weekly subteam meetings, and team-wide monthly project reviews ensure that the whole unit stays coordinated and aligned against its strategic question.

PROJECT MANAGEMENT IN A LEAN R&D COMMUNITY

Two interesting side issues arose for Lean practitioners in the area of project management. First, when a team achieves organic operation, it no longer *needs* a mechanically set cadence to coordinate fast learning. SPOT used weekly (subteam) and monthly (entire team) review cadences, but had no daily cadence. In fact, their redirection rate operated at a much higher-than-daily clock speed and, in any event, a mechanical cadence on a team as large as SPOT (officially, just fewer than 40 members) would make daily meetings unwieldy.

The second issue concerned the usefulness of a *future state* based on activities. Until SPOT, I was persuaded that activity-based planning was useful but not needed, but SPOT persuaded me that an activity-based future state and learning plan might actually hinder the top performance of an R&D team. SPOT's future-state map was so hopelessly out of date by 90 days that it was abandoned entirely.

In its stead, SPOT employed an *emergent* future state. Using the Critical Question Map as an enduring guide to the strategic issues, team members designed their experiments on a timescale appropriate to the needs of the team at the time such experimental plans were needed. The Critical Question Map then served as a project management tool, with the team conferring on elimination of open questions to mark progress. Thus, the team managed *knowledge creation* rather than activities, and activity planning became, like the experiments themselves, just another required, but nonvalue-added, step in their work.

Importantly, SPOT incorporated or exemplified all of the elements of a thriving, focused, Lean R&D community and a few besides. Respect for people was a defining factor in the team's *be state*, and was demonstrated and reinforced by managers and researchers alike. Managers shifted design and tactics entirely to the team, refusing pointedly to define research direction for researchers or to make technical decisions, on the premise that decisions were always best made closest to the data. This ensured that the best and freshest *data and context* would be used to answer technical questions, data that no manager would ever have at her fingertips and that no manager could ever amass in her office role. Managers, in fact, eschewed the problem-solving *role* itself, and began a new role of mentoring others in their efforts at solving problems and answering technical questions and facilitating the team and its subteams in research strategy. In that stroke, they moved their role one very large step upward in strategic value, and they regained a *tremendous* amount of time previously spent in telling others what to do. One manager estimated that she regained fully 50 percent of her time, which could be reapplied to more valuable work.

With the new level of common commitment, people had laid the foundation of trust to enable a different sort of building. They could give up fiefdom "ownership" of their work, since they no longer competed with each other. The competition had moved to the disease itself. As a result, sharing quickly escalated, enabling several unexpectedly valuable concepts to emerge. First, the team found that fast, direct sharing resulted in backup of function without significant time spent in cross-training or directly overlapping work. Coverage naturally resulted when people were unable to attend meetings or were away for extended periods on vacation or illness. A major internal project review was held successfully with half of the management and subteam project leadership called away on short notice. Several major management reviews of the project were successfully navigated under similar circumstances.

THE VALUE OF POINT-TO-POINT COMMUNICATION

The SPOT team demonstrated the value of point-to-point communications in R&D. If a researcher identifies new information that can shift the direction of one other researcher in the project, the SPOT scientist would *immediately* seek out that second researcher and engage a dialogue, whether the two scientists worked in the same functional area or reported to different managers. Another communication approach, taken before SPOT, would be for the first researcher to *go through channels*. Going through channels means that a researcher would describe her research to her manager. Her manager would identify the appropriate recipient of her new knowledge and set up a meeting with a manager in the recipient's function. At this point, if the recipient was in the same meeting, direct communications could commence. If not, the first researcher might describe the work to the recipient's manager in that meeting and set up a meeting with the recipient, where direct communication might finally occur. Only at the point where the recipient has in hand—and understands the implications of—the emerging data can the recipient redirect work to reflect the best knowledge.

From a Lean perspective, of course, all of the delay in the indirect route is waste. Moreover, the delay leaves the recipient progressing out-of-date research, hence the waste of delay causes a waste of research work that could be used to innovate.

The volume of this waste can be estimated through some simple mathematics. If a scientist with emerging data goes directly to the recipient, then the waste of innovation work is minimal. In SPOT, these conversations occurred typically within 5 minutes of emerging knowledge.

If a scientist with emerging data goes through channels, then the likely scenario is as follows: First, the communication to the manager will likely occur at scheduled one-on-one meetings. This is usually once or twice per week in many organizations, so we can estimate that two days are lost in initial reporting. The manager must then engage the second manager, and because managers are often busy and scheduling meetings can take time, there will be a week delay before the recipient's manager is informed. If each member of a 40 person team has one such item every week, 56 weeks of innovation work, more than one full scientist's effort will be lost to the organization. Another full week (×40 for the team as a whole) might be lost if the second manager does not bring the recipient to the meeting. In this case, 96 weeks, or two full scientist years of activity, will be lost.

Of course, in this case, we have not estimated the work required to prepare for meetings, which is probably a half hour per each meeting, nor the time taken in the actual meeting. These are small compared to the loss of two scientists, but even this is not the biggest effect. It turns out that small, actionable discoveries are made constantly through a large R&D organization. These discoveries not only help other scientists avoid blind alleys, but they spark creative thoughts that lead to breakthroughs. On an organization the size of SPOT, these discoveries are happening at a rate of at least several per day. It is easy to believe that productivity improvement, just through dynamic interaction, improved by a factor of two.

The same thing, by the way, is true of knowledge emanating from external sources. The delay between publication of an important research finding and the incorporation of that finding into new research is a potentially large source of waste within an organization. In SPOT, the lag time from data emergence to dissemination and reprioritization of work across the scientific community was negligible. Due to the tracking precision possible with electronic communication, the SPOT team showed that on *externally generated* data, their point-to-point communication approach reduced redirect lag time to somewhere between 20 minutes and two hours. In one example, a large academic research study readout appeared in a prominent scientific publication, and within 20 minutes, elements of the SPOT team had incorporated the published data into their records, analyzed the data against team hypotheses and empirical knowledge, and disseminated the implications to the broader team. In the ensuing two hours, team members sought each other out through e-mail and hallway conversations, and new strategies and work priorities were set. Within two hours of the publication time of the paper, SPOT was working on a newly adjusted research strategy.

In another instance that I witnessed personally, a colleague speculated on a hypothesis that could be tested with data available to the team. By the time he'd gotten back to his laboratory from the meeting, the comparison data were sitting in his electronic in-box, enabling him to immediately direct his work based on the latest thinking.

At best, through-channel communications cause significant lag time within the team. For emergent data, immediate communications are imperative and—with a knowledge of team roles and expectations—are easy to facilitate in a point-to-point fashion. At their worst, through-channel communication styles contribute to an unnecessary lack of trust. If researchers are unable to adequately discuss their work with other researchers, then that problem should be addressed by improving their capability, not by inserting management oversight.

RESULTS OF THE SPOT EXPERIMENT

The SPOT team performed significantly differently than its precursors would have projected. Normal pharmaceutical R&D projects take time. Target identification in particular takes a long time to progress, perhaps 18 to 36 months from inception to delivery of a large-enough body of evidence to make a solid proposal for moving forward on a single target. The SPOT team, on the other hand, developed and executed the science to interrogate and provide solid cause–effect data on *hundreds* of targets within six months, and then interrogated hundreds of targets for each of several disease hypotheses, perhaps one hypothesis per month, over the next several months. Although not exhaustive, in the first eight months the SPOT team identified several novel targets not being moved forward by any other company while ruling out as *unconnected to the disease* several targets that were being vigorously pursued in clinical trials. Performance measures are always tricky, but if you take just time and elucidation of a new target space, SPOT operated with a *demonstrable* three- to sixfold improvement speed, a 300- to 500-fold improvement in exploration of scientific space, and at least a six- to twelvefold improvement in innovation.

The power of community in creating environments in which researchers can flourish is immense. All SPOT did was to create an

□ Developed from Lean principles
□ Developed organically during
   implementation of SPOT

Learning Driver	SPOT Implementation
Strategic Alignment	• Critical scientific problems and their dependencies known to all • Timelines known to all
Ownership	• Everyone individually and collectively owns solving of all problems —on time and with required learning content • No timeline is *ever* missed!
Structured Problem Solving	• Common approach (A3), showing reasoning, is used by all • Data, interpreted results *and* reasoning are captured
Real-Time Adjustments	• To priority—most valuable problem is in play at all times • To resourcing—ensures progress never slows on critical science

Decision Making	• Made *only when needed*
	    • Ensures science develops fully
	    • Ensures dependent science is never delayed
	• Made by the person with the best data, not highest rank

Scale of Experimentation	• Small to support high learning tempo, acceleration of interdependent science

FIGURE 11.4
Elements of the fast-learning culture in the SPOT project.

environment in which their *be state* was as easy to embrace as command-and-control behavior was difficult, and to hold that tension until the team as a community realized the value in, and flipped to, a new model of thinking and operating. The drivers of that model generated the fast-learning culture of SPOT, and these are summarized in Figure 11.4.

CONCLUSIONS

SPOT did not prove that all elements of the Lean R&D, as described in this book, are required for success. Nor did the SPOT team prove that, engaged together, all elements of Lean R&D will create their level of capability. What SPOT did provide was a demonstration of what Lean R&D looks like, fully functioning as a system. It demonstrated that, operating as a system, Lean will create new tools that support the R&D environment. It demonstrated a new way of organic fast learning and project management that I, at least, have never witnessed. Finally, it demonstrated that almost unthinkable levels of improvement are possible, not merely in the *known* areas of normal science, but in the unexplored and fundamentally *unknown* areas of science, where new mental models are required for progress.

Since the completion of the SPOT project, we have used many of these same insights with other teams with varying levels of success. The most important factors we have found in our environment are (a) the design elements of A3 mentorship at all levels of the team and (b) whole-community involvement in the creation and implementation of the emerging Lean system.

12

Reflections

In building this book, I have focused very little on describing how tools of Lean manufacturing can apply to the innovation space. Instead, I have focused on the purpose of research and development (R&D) itself and have developed areas of Lean research that address, very specifically, the needs of innovation for both individuals and communities as well as the managers and systems that operate within them.

Lean invariably arises from purpose, and as we have seen, the purpose of R&D is different from that of manufacturing. It is different from every other business construct, in that its sole purpose is to innovate by creating new, valuable packages of knowledge that the company can use to (a) create, sell, or improve its existing products and processes or (b) sell, through license or direct means, to other people and organizations.

To serve this purpose well, we also went back to the basic core of Lean thinking and the purpose of Lean. In manufacturing, the purpose of Lean was to create clean (5S—sort, set in order, shine, standardize, sustain), effective (flow, Kanban, low waste), flexible, people-centric manufacturing environments. The purpose of Lean manufacturing is to create a manufacturing environment in which people (and their companies) can flourish. It does not take a lot of effort to generalize this purpose to Lean in any endeavor by stating simply that the purpose of Lean is to create environments in which people can flourish.

Taken together, Lean in R&D is the science of creating innovation environments in which people can flourish. Unfortunately, flourishing manufacturing environments have a different purpose than flourishing innovation environments, and concepts and tools that support the former do not always support the latter. As a result, I have described several ideas, some of them new, that specifically support the creation of an innovation environment. Each of these concepts, in its own way, supports creative thought, innovation, and/or the innovation community in a quest to build valuable knowledge packages that serve their purpose.

The first of these new Lean concepts is the seeing, reframing, experiencing, and growing learning loop. Like all learning loops, it describes, in a different way, the same underlying thought process that humans have always engaged in creating. But of course, language helps emphasize a new range, even in old concepts, and the "seeing, reframing, experiencing, and growing" learning loop emphasizes that our learning and innovation are *primarily hindered* by how we currently see the world and frame it in our minds. It is axiomatic that we cannot reframe our world in an easier and more effective way until we can see our assumptions about it and the context in which our current beliefs arise. That we can learn to see that context and its associated beliefs and assumptions in a structured and teachable way debunks the self-defeating belief that creativity, innovation, and flashes of brilliant thinking cannot be learned.

By keeping the "seeing, reframing, experiencing, and growing" construct in mind, the A3 process—already well established in the Lean community—takes on new and profoundly useful meaning within the R&D community. A3 is ideally suited to the improvement of scientific thought. It creates simultaneous rigor around the scientific learning loop, supporting rigorous "regular science" and, at the same time, the "eureka!" process represented in the "seeing, reframing, experiencing, and growing" learning loop. A3 is a fast, concise format that makes it easy to practice, easy to share, and easy to engage others. It serves to instill rigor; to create a thinking structure; and to support mentoring, scientific communications, and community building.

Creative, structured thinking, of course, is not enough to deliver good innovation. An innovation community must be able to integrate new knowledge from different experiments, usually developed by several researchers over the course of time. Many innovations, particularly those bringing basic research to the marketplace—whether in consumer, manufacturing, or pharmaceutical realms—integrate experiments over years and sometimes decades. Entire waves of researchers will work on such projects. These facts of R&D lead to information and coordination difficulties not generally seen in other areas of business. Moreover, research builds and integrates knowledge, ideas, and trains of thought more than it creates the activities, objects, and documents familiar to other areas of business.

Because of the differences and difficulties inherent in structuring and managing R&D projects, we developed a second new Lean construct, Critical Question Mapping[SM], to enable us to map, organize, and track the *learning* that must occur to deliver a successful innovation. No matter how well an activity train is designed, or how smoothly and effortlessly it is executed, if it does not yield the required learning, it cannot satisfy the innovation needs of the community. Question-based mapping and project management structures greatly reduce, and in many cases *eliminate*, the opportunity for a team to design a system that operates smoothly yet fails to deliver innovation.

The value of Critical Question Mapping to the Lean R&D community does not diminish the utility of value stream mapping; in fact, it puts value stream mapping in a unique context for "seeing" and "reframing" large, complicated work systems. As complexity arises, communities can easily lose their common focus and devolve into work silos that hinder the flow of innovation. By bringing them back together, enabling them to see how their work connects and integrates with others, value stream mapping provides a powerful tool for researchers to see not only barriers to their work, but also the barriers to thinking and social interactions that creep into their daily lives. By exposing these barriers, teams can easily see and remove them, delivering nearly effortless paths to twofold or greater operating improvements.

As Lean manufacturing developed entire suites of tools to promote flow (Kanban, work cells, Just-in-Time, one-piece flow, SMED, heijunka, supermarkets, and so on), so has Lean R&D. Flow is improved by many of the same factors as Lean manufacturing, including batch-free experimentation, fast changeovers, laboratory set-up to promote flow, and so on. But in R&D, the key factor is not speed of experimentation, but speed of learning. Critical to this process is good thinking (represented by our learning loop, by A3, and by conventional insight and scientific capability) as well as reducing blind alleys and suboptimal approaches.

Innovation flow is also supported by pursuing multiple options at the minimum possible scale to ensure that work always progresses on a good pathway. It is supported, when no viable pathway presents itself, by creating "good-better-best" ladders to take science from where we are now to the steps we *can* envision, and from there, or with a few more intervening steps, to that ultimate place where the innovation needs of the community are served but, at the moment, is completely beyond our grasp.

Of crucial importance to smooth flow and integration of innovation is the concept of cadence. A community cadence ensures that, at defined intervals, the community will integrate its knowledge, identify remaining gaps, and press forward again. Fast learning requires a high learning cadence. "Agile" programmers often integrate their work at hourly or faster cadences. High-cadence R&D operates at a daily or every-other-day tempo. With experiments reading out and results integrating with other research at that rate, a smooth, rapid growth of knowledge results, and improvements in innovation rates of more than two orders of magnitude have been observed.

Beyond cadenced research is "organically managed" research. Organic management applies the research activity of the currently available researchers and resources against the knowledge gaps facing the innovation community. What separates organic management from other forms of project management is twofold. First, the experiments that are progressed are optimized to give the most valuable contribution against the knowledge needs of the community using the resources currently available. Researchers, equipment, and materials are applied on an emerging basis as they become available from, or tied up by, research activities through the days, weeks, and months of work. Second, organic management differs from conventional management because this free flow of work, maximizing the total capacity of effort through the R&D community, *cannot* be planned. It can only happen through the simultaneous, self-directed activities of researchers interacting with each other. It requires real-time information sharing, experimental design, and cross-functional engagement.

Surprisingly, organic management is not *difficult* to achieve. In our experience, it happens naturally, but it does have some fairly substantial precursor requirements. Researchers must have a clear understanding of the knowledge gaps facing the community as well as the people and groups that are engaged most significantly in resolving those knowledge gaps. The researchers must have real-time knowledge of what others have accomplished, so that they build their future work on the most current and relevant knowledge base, not something that is a week, a day, or even 10 minutes old. The researchers must engage constantly with the other members of their community to coordinate activities and share information, and most importantly, each researcher must have a deep commitment to each member of the group and to the group's success. Since everyone's work must be relied on to be correct, each person must commit to delivering 100 percent complete and accurate results.

It is clear that organic management requires a solid, cohesive, and committed research community. It requires significant trust across the entire R&D community, so researchers have to be good and they have to be responsible. The advantage to organic R&D management is that almost no time is wasted on research that could, through knowledge already available to the system, have been avoided. Second, no time is wasted in coordinating activities through managers or other intermediaries. Third, people and equipment utilization rises dramatically. Fourth, collaboration increases across functional boundaries as well as within R&D functions. Fifth, the youngest and least experienced researchers can immediately contribute unexpected and unique talents to the group. Finally, with immediate project management tasks distributed throughout the system, managers can take on more valuable roles, such as mentoring, engaging in strategic questioning, and interfacing with the wider organization.

The total value of organic management is not easy to assess. Much of the value is in areas of the R&D enterprise that we do not normally measure. Nevertheless, the acceleration of science within an organically managed team using the A3, Critical Question Map, good-better-best, and other Lean R&D practices was well in excess of two orders of magnitude better than the same team prior to engagement of Lean. Importantly, despite many challenges—technical, managerial, and social—the team never missed a deadline, never delivered late on an innovation, and made radical improvements in their work as they progressed. Moreover, unlike the teams operating to a strict cadence, the organically managed teams *enjoyed* their work much more and were far more engaged, both at work and outside of work, with their coworkers.

In my mind, this is embodiment of a Lean R&D system. It is dynamic; it is integrated; it is engaged; and in the end, it is exceptionally capable in serving the innovation purpose of R&D. I believe that Lean R&D is every bit as big a leap for innovation over the corporate innovation models set forth by Edison and Bell as Lean manufacturing was over the mass production system that preceded it. Nevertheless, we should keep in mind that Lean R&D is not only an emerging science, but it is also a science in its infancy. There will be many more people who take these ideas and improve on them. There will be people who create new ideas to plug gaps or find opportunities that I have not, and cannot, envision. There will be people who integrate these ideas into a better and more complete understanding of how to create innovation environments in which people can flourish even more effectively. Lean R&D is a living science, and I look forward to your contributions to its growing body of knowledge.

Bibliography

Amabile, Teresa and Steven Kramer. *The Progress Principle: Using Small Wins to Ignite Joy, Engagement and Creativity at Work*. Harvard Business Review Press, 2011.

Coram, Robert. *Boyd: The Fighter Pilot Who Changed the Art of War*. New York: Back Bay Books, 2004.

Hounshell, David. *From the American System to Mass Production, 1800–1932*. Baltimore: Johns Hopkins Press, 1984.

IndustryWeek/Manufacturing Performance Institute, 2007 Census of U.S. Manufacturers.

Kuhn, Thomas. *The Structure of Scientific Revolutions*, (3rd ed.). Chicago: University of Chicago Press, 1996.

Lau Tsu, *The Tao Te Ching*, (trans. Stephen Aldiss and Stanley Lombardo). Boston: Shambhala, 2007.

Miller, D. "Successful Change Leaders: What Makes Them? What Do They Do That Is Different?" *Journal of Change Management*. 2 no. 4 (2002): 359–68

Musashi, Miyamoto. *The Book of Five Rings*, (trans. Thomas Cleary). Boston: Shambhala, 2000.

Ohno, Taiichi and John Miller. *Taiichi Ohno's Workplace Management*. Mukiteo, WA: Gemba Press, 2007.

Ohno, Taiichi and Norman Bodek. *Toyota Production System: Beyond Large-Scale Production*. Portland, OR: Productivity Press, 1988.

Osinga, Frans P. B. *Science Strategy and War: The Strategic Theory of John Boyd*. New York: Routledge, 2007.

Raps, A. "Implementing Strategy." *Strategic Finance*. 85, no. 12 (2004) 49–53.

Richards, Chester W. *Certain to Win: The Strategy of John Boyd Applied to Business*. Bloomington, IN: Xlibris, 2004.

Jaruzelski, Barry and Kevin Dehoff. "The Global Innovation 1000: How the Top Innovators Keep Winning." *Strategy and Business*. 61, Winter (2010)

Rother, Mike and John Shook. *Learning to See: Value Stream Mapping to Add Value and Eliminate Muda*. Cambridge, MA: Lean Enterprise Institute, 1999.

Senge, P. *The Dance of Change*. New York: Currency Doubleday, 1999.

Shimokawa, Koichi and Takahiro Fujimoto, eds. *The Birth of Lean* (trans. Brian Miller with John Shook). Cambridge, MA: The Lean Enterprise Institute, 2009.

Shingo, Shigeo and Andrew P. Dillon. *A Study of the Toyota Production System*. Portland, OR: Productivity Press, 1989.

Shingo, Shigeo. *A Revolution in Manufacturing: The SMED System*. Portland, OR: Productivity Press, 1985.

Shingo, Shigeo. *Zero Quality Control: Source Inspection and the Poka Yoke System*. Portland, OR: Productivity Press, 1986.

Shook, John. *Managing to Learn: Using the A3 Management Process*. Cambridge, MA: The Lean Enterprise Institute, 2009.

Spear, Steven J. and H. Kent Bowen. "Decoding the DNA of the Toyota Production System," *Harvard Business Review*, 1999 (September-October), 97–106.

Spear, Steven, J. *Chasing the Rabbit*. New York: McGraw Hill, 2009.

Stalk, Jr., George and Thomas M. Hout, *Competing against Time: How Time-Based Competition Is Reshaping Global Markets.* New York: Free Press, 1990.

Strebel, P. "Why Do Employees Resist Change?" *Harvard Business Review.* 74 no. 3 (1996): 86–92.

Taleb, Nassim Nicholas. Interview in *The Economist* (http://www.economist.com/blogs/multime-dia/2010/11/nassim_taleb_antifragility).

Ward, Allen. *Lean Product and Process Development.* Cambridge, MA: Lean Enterprise Institute, 2007.

Index

Printed in the United States
by Baker & Taylor Publisher Services

Printed in the United States
by Baker & Taylor Publisher Services